Culture and Communication: Signs in Flux

An Anthology of Major and Lesser-Known Works

by Yuri Lotman

Cultural Syllabus

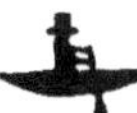

Culture and Communication: Signs in Flux

An Anthology of Major and Lesser-Known Works by Yuri Lotman

Edited by Andreas Schönle

Translated from the Russian by Benjamin Paloff

BOSTON
2020

The publication of this book is supported by the grant from the TRANSKRIPT program of the Mikhail Prokhorov Foundation.

Library of Congress Cataloging-in-Publication Data

Names: Lotman, I͡U. M. (I͡Uriĭ Mikhaĭlovich), 1922–1993, author. | Schönle, Andreas, editor. | Paloff, Benjamin, translator.
Title: Culture and communication: signs in flux: an anthology of major and lesser-known works/by Yuri Lotman; edited by Andreas Schönle; translated from the Russian by Benjamin Paloff.
Description: Boston: Academic Studies Press, 2020. | Series: Cultural syllabus | Includes bibliographical references.
Identifiers: LCCN 2020011311 (print) | LCCN 2020011312 (ebook) | ISBN 9781644693865 (hardback) | ISBN 9781644693872 (paperback) | ISBN 9781644693889 (adobe pdf)
Subjects: LCSH: Semiotics. | Culture--Semiotic models.
Classification: LCC P99 .L6625 2020 (print) | LCC P99 (ebook) | DDC 401/.4--dc23
LC record available at https://lccn.loc.gov/2020011311
LC ebook record available at https://lccn.loc.gov/2020011312

ISBN 9781644693865 hardback
ISBN 9781644693872 paperback
ISBN 9781644693889 ebook PDF
ISBN 9781644693896 ePub

Cover design by Ivan Grave
On the cover: Photograph by Malev Toom, Tartu Art Museum, Contemporary Art Collection. Reproduced by permission

Book design by PHi Business Solutions

Published by Academic Studies Press
1577 Beacon Street
Brookline, MA 02446, USA
press@academicstudiespress.com
www.academicstudiespress.com

Contents

PART TWO

Acknowledgments

We wish to express our gratitude to friends and colleagues who have helped shape and facilitate this project at various stages: Jonathan Bolton, Marina Grishakova, Mark Lipovetsky, Mikhail Lotman, William Mills Todd III, B. A. Uspensky as well as our two anonymous peer reviewers.

Thanks are also due to the supportive editorial team at Academic Studies Press, who have encouraged this project at every stage, including Jenna Colozza, Oleh Kotsyuba, Igor Nemirkovsky, Kira Nemirovsky, Faith Stein, and Ekaterina Yanduganova.

We are grateful to the Yuri Lotman Estate, Estonian Semiotics Repository Foundation (Eesti Semiootikavaramu) for the right to translate the texts included in this volume.

A Note on the Text

Lotman's original notes are reproduced here as endnotes referenced by Arabic numerals. We used footnotes, referenced by Roman numerals, for our editorial comments. Each article is introduced by a brief paragraph in italics explaining its source and significance, as well as placing it in a larger critical context.

The articles included in this collection reflect various scholarly styles, including some pieces that were initially presented as television programs and that accordingly present a more conversational style, with lighter referencing. Our translation has aimed to retain these inflections of tone and style.

A Note on Transliteration

This volume uses two different transliteration systems. For proper names occurring within the text, we have either used well-established English equivalents or applied simplified and anglicized spelling, writing, for example, Veselovsky instead of Veselovskii and Alexander instead of Aleksandr. In bibliographic references, we have consistently used the Library of Congress transliteration, even for proper names.

Introduction

ANDREAS SCHÖNLE

Yuri Lotman (1922–1993) is one of the most prominent and influential Russian scholars of the twentieth century.[1] A cofounder of the so-called Tartu-Moscow school of semiotics, he applied his mind to a wide array of disciplines, from aesthetics to literary and cultural history, narrative theory to intellectual history, cinema to mythology, not to speak of cybernetics. He advanced highly sustained theories on structural poetics, culture, and artificial intelligence, as well as the relationship between semiotics and neurology;[2] he proposed sweeping typological generalizations, such as his opposition between Russian and Western cultures; and he excavated layer after layer of Russian literary, cultural, and intellectual history. His interests ranged from how causal connections work in a semiotic series to the role of dolls in a system of culture. He touched on Freud, Charlie Chaplin, and Lenin. His semiotic analyses of Russian culture included studies of dueling, card-playing, and the theatricality of polite society. Considered groundbreaking in the context of Soviet disdain for the nobility, his thick description of aristocratic culture devoted appreciable attention to the situation of women and their contributions to culture (his long description of "A Woman's World" is translated in this volume for the first time). Along with numerous studies of Russian high literature from the Middle Ages to the twentieth century, he investigated the semiotics of St. Petersburg, the role of architecture in culture, and the symbolic construction of space. In a path-breaking interdisciplinary vein, he studied the interrelationship among various kinds of art, be it the impact of theater on painting or of landscape design on poetry. Perhaps his most influential ideas concerned the interpenetration of the arts and everyday life: along with several other articles, his biography of Alexander Pushkin, which demonstrated how the poet designed his social behavior as a work of art (*Aleksandr Sergeevich Pushkin: A Writer's Biography*) and his article on the ways in which the Decembrists plotted their lives according to codes derived from drama ("The Decembrist in Daily Life") spawned a series of studies on various cases of theatricality and "life-creation" [*zhiznetvorchestvo*] by Russian and American scholars of all stripes.[3] This conception took hold not the least because it resonated with Russian culture's recurrent valorization of art as an existential project, the notion that art formulates not only aesthetic values, but also desirable ways of living.

Lotman was both a theorist and a historian. His uncanny command of Russian print culture not only enabled him to introduce substantial revisions to Russia's historiographic paradigms, transforming the ways in which his readers thought of Russia's identity, but also stoked one of his most endearing talents—his knack for pointing to unexpected, poorly known facts of Russian and, sometimes, world culture in support of a theoretical position. Indeed, perhaps his greatest asset was the ability to underpin history with theory and substantiate theory with history, casting a new light on everything he touched. He was a daring and imaginative thinker. He did not shy away from speculation and sometimes was prone to confusing his erudition with a license to conjecture. His skill at finding patterns and subtexts, honed on the practice of literary analysis, served him less well when applied to social behavior: some of his last historiographic ventures (for example, his richly contextual biography of Nikolay Karamzin) smack of overreading. Yet, his theoretical investigation of the role of chance and unpredictability in history and culture, which he presented in his last theoretical book, *Culture and Explosion* [*Kul'tura i vzryv*], tempered this penchant for overdetermination. He died before he could consider how this new premise would transform his interpretations of distinct episodes of Russian literature and culture.

In many ways his career offered a palimpsest of his times. After serving six years in the army, including four in combat during World War II, Lotman came back a decorated soldier, one of an estimated five percent of the enlisted men born in 1922 to survive the war.[4] He enrolled in Leningrad State University to finish his undergraduate studies, but despite his brilliant performance and glowing recommendation from the army, he could not be admitted to graduate school on account of his Jewish background.[5] For the same reason, he experienced difficulties finding a job, until he landed a position as teacher of Russian literature in a two-year pedagogical institute in Tartu, Estonia. Annexed in 1940, the fifteenth Soviet republic needed russification, and local authorities did not deem Lotman's ethnicity a liability. Becoming a resident of Estonia proved to be a blessing in disguise. Lotman quickly began to teach classes in the Department of Russian Literature at Tartu University. In 1952, he finally was able to defend his dissertation at Leningrad University. By 1954, he was a regular faculty member at Tartu University. While ostensibly marginalized by this displacement from the two capitals, Lotman took advantage of the comparatively more relaxed atmosphere of Estonian intellectual life and progressively built the Department of Russian Literature into a pioneering theoretical and historical powerhouse.

In the 1950s Lotman worked on a reconceptualization of late eighteenth- and early nineteenth-century intellectual and literary history. Inspired by the emergence of structuralism in Moscow, he began publishing on theoretical issues in 1962 and the following year made contacts with Moscow colleagues.[6] The institution of biannual summer schools on "secondary modeling systems"[7] near Tartu helped establish intellectual and personal links with Moscow scholars, which enabled the Tartu-Moscow school of semiotics to coalesce.[8] In the 1950s and 1960s, Lotman's scholarship was first published in scientific journals at Tartu University, although Lotman was never completely barred from mainstream publication in Moscow or Leningrad. Despite small runs and poor distribution, his articles on semiotics drew the attention of elite intellectual circles in Moscow and Leningrad, and, subsequently, abroad. Starting in 1964, translations of his articles began to appear in various Western European countries, the United States, and Japan.[9] His reputation steadily grew over the years, and by 1988 he had become a TV star, presenting his study of the culture of the nobility in a series of televised lectures. When he died on October 28, 1993, Estonian president Lennart Meri interrupted his state visit to Germany to deliver an oration after the funeral: the Jewish scholar who had been hired to assist in russifying the Republic had become a pillar of Estonian national pride.[10]

Since then, Estonian and Russian academic circles have engaged in a lively and spirited reevaluation of Lotman's legacy. While his colleagues and former students at Tartu continued to work broadly within his conceptual frameworks, two different lines of succession coalesced institutionally and methodologically. Work on semiotics proceeded apace in the Department of Semiotics at the University of Tartu, while work on Russian cultural history was carried forward in the Department of Slavic Studies. This division reflected a breakdown of the unique synthesis between history and theory Lotman had attempted, as literary and cultural historians in the 1990s and 2000s in Russia engaged in much more empiricist, text- and archive-based, and theory-adverse studies. Lotman's semiotic legacy found a home on the pages of *Sign Systems Studies*, a journal

Lotman had founded in 1964 under the title of *Trudy po znakovym systemam* and which was rebranded as an English-language semiotics journal in 1998.[11] The work in literary and cultural history by Lotman's former students and colleagues was dispersed across various journals, but came together in the four thick issues of the *Lotman Volume* [*Lotmanovskii sbornik*].[12] Meanwhile, the history of the Tartu-Moscow school became a contested site, with various participants making contradictory claims about its emergence and development.[13] Nonetheless a series of recurring major conferences—the yearly "Lotman Seminars" in Tartu; the "International Lotman Congresses" in 2002 and 2012, also in Tartu; the "Annual Lotman Conference" in Tallinn; and the "Lotman Readings" [Lotmanovskie chteniia] in Moscow, which had their 26th occurrence in 2018—testify to Lotman's continuing relevance, even if not all the works presented at these meetings are directly indebted to his methodologies. In the last ten years, the Estonian Semiotics Repository Foundation, which holds Lotman's personal archive, has enabled the publication of archival texts and the incipient exploration of Lotman's yet unstudied international networks.[14]

In parallel with these scholarly developments, Lotman's public posture and ethical stance also began to attract scrutiny. Lotman's own self-fashioning strategies came into view, which helped debunk some of the partly self-forged mythology that surrounded his public aura. Andrey Zorin analyzed how Lotman's work on Karamzin was inflected by his carefully honed stance of stoic, if not heroic, disengagement from public affairs, while projecting a front of scrupulous moral integrity and commitment to preserving high culture's historical legacy for future benefit.[15] Some people tried, perhaps not quite successfully, to impugn this image of moral probity. Somewhat scabrous anecdotes about Lotman's everyday behavior at Tartu reached the pages of an elitist glossy magazine in 1998.[16] More recently, the publication of Faina Sonkina's memoirs revealed that from 1968 until his death, while married to Zara Mints, a fine scholar of the Silver Age, Lotman conducted an intense, if geographically distanced amorous relationship with Sonkina, one interlaced with earnest and agonizing reflections on morality.[17] From a sociological perspective, Maxim Waldstein drew an interesting if somewhat overwrought portrait of Lotman as a savvy operator working existing institutions and networks to carve out a position of power and relative freedom, in contrast to his more widespread image as a victim of state ostracization and as a heroic defender of core humanist values.[18]

During the 1970s and 1980s, Lotman's works and those of other Soviet semioticians became broadly influential in American and West European academia; next to Mikhail Bakhtin, Lotman was the most widely read and translated theorist of the former Soviet Union.[19] He spoke to an astonishing range of disciplines and authors: the philosopher Paul Ricoeur, new historicist Stephen Greenblatt, semiotician Umberto Eco, reception theorist Wolfgang Iser, feminist critic Julia Kristeva, and marxist critic Frederic Jameson, to name a few, have productively used Lotman's concepts. Nonetheless, his brand of semiotics never became as prominent in the English-speaking world as did French Structuralism, and Lotman received his most intense hearing in Germany and Italy, rather than in the United States or the United Kingdom. There are many reasons for this state of affairs, ranging from the fact that mainstream book-length translations of his works appeared after the structuralist wave had already swept over the United States, to his unique blending of theory with (Russian) history, which rendered access to his scholarship more difficult and less urgent to a non-Russianist.[20]

In the 1980s Lotman began to develop a theory of culture no longer based on the Saussurean distinction between code and utterance, but rather on how messages are embedded in a fluid semiotic environment from which they draw their meaning. Lotman calls this semiotic environment the *semiosphere*, a concept he developed in English translation in *Universe of the Mind*, a volume published in 1990. Internationally, however, Lotman's reputation was wedded to that of structuralist semiotics, and as a result, his later works have not found the audience they deserve. Most scholars continue to reference primarily his earlier pieces.[21] Yet, after the English publication of *Culture and Explosion* in 2009 and of *The Unpredictable Workings of Culture* in 2014, and with the republication of some sections from *Universe of the Mind* in semiotics anthologies, there are some signs that this is beginning to change.

Universe of the Mind presents a theory of cultural dynamics that results from interactions between non-homologous, that is, mutually untranslatable languages within a contentious field of discourses aspiring to move from the periphery to the center. Lotman's notion of the semiosphere, the semiotic environment in which communication occurs and from which it derives its codes, holds great interdisciplinary appeal. It tends to supersede the binary categories left over from structuralism (and sometimes retained in deconstruction) and to provide an underlying foundation for the local investigations undertaken by cultural studies. It emphasizes shifting boundaries and hierarchies, permutations between the center and the periphery, mediations and translations, isomorphic relations between events on the micro and macro levels, and unity through diversity. In that sense, the concept of the semiosphere is close to what Galin Tihanov has called "marginocentricity," defined as a regime in which "centre and periphery become fluid, mobile, and provisional, prone to swapping their places and exchanging cultural valences."[22] The organicist metaphor of the semiosphere serves not to essentialize discourse, but to restore to it a sense of unceasing life, of the continuous metabolic exchanges discourses undergo when they are thrown into the world.[23] In that sense, Lotman's semiosphere stands in sharp contrast with the notions of world literature developed by Franco Moretti and Pascale Casanova, for whom it is invariably at the center of culture that innovation happens, while the peripheries are confined to assimilating the forms imported from it.[24]

One of the attractive and unique dimensions of Lotman's theory is that it offers a way to conceptualize change and innovation, both on the individual and historical scales, but without lapsing into antiquated humanist or Romantic assumptions. *Culture and Explosion* explores two different types of change: continuous evolution and abrupt, unpredictable transformation (that is, "explosion") that turns a culture, especially a binary one, upside down. The existence of explosive changes throws an element of creativity and chance into history, thus calling into question meta-narratives that presume to encapsulate history's unfolding. Lotman thought that he was witnessing such a period of transformative change in the early 1990s, just as he was working on this book. Indeed, he ended this study on a plea to avoid "the historical catastrophe" that would result from missing the opportunity to abandon Russia's binaries and to join the more supple ternary system he ascribed to European culture. From the current perspective of rabid polarization between Russia and the notional "West," fostered by demagogues on both sides, Lotman's poignant hope highlights the extent to which he saw himself as a scion of European culture, not unlike the Russian noble elite he described in some of his later works.

For a reader accustomed, say, to French cultural theory, the works of Lotman will bring some surprise. While the likes of Barthes and Foucault were engaged in a sustained critique of prevailing ideologies, which they exposed in seemingly ordinary cultural formations and social processes, for example, in mass culture (Barthes) and clinical practice (Foucault), Lotman endeavored first and foremost to recover and protect the rich layeredness of high culture. There is a larger context to this, and to understand what is at stake we can draw on the productive opposition Caryl Emerson has proposed between the "hermeneutics of suspicion," a term coined by Paul Ricoeur, and the "hermeneutics of recovery of meaning," which Emerson identifies as a premise shared by Russian thinkers as diverse as Lotman, Bakhtin, Lev Vygotsky, and Lydia Ginzburg.[25] Whereas French theory took its impetus from the effort to unmask the false consciousness at work in cultural production ("suspecting" the ways it conceals the iniquities of the underlying system of economic production and of prevailing power relations), Emerson contends that what unifies these scholars is the belief that the word can change the world, and hence that culture is invested with a forward-looking responsibility to model desirable and morally sustainable behavior. For Lotman, this implicitly entailed foregrounding the world-making powers of prominent luminaries from the past, such as Karamzin, Pushkin, and the Decembrists (or their wives). Accordingly, Lotman's most innovative "move" in his treatment of literature consisted in analysing the ways in which it disseminates codes of behavior, as well as models of feelings, which can easily cross cultural and national boundaries and thus demonstrate their porousness (for an example, see his piece "A Woman's World" in this volume). In so doing, Lotman laid one of the foundations for the emotional turn in Russian history and culture.[26] His faith in the creative, that is, constructivist powers of high culture arose in the highly ideologized atmosphere of Soviet cultural politics, which tightly controlled innovative cultural production and, in particular, restricted how aristocratic culture of the eighteenth and nineteenth centuries could be received and understood. It thus acquired a tacit oppositional valence, which, however, could never become explicit or militant. While Lotman maintained an outward front of political aloofness, his concept of the semiosphere rests on a semiotic understanding of power: the discourses that vie for a position at the center shape our consciousness and constitute our reality. They exert, rather than transmit, power.[27]

Whereas Barthes was primarily interested in ideology, Lotman undertook the study of culture as a meaning-producing mechanism. There exists some superficial terminological overlap between Barthes and Lotman, which scholars have recently begun to explore, notably the notion of a "secondary modeling system," the ideological, artistic, or religious constructs that build on natural language as the primary system.[28] An important difference between the two semioticians lies in the fact that in his treatment of ideology, Barthes tended to assume a fairly homogenous and hierarchical discursive landscape, while Lotman foregrounded the interactions and exchanges between at least two heterogenous and intersecting systems. As Daniele Monticelli has usefully highlighted, when Barthes refers to culture, he means tradition and ideological conformity, while for Lotman culture is a dynamic landscape pervaded with languages that compete for ascendancy and whose seething activity is the very mechanism that enables the creation of (new) meaning.[29] The geological metaphors Lotman deploys to describe the semiosphere—a seething sun, layering in strata, cataclysmic events, the interaction between the mineral and the organic—describe a high-octane energetic framework that stands in sharp contrast with the stagnant political culture of the Brezhnev era during which he developed his theories. While Barthes was somewhat quicker than Lotman to "explode" the bounded and stable systems he described in his structuralist phase—for example, by introducing the difference between the self-contained "work" and the unpredictably limitless "text" in his famous article "From Work to Text" in 1971[30]—even in his earlier structuralist period, Lotman's understanding of the artistic text was always that of a dynamic system of inter-related binary oppositions, whose complex multi-layeredness enabled a degree of openness and variability that was subject to actualization by the readers in accordance with their own frames of reference.[31]

*****

The present collection of texts by Lotman aims to achieve several things. Firstly, it provides handy access to a broad range of his scholarly contributions, grouped under the two headings of Semiotics and Cultural History, thus presenting a self-standing overview of his works. In selecting texts for translation, emphasis was placed on his later, post-structuralist period, which is more attuned to contemporary concerns, although some earlier texts were also included, both to provide a fuller view of his intellectual development and because they have been influential. Secondly, it offers first or new translations of his works in a contemporary idiom that sought to remain faithful to the inflections of his syntactic cadences and to his metaphors, while conveying his thoughts through an approachable, non-scientist lexicon. We took the opportunity to bring heretofore untranslated works into the English-speaking world, but we also included well-known seminal pieces in a new translation, as consistency of terminology and style across various texts is key to enabling an adequate understanding of Lotman's scholarly legacy. This collection thus represents a stand-alone primer of his works. We should say that our decision to retranslate some pieces should not be read as a rebuke to our predecessors. We had initially considered including some existing translations into the volume, but the steep copyrights demanded by publishers quickly ruled this out, while consistency in the translation emerged as an important objective. Thirdly, the collection is aimed at an English-speaking audience of undergraduate and graduate students from a variety of disciplines, rather than at the narrow world of professional Russianists, so, to the extent possible, we chose texts that are accessible and do not require an extensive background in semiotics or in Russian literary history. Finally, this collection intends partly to bring Lotman into the orbit of contemporary concerns and debates such as gender, memory, performance, world literature, and urban studies. While Lotman approaches these themes from a standpoint and in a language that at first glance may feel alien and dated, we believe that his works still shed a distinctive light and thus continue to contribute to a pluralistic, multidisciplinary debate around these themes.

Lotman's gendered language triggered a lively exchange of views between us about the proper way to translate it. While Lotman clearly thought, with some justification, that his piece "A Woman's World," included in his *Conversations on Russian Culture*, was ground-breaking by the standards of Soviet historiography, given the latter's disregard for the life of the nobility and for the life of women in particular, it is also true that in it he deployed a language that is markedly gendered. References to *zhenshchina*, that is, "woman" in the singular, as a generic term applicable to all women, sound dangerously essentializing. Yet, the piece itself makes a constructivist argument, aimed at showing that women of the time were forged in their character and identities by the literature they read and thus changed profoundly over the period in question. Historians will be quick to point out that a substantial corpus of Lotman's evidence relies on literature itself, thus becoming circular, though in fairness he also draws on memoirs and biographies. The main interest of this essay lies precisely in the way it models the relationship between literature and the political and social behavior of its readers, along with their mental and emotional worlds. But Lotman also anchors his analysis of the identities and behavioral patterns of (noble) women in a more essentializing premise that men are more subject to social pressure than women, as the latter are more able to extricate themselves from social conventions due to their intimate ties with ahistorical dimensions of life, such as nature, processes of becoming, and emotions, an idea he draws from Leo Tolstoy and that looms large in Russian culture. This notion also explains, in his view, why women are quicker to respond to cultural solicitations than men and therefore can serve as a bellwether of intellectual and cultural change for the historian. In the final paragraphs of his article, Lotman raises what he sees as a distinctive mental perspective into some sort of anthropological and semiotic constant that supersedes actual gender differences: "women's culture is not merely the culture of women. It is a particular view of culture, an indispensable element of its multi-voicedness," pointing out that Pushkin identified himself with this perspective. Hence, this view of culture is no longer gendered, narrowly speaking, but a voice within the normal heteroglossia of culture to which men contribute as well. Indeed, in reading his glowing description of the fearless moral probity of the Decembrists' wives, it becomes clear that Lotman identified himself with this stance. Yet despite this fairly sophisticated recasting of gendered parameters, he nonetheless remains wedded to binary oppositions, even when these oppositions allow interesting, counter-intuitive permutations within them.[32] Ultimately the binary of man versus woman underpins his entire argument, in tribute to his times. His article is as much an analysis of the literary construction of female identity in the late eighteenth and early nineteenth centuries as a document about the gendered views of a sophisticated intellectual of the last Soviet period, and we ask readers to approach it in that spirit.

In discussing Lotman's views on gender, one should bear in mind the astonishingly dismissive analysis of Anna Labzina that Lotman gave in his essay "Two Women" [Dve zhenshchiny], which is also included in his *Conversations on Russian Culture.* As Gary Marker has astutely pointed out, here Lotman falls into the trap of taking entirely at face value the notion that Enlightenment necessarily implies moral probity.[33] In reading Labzina's memoirs, he dismisses as pure fantasy her account of her first husband Alexander Karamyshev, which depicts him as a depraved, womanizing, child-molesting, card-playing drunkard. Unable to reconcile this narrative with his high-minded vision of a Europeanized scientist, Lotman dismisses her tale of woes as the fabrication of a woman wholly given to a literary masterplot of martyrdom and thus unable to recognize her husband's attempts to educate her in the ways of the Enlightenment for what they were. Whereas Marker carefully teases out—on the basis of her memoirs, diary, and external evidence—the traces of Labzina's own resourceful agency and coping strategies, Lotman confines her to the role of a hallucinating girl incapable of receiving the gift of knowledge (even though she was in her fifties when she wrote her memoirs). While the gendered optics of Lotman's misreading are truly alarming, this passage can also alert us to the pitfalls of assuming that people thought exclusively through literary paradigms.

All things considered, how then should one translate *zhenshchina*? Given that in Russian this generic use of the singular sounds entirely neutral, should one gloss over its essentializing implications by adopting the current English-language norm of using the plural instead? Or, on the contrary, should one draw specific attention to the way Lotman's language embeds gendered assumptions, for example by using the archaizing "woman" without article, making him even more essentializing than he was (or at least sounded in Russian), at the risk of putting off the English-speaking readers we address with this translation? Or would the compromise position "a woman" both convey the gendered language, while also implying the neutrality of its expression in Russian? Ultimately such decisions can only be adjudicated on the basis of an agreed understanding of the role of the translator, which can range from that of an invisible, or inaudible (if duly credited) conveyor of the thoughts expressed in the original into a fluid idiom of the target language, through that of a transcriber and performer attentive to the inflections and cadences of the original and willing to "foreignize" the target language accordingly, to that, ultimately, of an interventionist broker who conveys through translation an interpretation that both historicizes and actualizes the original in varying measures. Priorities will change depending on whether one aims for semantic equivalence, faithfulness to the distinctive form and style of the original, equivalence of effect or impact, or creative and critical reinsertion into a new discursive context. Do we agree with Walter Benjamin that the responsibility of the translator is to retain as much difference as possible, even at the risk of stretching the norms of the target language?[34] Given that with Lotman we deal with expository rather than artistic prose, and given the instrumental aims of this translation of making his ideas more widely accessible, it seemed appropriate to err on the side of intelligibility and fluidity, while also recognizing that Lotman's "otherness," his distinctive syntax and metaphors, are intrinsic to the meanings he constructs and therefore also worth smuggling through the checkpoints of linguistic boundaries, striking some uneasy balance between domestication and foreignization.[35] In the end, we settled for "a woman" as a reasonable compromise that does not disguise the gendered tone of Lotman's prose, but avoids blatant reification and essentializing. The same principles also determined how we conveyed pronouns, inducing us to avoid modernizing turns such as "s/he." Thus, in Lotman's model of communication, the addressee in the I—HE channel remains a HE, and does not become a S/HE. The capital letters here clearly indicate that we deal with an abstract model, not with a representational icon. Avoiding the s/he binary also has the advantage of eschewing the imposition of a binary at a time when fixed gendered binaries have themselves become problematic. We trust the readers will understand that for Lotman, as much as for us, the translator and editor of this volume, the use of the male pronoun is a manifestation and recognition (on our part) of a historical convention that has now thankfully been superseded.

To facilitate comprehension, especially among readers not specialized in Russian history and culture, it seemed essential to elucidate some of Lotman's rich cultural references. At the same time, doing so in an exhaustive fashion would have laden this edition with an overly ponderous apparatus. I aimed to cut a middle way, appending a commentary where some additional information was required for full comprehension, while leaving alone many references that could easily be illuminated through a couple of internet clicks. There are many personalities making brief appearances in Lotman's prose, and I have dwelt on them only where a conceptual understanding of their roles in the text contributed to its understanding. Each piece is introduced by a brief paragraph in italics, in which I took the liberty to highlight some of Lotman's core ideas, or place them in a larger critical context, which I did partly to account for my selection of works, and partly to aid understanding and gesture at the internal coherence of Lotman's thinking. Indeed, while the division between the structuralist and the post-structuralist periods in Lotman's intellectual career is a well-established proposition (and one to which I have contributed myself in my previous works on him), what emerged here, to my surprise, is the consonance and interconnectedness of his oeuvre, despite superficial shifts of emphasis, even across the two broad spheres of semiotics and cultural history. As we worked on the translation, we also noticed a few mistakes. The trivial ones were corrected silently, while we left a trace of our corrections where the matter seemed more consequential or served to illustrate Lotman's method.

Translator's Note

BENJAMIN PALOFF

From its inception, the project of offering a representative selection of Yuri Lotman's work in a new English translation, one that would be both true to the peculiarities of the author's style and accessible to an audience potentially unfamiliar with it, posed serious challenges that the reader would do well to consider. First among these is Lotman's often knotty language, which wends between conversational intimacy and dense theoretical jargon. Second is how Lotman quotes liberally (and sometimes inaccurately) from a wide variety of sources, in prose and in verse, in Russian, French, German, and English, from the Middle Ages to the present, each having their own formal and stylistic virtues to which the new readership also deserves access. Finally, there is Lotman's fondness for wordplay, which ranges from the occasional witticism to a truly generative paronomasia.

We have approached each of these challenges with the intention of replicating for the Anglophone reader the experience of reading Lotman in Russian, within the limits of language and the translator's own facility with it. Wherever appropriate, proper names appear in their most familiar Anglicized form rather than in scholarly transliteration (for instance, *Tolstoy* rather than *Tolstoi*), and we have reined in the occasional superfluous transition that might grate against the economies of English style. While not always precisely replicating that of the Russian original, we have tried to mirror Lotman's punning to allow the reader access to those instances when one notion grows organically from the expression of another.

Verse, meanwhile, is rendered as verse. This strategy, whereby the reader encounters the lyric poems frequently cited by Lotman in English renderings whose meter and rhyme convey that of the original texts, runs counter to the convention, long current in the field of Slavic studies, of providing literal prose glosses that often seem to go out of their way to deprive the reader of even a glimpse of what makes the poem a poem. The editor and translator have determined that such studied artlessness does a serious injustice, if not to the long-dead poet, who is unlikely to object, then to the reader thus left to take the admiring critic's word for it. For those who might prefer to read the poems in the original, however, in each instance this is provided after the English translation.

If every translator also edits, retooling the text to serve a new audience in their own language and to their own purposes, then it is equally true that the engaged editor of a translation also translates. That is certainly the case here. Andreas Schönle not only conceptualized the project, selecting its constituent texts and their arrangement, but throughout the process of pulling these texts into English he has been the translator's close collaborator, interlocutor, and—occasionally, and in the very best spirit—sparring partner. He has rescued the effort from my numerous oversights, misjudgments, and outright errors. The fault for any that remain rests with me alone.

Part One

SEMIOTICS

CHAPTER 1

From *Universe of the Mind*

This section and the next two are from a monograph, composed partly from previously published articles, which came out first in English translation in 1990 under the title of Universe of the Mind, *trans. Ann Shukman (Bloomington: Indiana University Press, 1990), and in Russian in 1999. Our translation is based on the version included in Iu. M. Lotman,* Semiosfera *(St. Petersburg: Iskusstvo-SPB, 2000), 163–177, itself based on the manuscript copy of Lotman's text. In this section we see Lotman grapple with an important issue, rarely addressed, which is how semiotics can account for the production of new ideas and information, as opposed to the actualization of meanings already encoded in the linguistic structure. Lotman derives novelty from the interaction between two differently coded semiotic systems, placing heterogeneity at the heart of his theory, which lends it dynamism and openness to change. In the previous section in* Universe of the Mind, *Lotman had questioned Ferdinand de Saussure's premise that what matters for linguistics is only the underlying semiotic structure, and not actual utterances. For Lotman, this reflects an impoverished understanding of the function of language as merely a conveyor of pre-existing information. Instead he argued for a broader view, which takes into account the "creative function" of languages, as well as their capacity to condense cultural memory.*

AUTOCOMMUNICATION: "I" AND "OTHER" AS ADDRESSEES

(On the Two Models of Communication in the System of Culture)

The organic connection between culture and communication forms one basis of contemporary cultural studies. A consequence of this is the transfer of models and terms adopted into the cultural sphere from communication theory. Applying the basic model elaborated by Roman Jakobson has allowed us to connect the broad range of problems in language, art, and culture more broadly with the theory of communicative systems. As we know, the model laid out by Jakobson is as follows:[1]

context
message
addresser .... addressee
contact
code

The creation of a unified model of communicative situations has been a substantial contribution to the study of the semiotic cycle and has provoked a response in many scholarly works. Yet the automatic transfer of established ideas into the realm of culture creates a raft of difficulties. The most basic of these is the following: in the mechanics of culture, communication operates through a minimum of two channels that are differently constructed.

We will have an opportunity later to turn our attention to how the unified mechanism of culture must have both visual and verbal connections, which can be regarded as two differently constructed channels for information transfer.[i] Both of these channels, however, can be described by Jakobson's model, and in this respect they are of one kind. But if we were to task ourselves with constructing a model of culture on a more abstract level, it would be possible to separate the two kinds of communicative channel, only one of which would be described by the classic model used till now. Doing so would first require that we separate two potential directions for transferring a message. The most typical case is the direction "I—HE," in which the "I" is the subject of the transmission, the one who possesses the information, and "HE" is the object, the addressee. In this instance, it is assumed that until the act of communication begins a certain message is known to "me" and unknown to "him."

In the culture to which we are accustomed, the prevalence of communications of this kind overshadows another channel of communicative transmission, one that one could characterize schematically as the "I—I" channel. A case of the subject delivering a message to himself—that is, to the person who already knows the message in the first place—seems paradoxical. In actual fact, however, it is not really so rare, and it plays a not insignificant role in the general system of culture.

---

i Lotman's discussion of the relationship between the verbal and the visual (iconic) can be found in *Universe of the Mind*, trans. Ann Shukman (Bloomington: Indiana University Press, 1990), 54–62. Lotman's core idea is that verbal and iconic signs (the latter, for example, expressed in metaphors or symbols) are mutually untranslatable, which, when combined within a text, opens up a productive indeterminacy conducive to the creation of new meaning.

When we speak of transmitting a message through the "I—I" system, we have in mind, firstly, not those instances when the text fulfills a mnemonic function. Here, the second, recipient "I" is functionally equivalent to the third person. The distinction comes down to the fact that in the "I—HE" system, information circulates in space, whereas in the "I—I" system it does so in time.[2]

What interests us first of all is the instance when the transmission of information from "I" to "I" is not accompanied by a gap in time and serves not a mnemonic function, but some other cultural function instead. Communicating to oneself information that one already knows occurs, first of all, whenever the communicative register is elevated in the process. Thus when a young poet reads his own poem as it is printed, the message remains textually the same as the manuscript text he knows. But once it is transcribed into a new system of graphic signs that possess another level of authority in the given culture, it receives a certain added significance. Analogous instances are those where the veracity or falsehood of the communication is conditional on whether it has been articulated in words or is merely implied, spoken or written, written or printed, and so on.

But we are dealing with the transmission of a message from "I" to "I" in many other instances as well. These include every instance where a person addresses himself, in particular those diary entries that are recorded not with the goal of memorializing specific data, but rather, for example, of elucidating the writer's interior state, an elucidation that does not occur without the entry. Addressing oneself—in text, in speech, in argument—is an essential fact not only of psychology, but of the history of culture as well.

In what follows we shall strive to demonstrate how the place of autocommunication in the system of culture is much more significant than one might suppose.

But how does such a strange situation arise, that a message transmitted within the "I—I" system not only doesn't become completely superfluous, but acquires some new, additional information?

In the "I—HE" system, the model's framing elements are variable (the addresser changes places with the addressee), while the code and message are stable. The message and the information it contains are constant, whereas the carriers of that information change.

In the "I—I" system, the carrier of information remains the same, but the message is reformulated and assumes a new meaning in the process of communication. This occurs due to the fact that a second, supplementary code is introduced, and the initial message is recoded in the units of that code's structure, acquiring the features of a new message.

In this instance, the communicative schema looks like this:

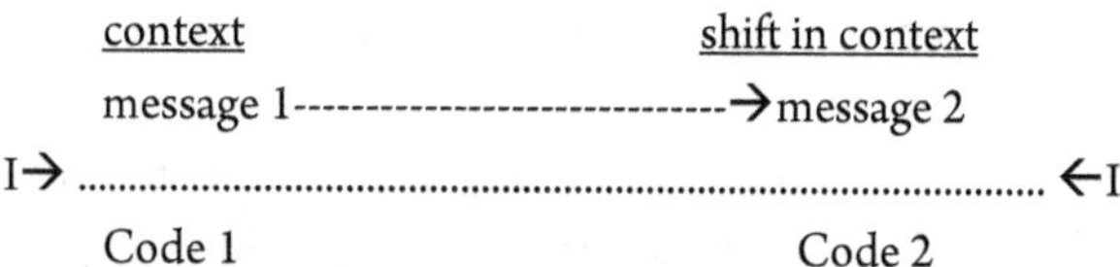

If the "I—HE" communicative system secures only the transmission of a certain constant informational content, then what happens in the "I—I" channel is its qualitative transformation, which leads to the reformation of the "I" itself.[ii] In the first instance, the addresser transmits a message to someone else, the addressee, and remains unchanged in the course of the act. In the second, in broadcasting to himself, he reforms his own essence internally, insofar as one can regard one's personal essence as one's individual store of socially meaningful codes, and here this store of codes changes in the process of the communicative act.

A message's transmission through the "I—I" channel has no immanent character, insofar as it is conditioned by the encroachment of certain additional codes from outside and by the presence of external shocks that shift the contextual situation.

A typical example would be the effect of metered sounds (the beat of wheels turning; rhythmic music) on a person's interior monologue. One could name a whole range of artistic texts in which rich and unbridled fantasy is conditioned by the metered rhythms of riding on horseback (Goethe's "Erlkönig," a number of poems from Heine's *Lyrical Intermezzo*), the rocking of a ship (Fyodor Tyutchev's "Dream upon the Sea" [Son na more]), the rhythms of the railroad (Mikhail Glinka's "Travelling Song" [Poputnaia pesnia], with words by Nestor Kukolnik).

Let us consider Tyutchev's "Dream upon the Sea" from this perspective:

Dream upon the Sea

Both sea and the storm held our bark in its sway;
And, sleepy, I felt at the whim of each wave.
Infinitudes two I possessed deep within,

ii In the schema printed in *Universe of the Mind*, this transformation of the subject is marked graphically by a transformation from I to I′ as a result of the communicative process.

And they made of me a most trifling thing.
So like cymbals, around me, the rock cliffs did crash,
The swells singing their part, the winds answering back.
And I in the chaos of sound lay there stunned,
But then over the chaos of sound came my dream.
A shock to behold, and yet magically mute,
O'er fulminous mist it plotted its route.
In feverish rays it unfolded its world,
The green earth grew greener as the ether glowed,
Circuitous gardens, rich halls, colonnades,
Assemblages seething in unspeaking crowds.
And many a stranger's new face I observed,
Saw sorcerous creatures, mysterious birds,
On the heights of creation, like God, I did tread,
And the world underneath me still shone, as if dead.
But like sorcerers' howling, in these reveries,
I hearkened the rumbling of unfathomed seas,
And visions and dreams, all my quiet domain
Was breached by the swells and the blasting of foam.[3]

И море, и буря качали наш челн;
Я, сонный, был предан всей прихоти волн.
Две беспредельности были во мне,
И мной своевольно играли оне.
Вкруг меня, как кимвалы, звучали скалы́,
Окликалися ветры и пели валы.
Я в хаосе звуков лежал оглушен,
Но над хаосом звуков носился мой сон.
Болезненно-яркий, волшебно-немой,
Он веял легко над гремящею тьмой.
В лучах огневицы развил он свой мир –
Земля зеленела, светился эфир,
Сады-лавиринфы, чертоги, столпы,
И сонмы кипели безмолвной толпы.
Я много узнал мне неведомых лиц,
Зрел тварей волшебных, таинственных птиц,
По высям творенья, как бог, я шагал,
И мир подо мною недвижный сиял.

Но все грезы насквозь, как волшебника вой,
Мне слышался грохот пучины морской,
И в тихую область видений и снов
Врывалася пена ревущих валов.

We are not interested here in that aspect of the poem that is connected with what is for Tyutchev an essential juxtaposition ("Thought upon thought, wave upon wave" [*Duma za dumoi, volna za volnoi*]) or the opposition ("A melody found in the waves of the sea" [*Pevuchest' est' v morskikh volnakh*]) between the life of the soul, on the one hand, and the sea, on the other.

Insofar as the text is evidently rooted in a real experience—the recollection of a four-day storm in September 1833, as he was voyaging around the Adriatic—it interests us as a monument to the author's psychological self-observation (one can hardly deny the legitimacy of such an approach to the text, among others).

The poem lays out two components of the author's spiritual state: the soundless dream and the storm's metrical roar. The latter is marked in the original by the unexpected insertion of an anapestic line into an amphibrachic text:

So like cymbals, around me, the rock cliffs did crash,
The swells singing their part, the winds answering back …
But then over the chaos of sound came my dream …
But like sorcerers' howling, in these reveries …

The anapestic lines are devoted to the rumbling of the storm, and the two symmetrical verses beginning with "but" portray the dream erupting through the storm's noise, or else the noise of the storm erupting through the dream. The verse dedicated to the philosophical theme of the "double abyss" ("infinitudes two") and connecting the text to other Tyutchev poems is set off by the sole dactyl.[iii]

The abundance of sonic features makes the noise of the storm stand out just as sharply against the backdrop of the soundless world of the dream ("magically mute," populated by "speechless crowds"). But it is precisely these metrical, deafening sounds that become the rhythmic backdrop that occasions the liberation of thought, its ascent and brilliance.

---

iii The two infinitudes or infinities in Tyutchev's poem are usually construed as a reference to the Early Modern French philosopher Blaise Pascal and refer to the infinitely small and infinitely large, which human beings are equally unable to contemplate. See Blaise Pascal, *Pensées*, par. 72.

Let us bring in another example (Alexander Pushkin's *Eugene Onegin*, chapter 8):

XXXVI
And so? While eyes continued reading,
His thoughts remained yet far away;
His dreams, desires, as well as grieving
Were crammed deep in his soul today.
Among the lines in plain print visible,
And with the spirit's eyes perceptible,
Were others. Those were what for verse
He took, now utterly immersed.
'Twas secret lore of deep tradition,
Obscure, sincere, from olden times,
And disconnected, muddled dreams,
A dread, and mumblings, premonitions,
Just living nonsense in a fairy's land
Or correspondence in girlish hand.

XXXVII
And gradual pacification
Of thoughts and feelings now holds sway,
And before him his imagination
Its motley pharaoh sets to play ...

XXXVIII
... How much when in a corner, solo,
Did he look like a poet inspired,
And sat he near the blazing fire,
And to himself hummed "Idol mio"
Or "Benedetta," while up the flue
Burned now a paper, now a shoe.
(VI, 183–184)[4]

XXXVI
И что ж? Глаза его читали,
Но мысли были далеко;
Мечты, желания, печали
Теснились в душу глубоко.

Он меж печатными строками
Читал духовными глазами
Другие строки. В них-то он
Был совершенно углублен.
То были тайные преданья
Сердечной, темной старины,
Ни с чем не связанные сны,
Угрозы, толки, предсказанья,
Иль длинной сказки вздор живой,
Иль письма девы молодой.

XXXVII
И постепенно в усыпленье
И чувств и дум впадает он,
А перед ним воображенье
Свой пестрый мечет фараон …

XXXVIII
… Как походил он на поэта,
Когда в углу сидел один,
И перед ним пылал камин,
И он мурлыкал: *Benedetta*
Иль *Idol mio* и ронял
В огонь то туфлю, то журнал.

In this instance, we have three external rhythm-forming codes: the printed text, the measured flickering of the fire, and the "humming" motif. It is quite typical that the book appears here not as communication—it is read without its content being noticed ("While eyes continued reading,/His thoughts remained yet far away")—but as something that stimulates the development of an idea. And, crucially, it stimulates not with its content, but through the mechanistic automaticity of reading. Onegin "reads without reading," just as he looks at the fire without seeing it and hums without noticing. None of these three rhythmic sequences, each perceived by different organs, has an immediate semantic relationship to what he is thinking, his imagination's game of "pharaoh."[iv] And yet they are indispensable if he is to read the "other" lines "with

iv Pharaoh, or Faro, was a betting card game of French origin widely popular in Europe and the United States in the nineteenth century.

the spirit's eyes." The external rhythm's intrusion organizes and stimulates the interior monologue.

Finally, a third example we would wish to introduce is the Japanese Buddhist monk contemplating a "rock garden."[5] Such a garden consists of a modest, gravel-strewn square with stones arranged according to a complex mathematical rhythm. Contemplating these complexly arranged pebbles is supposed to create a certain mood that fosters introspection.

* * *

Various systems of rhythmic series, from musical repetitions to repeating ornamental patterns—constructed according to clearly marked syntagmatic principles, but deprived of their own semantic content—can appear as the external codes by which the verbal message is reconstructed. For comparison, see also Yuri Knorozov's notion of a correlation between information and fascination.[6 v] In order for the system to work, however, two heterogeneous fundamentals must collide and interact: the message, in some semantic language, and the intrusion of an additional, purely syntagmatic code. Only the combination of these fundamentals gives rise to a communicative system that one might characterize as "I—I."

Thus we can regard the existence of a special channel for autocommunication as well-established. And it happens that this question has already drawn scholarly attention. We find an indication of the existence of a special language specifically designed for autocommunication in L. S. Vygotsky, who describes it as "inner speech."[vi] And here we also find an indication of its structural markers:

> The basic distinction between inner and outer speech is the absence of vocalization.
>
> Inner speech is mute, silent speech. This is its fundamental distinction. But it is in precisely this respect, meaning the gradual increase of this

v Yuri Knorozov (1922–1999) was a Soviet historian, ethnographer, and linguist, known most prominently for his ground-breaking deciphering of the Mayan script. The Russian edition has *fastsiatsiia* [fasciation], which is evidently a typo, as Knorozov proposed a theory of fascination, by which he meant the change of consciousness resulting from participation in collective rituals.

vi Lev Vygotsky was a leading Soviet psychologist of the 1920s and 1930s, who worked in sociocultural developmental psychology and focused in particular on the relationship between language and thought. His ideas about "inner speech" as a qualitatively distinct form of language use, a "conversation with the self" crucial to self-regulation and close to thinking, are laid out in his influential *Thinking and Speech* (1934).

> distinction, that egocentric speech undergoes an evolution. ... The very fact that this marker develops gradually, that egocentric speech makes itself known sooner in function and structure than in vocalization, indicates only that upon which we have based our hypothesis about how inner speech develops, namely, that inner speech develops not through the outer weakening of its vocal aspect, passing from speech to whisper and from whisper to mute speech, but through the functional and structural separation from outer speech, passing from it to the egocentric, and from egocentric to inner speech.[7]

Let us try to describe some features of the autocommunicative system.

The first marker distinguishing it from the "I—HE" system will be such language's reduction of words: they will tend to turn into signs of words, indices of signs. On this score, Wilhelm Küchelbecker has an excellent note in his fortress diary: "I have noted something strange, a curiosity for psychologists and physiologists alike: for some time I have been dreaming not of things, not of incidents, but of these wondrous sorts of abridgements that are related to them, as a hieroglyph is to a picture, as a book's table of contents is to the book itself. Does this not proceed from the paucity of things around me and of incidents that befall me?"[8]

The tendency toward reduction in "I—I" language is manifest in the shorthand that forms the basis of notes to oneself. Ultimately, the words of such notes constitute indices that one might decipher only by knowing what was written. Consider how the scholar I. Iu. Krachkovsky characterized the early script tradition of the Koran: "*Scriptio defectiva.* Absence not only of short vowels, but also of long ones, and of diacritical marks. *Can only be read if you know it by heart.*"[9]

We find a striking example of this kind of communication in *Anna Karenina,* in the famous confession scene between Kitty and Konstantin Levin, which is all the more interesting for recalling the episode of Leo Tolstoy's confession to his fiancée Sofya Bers:

> "Right," he said, and he wrote the initials *w, y, r—i, c, b—d, t, m, n, o, t?* These letters meant: *When you replied, "It cannot be," did that mean never, or then?* ...
>
> "I got it," she said, blushing.
>
> "What word is this?" he asked, pointing to the *n,* which signified *never.*
>
> "That one means *never,*" she said.[10]

In all of these examples we are dealing with a case where the reader understands the text only because he or she knows it in advance (in Tolstoy, because of the fact that Kitty and Levin are spiritually already one; the conflation of the addresser and addressee occurs before our very eyes).

Word-indices formed through such reduction tend toward isometry. Also connected with this is the fundamental peculiarity of syntax in this kind of speech: it does not form complete propositions, but moves toward infinite chains of rhythmic repeatability.

The majority of the examples we have introduced are not "I—I" communications in the pure sense, but constitute a compromise that arises because the laws governing the text deform its usual language. Accordingly, one ought to distinguish between two instances of autocommunication: one having a mnemonic function, the other not.

As an example of the first, one might turn to Pushkin's note to the final draft of his poem "Beneath the Blue Sky of One's Native Land" [Pod nebom golubym strany svoei rodnoi]:

Hear of d. 25
H of d. R. P. M. K. B.: 24.

It can be deciphered as follows:

Hear[d] of d[eath of] [Riznich] 25 [July 1826]
H[eard] of d[eath of] R[yleev], P[estel], M[uravyov], K[akhovsky], B[estuzhev]: 24 [July 1826].[11 vii]

The note serves a distinctively mnemonic function, though one ought not to forget the other as well: to a significant degree, by virtue of the sporadic connection between the signified and the signifier in the "I—I" system, it turns out to be significantly better suited to cryptography, insofar as it is constructed according to the formula of being "understood only by those who understand." As a rule, the text's secret encoding is connected to its transfer from the "I—HE" system to the "I—I" one. (Members of a collective using cryptography are regarded

vii Amaliya Riznich (1803?–1825) was a woman of striking beauty with whom Pushkin briefly conducted an affair in Odessa in 1823 during the period of his southern exile to the city. She was married to the Serbian merchant Ivan Riznich. Kondraty Ryleev, Pavel Pestel, Sergei Muravyov-Apostol, Petr Kakhovsky, and Mikhail Bestuzhev-Ryumin were the five Decembrists executed in 1826 for their participation in the uprising against the Tsar in December 1825.

in this case as a single "I," relative to which those from whom the text should be concealed compose a collective third person.) True, what occurs here, too, is clearly an unconscious act that can be explained by neither the mnemonic-memorial function of the note, nor by its nature as secret: the words in the first line are shortened into groups consisting of a few graphemes, and in the second the group is composed of single letters. Indices gravitate toward equal length and rhythm. In the first line, insofar as the preposition feels a pull to merge with the noun, two groups are formed that, in the phonological parallelism of *u* and *o* in the original Russian, on the one hand, and *l* and *m*, on the other, display not only rhythmic features, but a phonological organization as well. In the second line, the need to shorten surnames to one letter for conspiratorial reasons has established a second, internal rhythm, and all remaining words have been equally reduced. It would be strange and monstrous to suggest that Pushkin had structured this note, one that he would have found tragic, with conscious care for its rhythmic or phonological organization; the point, rather, is that the immanent and unconsciously operative laws of autocommunication display certain structural features that we commonly observe in the example of a poetic text.

These peculiarities are even more noticeable in the following example, stripped of both the mnemonic and the conspiratorial functions and presenting auto-messaging in its purest form. We are speaking here of the unconscious notes that Pushkin made in the process of reflection, quite possibly without realizing he was doing so.

On May 9, 1828, Pushkin wrote the poem "Alas! The Language of Garrulous Love" [Uvy! iazyk liubvi boltlivoi], dedicated to Anna Alexeevna Olenina, whom he was then courting. There we find the following note:

ettenna eninelo
eninelo ettenna.[12]

Beside the note: "Olenina Annette." Over "Annette," Pushkin had jotted "Pouchkine." It is not difficult to reconstruct the line of thought: Pushkin was thinking about Annette Olenina as a fiancée and wife (the note "Pouchkine"). The text presents anagrams (one reads them right-to-left) of A. A. Olenina's first and last name as he was thinking of her in French.

The note's mechanics are interesting. Initially, the name is transformed through its reverse reading into a conventional index, and then the repetition establishes a certain rhythm, while the transposition rhythmically disturbs that rhythm. The poem-like character of such a construction is obvious.

* * *

One can represent the mechanism for information transfer along the "I—I" channel as follows: a certain message is introduced in a natural language, then a certain supplemental code is introduced that constitutes a purely formal organization, one that is constructed syntagmatically in a specific way and is simultaneously either liberated completely from semantic meanings or strives toward such liberation. A tension arises between the initial message and the secondary code, fostering a tendency to interpret the text's semantic elements as having already been included within the supplemental syntagmatic construction and now receiving new—relational—meanings from their mutual correlation. However, while the secondary code strives to liberate the primarily signifying elements from the general semantic embedded in the primary code, this does not occur. The shared semantics remains, but they are overlaid with a secondary semantics formed on account of those shifts that arise out of using signifying units to construct a language of different kinds of rhythmic series. But the text's semantic transformation does not end there. The proliferation of semantic connections within the message muffles the primary semantic connections, and the text can behave, at a given level of perception, as a complexly organized, asemantic message. But highly organized, asemantic texts tend to become the organizers of our associations. We ascribe them associative meanings. Thus, in scrutinizing the pattern on the wallpaper or listening to non-program music, we ascribe specific meanings to the elements of these texts. The starker the syntagmatic organization, the more associative and free the semantic connections will become. Accordingly, the text along the "I—I" channel tends to become overgrown with individual meanings, and it begins to serve as an organizer of the scattered associations that accumulate in a given person's consciousness. It restructures the personality that has been involved in the autocommunicative process.

In this way, the text carries a threefold significance: the primary level is in the language itself; the secondary comes about on account of the text's syntagmatic reorganization and the tension among its primary units; and the third level arises from extratextual associations of varying degrees—from the most general to the extremely individual—being drawn into the message.

There is no need to prove that the mechanism we have described can simultaneously be presented as typical of the processes that form the basis of poetic creation.

The poetic principle, however, is one thing, but actual poetic texts are another. It would be an oversimplification to identify the latter with the messages being broadcast along the "I—I" channel. An actual poetic text is broadcast along two channels simultaneously (the exceptions being experimental texts, glossolalia, texts like asemantic children's school rhymes and *zaum*,[viii] as well as texts in languages their audiences do not understand). It oscillates between the meanings transmitted across the "I—HE" channel and those formed in the process of autocommunication. Depending on its movement toward one axis or the other, and on the text's orientation toward one kind of transmission or the other, it is taken to be a "poem" or "prose."

Of course, the text's orientation toward the primary linguistic message or a complex restructuring of meanings and the proliferation of information in itself does not mean that it will function as poetry or as prose: what comes into play here is the correlation with these concepts' general cultural models within a given era.

And so we can conclude that the system of human communication can be constructed in two ways. In one instance, we are dealing with certain information given in advance and traversing from one person to another, and with a code that is constant within the limits of the entire communicative act. In the other, we have an increase in information, its transformation, its reformulation, during which it is not new messages but new codes that are introduced, and the receiver and the transmitter are combined in one person. In the process of such autocommunication the individual personality is itself reformulated, and a rather broad range of cultural functions is tied to this, from the sense of your own separate being that a person needs to have in certain kinds of culture, to self-consciousness and autopsychotherapy.

The role of such codes can be played by various kinds of formal structure—the more asemantic their organization, the more successfully they serve the function of reorganizing meanings. Such are spatial objects that, like patterns or architectural assemblages, are destined to be contemplated, or temporal ones, like music.

Verbal texts present a more complex issue. Insofar as the autocommunicative nature of a transmission can be masked by its assuming the forms of other aspects of communication (for example, a prayer can be perceived as a

---

viii *Zaum*, often translated as transrational language, is an invented language, often based on deformations of an existing language on the phonetic and morphological levels. Although deployed as an artistic device first by Russian Futurist poets Velimir Khlebnikov and Alexey Kruchenykh, elements of it can be discerned in folklore and religious glossolalia. See Gerald Janecek, *Zaum: The Transrational Poetry of Russian Futurism* (San Diego: San Diego State University Press, 1996).

communication not with oneself, but with an external, almighty power; a repeat reading, the reading of a text that is already familiar—by analogy with the first reading—as a communication with the author, and so on), the addressee who is receiving the verbal text must decide what it is that has been transmitted to him—a code or a message. Here, to a significant degree, it will be a question of the receiver's frame of mind, insofar as one and the same text can serve as message or code or, oscillating between these poles, one and the other simultaneously.

Here one ought to distinguish between two facets—the properties of the text that allow it to be interpreted as a code, and how the text functions, which allows it to be used in this way.

In the first case, the need to receive the text not as a usual message but as some coded model is marked by the formation of rhythmic series, of repetitions, by the appearance of supplemental patterns that are completely superfluous from the point of view of communication within the "I—HE" system. Rhythm is not a structural level in the construction of natural languages. It is no accident that while the poetic functions of phonology, grammar, and syntax find their bases and analogues in corresponding, non-artistic levels of the text, one can point to no such parallel for meter.

The rhythmic-metrical systems are transferred not from the "I—HE" communicative structure, but from the "I—I." The projection of the principle of repetition into the phonological and other levels of natural language constitutes autocommunication's aggression toward any linguistic sphere that is alien to it.[ix]

Functionally, whenever it adds no new information to what we already have and transforms the self-awareness of the individual who generates texts and transfers messages already in hand to a new system of meanings, the text is used not as a message but as a code. If Reader N is informed that a certain woman named Anna Karenina has thrown herself in front of a train because of a tragic love affair, and instead of attaching that message to those she already has in her memory she concludes, "Anna Karenina—that's me," and she reconsiders

---

ix Lotman builds here on Roman Jakobson's famous definition of the "poetic function" as "the projection of the principle of equivalence from the axis of selection to the axis of combination," that is, the imposition of a pattern of recurrences on the unfolding of the text (R. Jakobson, "Linguistics and Poetics," *Language in Literature*, ed. Krystyna Pomorska and Stephen Rudy [Cambridge, MA: Harvard University Press, 1987], 62–94). However, from the sphere of rhetoric Lotman expands the significance of this device to that of an anthropological constant, constitutive of a particular form of communication intrinsic to all human communicative systems and available to all cultures.

her own understanding of herself, her relationships with others, and sometimes even her own behavior, then it is obvious that she is using the text of the novel not as a message like any other, but as a kind of code within the process of communicating with herself.[x]

This is precisely how Pushkin's Tatyana reads novels:[xi]

X
Imagining each heroine
Of her own most belovèd authors,
Clarissa, Julie, and Delphine,
Tatyana silent forests wanders,
In hand a risky volume caught,
In which she finds, there having sought,
Her secret ardor, reveries,
The fullest fruits of heartfelt dreams,
She sighs to make of stranger's sorrow,
Of stranger's rapture, her own plight,
And in absent whisper she recites
A letter to a tender hero ...
Our hero, though, a man such as he
A Grandison could never be. (VI, 55)

X
Воображаясь героиней
Своих возлюбленных творцов,
Кларисой, Юлией, Дельфиной,
Татьяна в тишине лесов
Одна с опасной книгой бродит,
Она в ней ищет и находит

x The ability of any message to become a code is crucial to Lotman's rethinking of the Saussurean *langue–parole* dichotomy. This ability is predicated on activating the syntagmatic patterns inherent in the message, so that it becomes a model that informs the production of other messages.

xi Refers to chapter 3 of Pushkin's novel in verse *Eugene Onegin*. The novel recounts the unhappy relationship between Eugene Onegin and Tatyana Larina. Vladimir Lensky, mentioned further down, is likewise a protagonist of the novel, Onegin's friend and a card-carrying Romantic poet, who ends up being killed by Onegin in an unnecessary duel over a trivial matter.

Свой тайный жар, свои мечты,
Плоды сердечной полноты,
Вздыхает и, себе присвоя
Чужой восторг, чужую грусть,
В забвенье шепчет наизусть
Письмо для милого героя …
Но наш герой, кто б ни был он,
Уж верно был не Грандисон.

The text of the novel she has read becomes a model for rethinking reality. Tatyana has no doubt that Onegin is a novelistic character; what is not clear to her is which type she ought to identify him with:

What are you, angel my protector,
Or else perfidious seducer … (6, LXVII)

Кто ты, мой ангел ли хранитель,
Или коварный искуситель …

In Tatyana's letter to Onegin, it is characteristic that the text splits into two parts: in the frame (the first two stanzas and the last), where Tatyana writes as a lady in love with the lord of the neighboring estate, she naturally addresses him formally, but the middle portion, where she models both him and herself against novelistic schemata, is written in the informal. Given that the letter had originally been written, as Pushkin has advised us, in French, where in both cases one would only use the pronoun *vous*, the form of address in the letter's central passage is merely a sign of the bookish, non-experiential—coded—nature of the given text.

It is interesting that Lensky, a Romantic, likewise explains people (including himself) to himself by identifying them with certain texts. Here, too, Pushkin makes demonstrative use of the same set of clichés: "savior" (= "protector"), "tempter" (= "seducer"):

He thinks: For her I'll be a savior.
I will not suffer that some tempter … (6, CXXIII)

Он мыслит: «Буду ей спаситель.
Не потерплю, чтоб развратитель …»

It is obvious that in all these instances the texts function not as messages in a given language (not for Pushkin, but for Tatyana and Lensky), but as codes that incorporate information about what kind of language they are.

We have been borrowing examples from artistic literature, but it would be erroneous to conclude from this that poetry constitutes a pure form of communication within the "I—I" system. This principle is applied in a more consistent form not in art, but in moralistic and religious texts like parables, in myths, in proverbs. It is characteristic that repetitions penetrated proverbs well before they were treated chiefly in an aesthetic way and still served a much more substantial mnemonic or moral-normative function.

Repetitions of specific constructive (architectural) elements in a temple interior compel us to perceive its structure as something not bound to practical, constructive, technical needs, but, we might say, as a model of the universe or of human individuality. It is precisely because the temple interior in this case is a code, and not just a text, that it is perceived not only aesthetically (only a text, and not the rules of its construction, can be perceived aesthetically), but religiously, philosophically, theologically, or in some other, non-artistic way.

Art arises not among texts of the "I—HE" system or the "I—I" system. It uses both communicative systems in oscillating across the structural tension between them. The aesthetic effect arises at the moment when the code starts to be used as a message, and the message as a code, that is, when the text switches from one communicative system to the other while preserving the connection between them in the audience's consciousness.

The nature of artistic texts, as a variable phenomenon connected to both kinds of communication, does not exclude the fact that separate genres are oriented to a greater or lesser degree toward the reception of texts as messages or codes. Of course, the lyric poem and the sketch do not correspond equally to one system of communication or the other. Besides the orientations of genres, however, at specific moments, due to historical, social, or other causes of an epochal nature, one literature or another (or, more broadly, art as a whole) can be wholly characterized as an orientation toward autocommunication. It is evident that a negative attitude toward the text/cliché will be a good working criterion for a literature's general orientation toward the message. Literature oriented toward autocommunication will not only not avoid clichés, but will display a gravitation toward transforming texts into clichés and identifying the "high," "good," and "true" with the "stable," the "eternal"—that is, with cliché.

And yet moving away from one pole (and even consciously polemicizing with it) in no way means casting off its structural influence. No matter how much the literary work imitates the text of a newspaper report, it retains, for example, so typical a feature of autocommunicative texts as the multiple repeatability of its reading. Rereading *War and Peace* is a significantly more natural activity than rereading the historical sources that Tolstoy used. At the same time, no matter how the artistic text strives, for polemical or experimental reasons, no longer to be a message, this is impossible, as the whole experience of art convinces us.

Poetic texts are apparently formed through a distinctive "swinging" between structures: texts created within the "I—HE" system function as autocommunications, and the other way around—texts become codes, and codes become messages. Obeying the laws of autocommunication—the separation of the text into rhythmic segments, the reduction of words to indices, the weakening of semantic connections while underscoring the syntagmatic ones—the poetic text comes into conflict with the laws of natural language. And yet, without being perceived as a text in natural language, poetry could not exist and fulfill its communicative function. But if one were to view poetry as nothing more than a message in natural language, its specificity would be lost. Poetry's high capacity for modeling behavior is connected to its transformation from message to code. The poetic text swings like a peculiar pendulum between the "I—HE" system and the "I—I" system. Rhythm is elevated to the level of meaning, and meanings fall into a rhythm.

To a considerable degree, the laws for the construction of the artistic text come down to those for constructing culture as a whole. This has to do with the fact that culture itself can be regarded as the sum of messages exchanged among various addressers (each of whom, to an addressee, is the "other," "he"), and as the single message that the collective "I" of humanity is sending to itself. From this perspective, the culture of humanity is a colossal example of autocommunication.

* * *

Transmitting simultaneously along two communicative channels doesn't belong to artistic texts alone. It is a typical feature of culture, if one treats it as a single message. In this regard, one can single out the cultures where the dominant message will be the one transmitted along the general "I—HE" channel and those aiming toward autocommunication.

Insofar as a wide swath of the information that does in fact make up the specifics of a given personality can serve as "message 1," restructuring that information leads to a change in the structure of the personality. One ought to mention that if the "I—HE" communicative scheme implies a *transmission* of information while maintaining its constant capacity, then the "I—I" scheme is aimed at *increasing* information (the appearance of "message 2" does not destroy "message 1").

In modern times, European culture has been consciously oriented toward the "I—HE" system. The consumer of culture finds himself in the position of ideal addressee; he receives information from outside. Peter the Great formulated such an attitude quite precisely when he said, "I am at the rank of those who are taught, so I demand teachers." *The Honest Mirror of Youth*[xii] prescribes young people to approach education as receiving knowledge, "... wishing to learn from everything, and looking not in cursory fashion. ..."[13] We are talking here precisely of orientation, insofar as on the level of textual reality any culture is composed of both aspects of communication. Besides, the feature I have noted is not peculiar to culture in modern times; one can find it in various forms in different eras. Emphasizing the European culture of the eighteenth and nineteenth centuries is necessary because it has conditioned our customary scientific assumptions, specifically, our identifying information as an act, with reception, with exchange. Still, it is hardly the case that every phenomenon in the history of culture can be explained from these positions.

Let us consider the paradoxical position we find ourselves in when studying folklore. We know that it is precisely folklore that offers the greatest bases for structural parallels with natural languages, and that it is precisely in folklore that applying linguistic methods has met with the greatest success. Indeed, here the researcher can observe a limited number of systemic elements and of easily articulated rules for combining them. Yet there is also a profound difference: language provides a formal system of expression, but the realm of content remains, as far as concerns language as such, extremely free. Folklore, especially in such forms as the fairytale, automatizes both spheres to an extreme. But such a circumstance is paradoxical. If the text were truly constructed in such a way, it would be completely redundant. One could say the exact same thing, too, of other artistic modes oriented toward canonical forms, toward the implementation, and not the violation, of norms and rules.

The answer apparently consists in the fact that if these kinds of texts possessed a particular semantics at the instant of their conception (the semantics of the fairytale was apparently tied to its relationship with ritual), then these connections were subsequently lost, and texts started to acquire the features of

xii *The Honest Mirror of Youth* (1717) is an etiquette book prepared by an unknown author under instruction from Peter I.

purely syntagmatic organizations. If, at the level of natural language, they indisputably possess a semantics, then as manifestations of culture they gravitate toward the purely syntagmatic, that is, the texts become instances of "code 2." This tendency of myth to transform into a purely syntagmatic, asemantic text, not a message about certain events, but the scheme by which the message is organized, is what Claude Lévi-Straus had in mind when he spoke of its musical nature.

For culture to exist as a mechanism that assembles a collective personality with a shared memory and collective consciousness, it apparently demands the availability of paired semiotic systems, with the later potential for the texts' subsequent translation.

This is the kind of structural pair that takes shape in "I—HE" and "I—I" communicative systems (we must note parenthetically that the rule that one part of any culture-formative semiotic pair be presented in natural language or contain natural language appears to be the law, one that, it seems, we can take for a universal feature of culture on earth).

Actual cultures, like artistic texts, are constructed according to a principle of a pendular swinging between these systems. Yet the orientation of one or another kind of culture toward either autocommunication or receiving the truth from outside in the form of a message becomes a dominant tendency. The orientation is especially pronounced in the mythological image that every culture creates as its own ideal self-portrait. This model of oneself has an impact on cultural texts, but it cannot be conflated with them, as it is sometimes the generalization of structural principles hidden behind textual contradictions and sometimes a representation of their direct opposition. (In the realm of cultural typology, it is possible for a grammar to emerge that essentially does not apply to texts in the language it pretends to describe.)

Cultures focused on messages have a more mobile, dynamic nature. They tend to multiply the number of texts infinitely and provide for a rapid increase in knowledge. The classic example might be European culture of the nineteenth century. The reverse side of this kind of culture is the society's sharp split into transmitters and receivers, the appearance of a psychological predisposition to receive the truth in the form of a readymade message about someone else's mental effort, and the rise in social passivity among those who find themselves in the position of the message's recipients. It is obvious that the reader of the European novel in the modern era is more passive than he who listens to a fairytale, who is still faced with having to transform the clichés he has received into the texts of his own consciousness, just as one who visits the theater is more passive than one taking part in the carnival. The tendency toward mental consumerism constitutes the precarious side of a culture focused unilaterally on receiving information from outside.

Cultures focused on autocommunication are capable of developing great spiritual activity, yet they frequently turn out to be significantly less dynamic than the needs of human society demand.

Historical experience shows us that the systems that turn out to be most vigorous are those in which the struggle between these structures does not lead to the unconditional victory of one over the other.

At present, however, we are still quite far from the possibility of providing anything like a sound forecast of which cultural structures are optimal. Before that day comes, we must still understand and describe their mechanisms, if only in their most typical manifestations.

SEMIOTIC SPACE

Translated from Iu. M. Lotman, "Semioticheskoe prostranstvo," in Semiosfera, *250–256. Lotman first proposed the concept of the semiosphere in an article published in* Sign System Studies [Trudy po znakovym sistemam] *in 1984. The flexibility of this model, in the way it pits highly structured metalanguages produced from the center against displacements, disruptions, and recodings from the peripheries, can be highly productive, and the model has been used extensively. It presumes a degree of semiotic fluidity that renders justice to the complex ways in which communication circulates within a society. However, it may be less applicable to such cases, where the semiotic traffic is between plural centers, or directly between peripheries, however construed. Ultimately, the dialectic of center and periphery remains dependent on a monocentric view of communication. This has the advantage of implicitly incorporating a consideration of the semiotic ways in which political and social power are manifest in society, but it risks eclipsing communications that elude this dialectic. On Lotman's concentric view of culture, see also Semenenko,* The Texture of Culture, *51–54.*

Our discussions up to this point have been constructed according to a standard scheme: first we have the discrete, isolated communicative act, and then we examine the relationship between addresser and addressee that arises from it. This approach assumes that studying an isolated fact reveals all the basic features of semiosis that can then be extrapolated into more complex semiotic processes. Such an approach satisfies the famous third rule from Descartes's

Discourse on Method, "to adhere to a certain order of thought, beginning with the simplest and most easily recognized of objects and proceeding gradually to know the more complex. ..."[1]

In addition, this speaks to the scientific habit, a product of the Enlightenment, of performing a Robinsonade: singling out an isolated object and later imparting the significance of the general model to it.[i]

However, in order for such singling out to be appropriate, it is necessary that the isolated fact allow us to model all the properties of the phenomenon to which conclusions will be extrapolated. This cannot be said of this instance. A setup consisting of an addresser, addressee, and the sole channel connecting them will not yet work. For that, it should be immersed in semiotic space. All those who participate in communication should already have some kind of experience, some practice at semiosis. In this way, paradoxically, semiotic experience should precede any semiotic act. Were we to zero in on the semiosphere through an analogy with the biosphere (Vladimir Vernadsky's concept), it would become obvious that this semiotic space is not the sum of separate languages but rather consists of the condition for their existence and operation and, in a certain respect, precedes them and constantly interacts with them.[ii] In this respect, language is a function, a concentration of semiotic space, and the boundaries between them, however stark in the language's grammatical self-description, appear in semiotic reality as blurry and replete with transitional forms. There is neither communication, nor language, outside of the semiosphere. Of course, a single-channel structure also exists in reality. A self-sufficient, single-channel system is an acceptable mechanism for transmitting exceedingly simple signals and, in general, for actualizing the first function, but it is decisively inadequate to the task of generating information. It is no accident that we can view such a system as an artificial construct, but under natural conditions working systems of a completely different kind emerge. The

---

i Reference is to Daniel Defoe's novel *Robinson Crusoe*, the prototype and model of the desert island story.

ii Vladimir Vernadsky (1863–1945) was a Russo-Ukrainian and Soviet geochemist, known primarily for his concept of the biosphere, which can be understood as a global ecosystem, internally organized and constant. The biosphere contains the totality of living organisms in their interrelations and mutual dependence and conditioning. The concept of the biosphere goes back to Jean-Baptiste Lamarck in *Hydrogeology* (1802), but Vernadsky gave it new prominence and meaning. This concept is attractive to Lotman as it emphasizes not only the totality of living matter, but the unceasing transformations undergone by its many elements, while featuring a degree of self-organization and remaining constant to itself. Furthermore, it operates according to mechanisms that, in principle, can be described.

very fact that the dualism of arbitrary and figurative signs (or, more precisely, of arbitrariness and figuration, which are present to varying degrees in these signs or others) is universal in human culture can be regarded as a clear example of how semiotic dualism is the minimal organizational form of a working semiotic system.

Binarity and *asymmetry* are the obligatory laws for constructing a real semiotic system. Binarity, however, ought to be understood as a principle that is actualized as multiplicity, insofar as every newly formed language is fragmented binarily in turn. All living culture has a "built-in" mechanism for multiplying its languages (we will see later that in parallel there is a mechanism of unifying languages that works in the other direction). Thus, for example, we are constantly witness to a proliferation in the languages of art. This is especially noticeable in the culture of the twentieth century and in past cultures to which it is typologically comparable. Under conditions where basic creative activity shifts into the audience's camp, the following slogan becomes operative: art is anything that we take for art. At the beginning of the twentieth century, cinema turned from a fairground amusement into high art. It was not alone, but was accompanied by a whole cortege of traditional and newly invented spectacles. Back in the nineteenth century, no one would have considered the circus, the spectacles of the fairground, folk toys, signboards, or the shouts of street merchants as artforms. Once it became art, filmmaking immediately split into narrative and documentary, live-action and animated, each having its own poetics. And in the present time yet another opposition has been added: cinema versus television. True, at the same time as the range of languages of the arts has been expanding there has also been a contraction: certain arts are almost dropping out of the active repertoire—so much so that one ought not be surprised if a more thorough study were to discover that the diversity of semiotic means within one or another culture remains relatively constant. But the essential thing is that the composition of languages entering into the active cultural field is continually changing, and what is subject to even greater changes is the axiological appraisal and hierarchical position of the elements entering that field.

At the same time, in the entire space of semiosis—from social, age-specific, and other jargons, to fashion—there is also a continuous renewal of codes. In this way, any discrete language turns out to be immersed in some semiotic space, and it is only by virtue of its interaction with this space that it is able to function. We ought to regard as an indivisible working mechanism—a unit of semiosis—not the discrete language, but the entire semiotic space inherent to a given culture. It is this space that we define as the *semiosphere*.

Such a designation is justified, insofar as, like the biosphere—which is, on the one hand, the aggregate and the organic unity of living matter (as defined by Vladimir Vernadsky, who introduced this concept), and on the other the condition for the continued existence of life—the semiosphere is both the result of and condition for the development of culture.

Vladimir Vernadsky wrote that all "concentrations of life are intimately connected. One cannot exist without the other. This connection between different living strata and concentrations, as well as their unchanging nature, are the perennial feature of the mechanism of the earth's crust, manifest within it across all geological eras."[2]

This notion is expressed with particular specificity in the following formula: "… the biosphere has a quite specific structure, one that defines *everything occurring within it, without exception.* … Man, as he is observed in nature, is, like all living organisms, a specific *function of the biosphere* within its specific space–time."[3]

As early as his notes from 1892, Vernadsky pointed to man's (mankind's) intellectual activity as an extension of the cosmic conflict between life and inert matter:

> … the lawlike nature of conscious labor in national life has led many to deny individual influence in history, though in essence we see throughout history the continuous struggle of the conscious (that is, "not natural") ways of life against the unconscious order of nature's dead laws, and within this exertion of consciousness is the entire beauty of historical manifestations, their original place among all other natural processes. One can use this exertion of consciousness to appraise the historical era.[4]

The semiosphere is distinguished by its *nonuniformity.* The languages that fill semiotic space are diverse by nature and related to each other along a spectrum from complete mutual translatability to equally complete mutual non-translatability. The nonuniformity is shaped by the languages' heterogeneity and heterofunctionality. In this way, if we, as a thought experiment, were to picture a model of semiotic space in which all the languages appear at the very same moment and are compelled by identical impulses, we would still be faced not with one coding structure, but by some plurality of connected, yet diverse, systems. Let's say, for example, that we build a model of the semiotic structure of European Romanticism, arbitrarily delineating its chronological boundaries. Even within such a space, which is completely artificial, we will not achieve uniformity, insofar as a different measure of iconism will inevitably create a situation of notional correspondence rather than of mutually unambiguous semantic translatability. Of course, Denis Davydov, the poet-partisan of 1812, could compare the tactics of partisan warfare to Romantic poetry when he demanded that as leader of a partisan detachment one should appoint "not a *methodist* of calculating mind and cold spirit. ... This walk of life, imbued with poetry, demands a Romantic imagination, a passion for adventure, and this is not supplied by dry, prosaic daring. It's a stanza from Byron!"[5]

However, one need only look at his historical-tactical study *Toward a Theory of Partisan Action* [*Opyt teorii partizanskogo deistviia*], which is full of plans and maps, to be convinced that this beautiful metaphor speaks only to the conjoining of the incommensurate within this Romantic's contradictory consciousness. The fact that the unity of diverse languages is established through a metaphor speaks better than anything else to their fundamental difference.

But one must also account for the fact that different languages possess varying periods of circulation: clothing fashion changes with a rapidity incomparable to the rate of change in the manifestations of literary language, and Romanticism in dance is not synchronous with Romanticism in architecture. In this way, at the same time as some segments of the semiosphere will be experiencing the poetics of Romanticism, others might already be moving toward post-Romanticism. Accordingly, even this artificial model will not provide a homologous picture in a strictly synchronous cross-section. It is no accident that when people endeavor to provide a synthetic picture of Romanticism that characterizes all the forms of art (and at times adding still other spheres of culture), chronology is decisively sacrificed. The same applies to the Baroque, Classicism, and many other "isms."

If, however, we were to speak not of artificial models, but of the modeling of a real literary (or, more broadly, cultural) process, then we will have to admit that—continuing with our example—Romanticism encompasses only a certain segment of the semiosphere, wherein diverse traditional structures, which at times reach deep into antiquity, continue to exist. Beyond that, none of these stages of development is free from collision with texts that enter from outside, from cultures generally situated up to that point beyond the horizon of a given semiospshere. These incursions—sometimes individual texts, sometimes whole strata of culture—exert diverse disturbing influences on the internal order of a given culture's "world picture." In this way, in any synchronous cross-section of the semiosphere we see a tension among various languages, various stages of their development, some texts turn out to be submerged in languages that are inappropriate to them, and the codes that would decipher them may be quite absent. Let's imagine, as a kind of uniform world caught in a synchronic cross-section, a museum hall where exhibits for different eras are displayed in different windows, and there are captions in familiar and unfamiliar languages, instructions on how to decipher them, explanatory notes to the exhibition formulated by pedagogues, diagrams for walking tours and the regulations for visitor conduct. Let's go on to furnish this hall with guides and visitors, and let's picture all of this as a unified mechanism (which is what, *in a certain respect*, it is). We will have an image of a semiosphere. In doing this, one ought not to lose sight of the fact that every element of a semiosphere is not static, but in fluid, dynamic correlation, constantly changing the formulae of their mutual relations. This is especially noticeable in traditional instances drawn from the culture's earlier manifestations. The evolution of culture differs radically from biological evolution, and here the word "evolution" often performs a poor, misleading service.[iii]

Evolutionary development in biology has to do with the extinction of species rejected by natural selection. Only that which is synchronic with the researcher is alive. Somewhat analogous is the situation of technological history, where the instrument that technological progress has pushed out of use finds refuge only in the museum. It is transformed into a dead exhibit. In the history of art, works related to a culture's long-past epochs continue to take an active part as living factors in its development. The work of art can "die" and be reborn; having grown obsolete, it can be made contemporary or even prophetically indicative of the future. What is "operative" here is not the last temporal cross-section, but the whole depth of the culture's texts. The model of the history of literature built according to the evolutionary principle was created under the influence of concepts from the natural sciences. Consequently, what is considered to be the synchronic state of literature in any given year is the roster of works *written* in that year. Meanwhile, if one were to draw up lists of what *had been read* in that year or another, the picture would likely be different. And it is difficult to say which of the lists would most characterize the culture's synchronic condition. Thus, for Pushkin in 1824 and 1825, the most current writer was Shakespeare, Bulgakov experienced Gogol and Cervantes as writers contemporaneous with himself, and Dostoevsky seems no less current at the end of the twentieth century than he did at the end of the nineteenth. In effect,

iii Lotman considers different modes of cultural evolution in greater detail in the sections from *Culture and Explosion* translated in this volume.

everything contained in the current memory of a culture partakes, directly or indirectly, of its synchrony.

The semiosphere's structure is asymmetrical. This is expressed in the directional system of internal translations permeating the whole depth of the semiosphere. Translation is the fundamental mechanism of consciousness. The expression of some essence by means of another language is the basis by which the nature of this essence is revealed. And insofar as the various languages of the semiosphere are semiotically asymmetrical in the majority of cases—that is, they do not possess mutually unambiguous signifying correspondences—the entire semiosphere can be regarded in its totality as an information-generator.

The asymmetry manifests itself in the relation between the semiosphere's center and its periphery. The languages that show the most development and structural organization constitute the center of the semiosphere. First and foremost, this includes the given culture's natural language. One can say that if no one language (the natural language among them) can function, not being immersed in a semiosphere, then no semiosphere, as Émile Benveniste has noted, can exist without a natural language as its organizing core. The point is that alongside structurally organized languages, in the space of the semiosphere specialized languages are jostling for position, languages capable of serving only discrete cultural functions and quasi-lingual, half-shaped formations that can be carriers of semiosis if they are inserted into a semiotic context. This can be compared to the fact that a stone or fancifully twisted tree trunk can function as a work of art. The object assumes the function that is ascribed to it.

In order to perceive the whole mass of these constructions as carriers of semiotic meaning, one must hold "the presumption of semioticity": the potential of meaningful structures should be a given in one's consciousness and in the semiotic intuition of the collective. These qualities are produced through the use of natural language. Thus, for example, it appears obvious that, in some cases, the structure of the "family of gods" or other basic elements of a world picture depends on the language's grammatical composition.

The highest form of structural organization of a semiotic system is the self-descriptive phase. The very process of description is the ultimate level of structural organization. The creation of grammars, much like the codification of customs or of juridical norms, raises the descriptive object to a new level of organization. That is why a system's self-description is the last stage in the process of its self-organization. Meanwhile, the system gains in its level of structural orderliness, but it loses the inner stores of indeterminacy to which its flexibility, its ability to increase its informational capacity, and the reserve of its dynamic development are bound.

The need for a self-descriptive stage is connected to the threat of excessive diversity within the semiosphere: the system can lose its unity and distinctiveness and can "fray." Whether we are talking about linguistic, political, or cultural aspects, we are facing analogous mechanisms in all cases: some one segment of the semiosphere (as a rule, one that falls within its core structure) creates its own grammar in the course of its self-description—real or ideal, this depends on the description's inner orientation toward the present or the future. Next, attempts are made to extend these norms across the entire semiosphere. The local grammar of a single cultural dialect becomes the metalanguage for the description of culture as such. Thus, during the Renaissance, the Florentine dialect is made into the literary language of Italy, the juridical norms of Rome into the laws of the entire Empire, and court etiquette in the era of Louis XIV into the court etiquette for all of Europe. There arises a literature of norms and prescriptions in which the later historian sees the real portrait of actual life in this era or another, its semiotic praxis. This illusion is supported by the testimonies of contemporaries, who are actually convinced that this is precisely how they conduct themselves. The contemporary argues roughly as follows: "I am a person of culture (meaning, an Athenian, a Roman, a Christian, a knight, an *esprit fort,* an Enlightenment philosopher, or a Romantic genius). As a person of culture I enact the behavior that is prescribed by such-and-such norms. It is only that portion of my behavior that corresponds with those norms that one can consider an *action.* Yet if I, out of weakness, illness, inconsistency, or other reasons somehow deviate from the given norms, it is meaningless, irrelevant, it simply *does not exist.*" The list of what "does not exist" in a given system of culture, despite its happening in praxis, is always an essential typological feature of the accepted semiotic system. Thus, for example, the famous Andreas Capellanus, author of *De Amore* (between 1175 and 1186), a tractate about the norms of *fin'amor,* in subjecting courtly love to thorough codification and demanding of the lover faithfulness toward his lady, silence, attentive *servir,* chastity, chivalry, and so forth, blithely permits violence towards a female peasant, since in this world picture she is "as if nonexistent"; what is done to her stands outside of semiotics—that is, it is "as if it never happened."

The world picture created in such a way will be perceived by contemporaries as reality. What is more, it will even *be* their reality, inasmuch as they have accepted the laws of the given semiotics. But subsequent generations (including scholars), reconstructing life according to texts, will adopt the notion that this is also precisely how lived reality had been. And yet, how such a metaplasm of the semiosphere relates to the real picture of its semiotic "map," on the one hand, and the lived everyday reality that lies beyond semiotics, on the other, will be rather complex. First, if, in the core structure where the given self-description has been created, it has actually presented an idealization of some real language, then on the semiosphere's periphery the ideal norm has contradicted the semiotic reality located "underneath it"; it has not emerged from it. If the texts' self-description has engendered norms at the center of the semiosphere, then on the periphery the norms, actively invading the "incorrect" praxis, have engendered "correct" texts that correspond to them. Second, whole strata of cultural formations that are marginal from the perspective of a given metastructure are in no way correlated with the culture's idealized portrait. They have been declared "nonexistent." Beginning with the works of the cultural-historical school, a favorite genre of many scholars has been articles with titles like "An Unknown Poet of the Twelfth Century" or "Another Forgotten Author of the Enlightenment," and so on. Where does this unlimited store of the "unknowns" and the "forgotten" come from? These are the ones who in their own era had slipped in among the "nonexistent" and were ignored by science, since its point of view had fallen in line with the normative views of the era. But points of view shift—and the "unknowns" are suddenly revealed. People remember that the "unknown philosopher" Louis Claude de Saint-Martin was already thirty-five in the year that Voltaire died; that Nicolas-Edme Rétif[iv] wrote over 200 volumes that continue to stump historians of literature when they call their author now "a minor Rousseau," now "the Balzac of the eighteenth century"; that during the Romantic era in Russia there lived a Vasily Narezhny, who wrote about two dozen novels that went "unnoticed" by his contemporaries, since they already displayed features of Realism.

In this way, a picture of semiotic unification is created on the meta-level, while a diversity of tendencies seethes on the level of the semiotic "reality" it is describing. If the map of the surface layer is painted a uniformly even color, the bottom layer is brightly mottled and has a multitude of intersecting boundaries. When, at the close of the eighth century, Charlemagne raised the cross and sword to the Saxons, and St. Vladimir baptized Kievan Rus a century later, the great barbarian empires of the West and the East turned into Christian states.

iv Also known as Nicolas Rétif de la Bretonne (1734–1806), an extremely prolific writer, author, among other genres, of a fourteen-volume autobiography *Mr Nicolas, or the human heart exposed* [*Monsieur Nicolas, ou Le coeur humain dévoilé*].

Their Christianity, however, suited their self-characterization and was situated on a political and religious meta-level, with language traditions and diverse everyday compromises seething beneath it. It could not have been otherwise under the conditions of mass and, at times, forced baptism. The horrifying massacre that Charlemagne inflicted upon the captive pagan Saxons at Verden could hardly foster the propagation of the principles of the Sermon on the Mount among the barbarians.[v]

And yet it would be wrong to suggest that even a simple change of self-identification held no sway on "lower" levels, that it didn't foster a transformation of Christianization into Evangelism, that it didn't unify the cultural space of these states, now at the level of "real semiotics." In this way, currents of meaning flow not only along the horizontal layers of the semiosphere, but also act along the vertical, forming complex dialogues among its various layers.

Yet the unity of the semiosphere's semiotic space is achieved not only through metastructural constructions, but, even to a significantly greater degree, through the unity of the relation to the boundary that divides the semiosphere's inner space from the outer, its *in* from its *out*.

THE IDEA OF BOUNDARY

Translated from Iu. M. Lotman, "Poniatie granitsy," in Semiosfera, *257–268. The notion of the boundary as a site of semiotic translation, rather than obstruction, offers interesting extensions. It bears, of course, on the emergent field of Boundary Studies, which incorporates the study of border areas, but it also applies more broadly to approaches that aim to conceptualize the contact between cultures and the transfer of ideas and values across their borders, such as Transfer Studies, Transnational History, or Histoire croisée. For a good overview and critical discussion of these various approaches, see Sebastian Conrad,* What is Global History *(Princeton: Princeton University Press, 2016). In its emphasis on the transformations that occur in the act of translation, Lotman's expansive understanding of translation resonates with current debates in Translation Studies and Cultural Anthropology about cultural translation. See, for example, Emily Apter,* The Translation Zone: A New Comparative Literature *(Princeton: Princeton University Press, 2006).*

v The massacre of some 4500 Saxons, ordered by Charlemagne as a response to an attempted rebellion against the occupying Franks, took place in 782. It is attested in the Royal Frankish Annals, as well as in other annals. The insurrection arose in the context of Charlemagne's attempts to Christianize the Saxons, which included destroying their devotional objects, such as the Irminsul, a sacred pillar.

The semiosphere's inner space is, in a paradoxical way, simultaneously both uneven, asymmetrical, and unified, uniform. Consisting of structures in conflict, it possesses an individuality as well. This space's self-description implies a first-person pronoun. One of the basic mechanisms of semiotic individuality is the boundary. And one can define this boundary as the feature where periodic form ends. This space is defined as "ours," "one's own," "cultural," "safe," "harmoniously organized," and so forth. It is opposed by that which is "their space," "foreign," "enemy," "dangerous," "chaotic."

Any culture begins by dividing the world into inner ("one's own") and outer ("their") space. How this binary separation is interpreted depends on the culture's typology. Such division itself, however, belongs to universals. The boundary can separate the living from the dead, the settled from the nomadic, the city from the steppe, it can have a governmental, social, national, confessional, or some other character. It is striking how unconnected civilizations find convergent expressions for characterizing the world beyond the boundary. This is how a Kievan monastic chronicler in the eleventh century described the lives of other, still-pagan East Slavic tribes:

> ... the Drevlyans live in a beastly manner, living brutishly: they kill one another, they eat all in filth, and hold no wedding, but abduct maidens by the water. And the Radimichi, and the Vyatichi, and the Northerns all keep the same custom: they live in the forest like any beast, they eat everything in filth, and speak foul before their fathers and before their daughters-in-law, and there are no wedding feasts among them, but festivities between the villages, they get together for festivities, dancing, and all manner of demonic songs. ...[1]

And here is how, in the eighth century, a Frankish chronicler—a Christian—described the mores of the pagan Saxons: "Vicious by nature, devoted to a demonic cult, enemies of our religion, they respect the laws neither of men, nor of God, what is not permitted they permit themselves."[2]

These last words offer a clear expression of how "our" world and "theirs" mirror each other: what is not permitted to us, is permitted to them.

Any existence is possible only in the forms of a given spatial and temporal concreteness. Human history is only a particular instance of this law. A person is immersed in the real, the space that nature has given him. The constants of the earth's rotation (the sun's movement across the sky), of the movement of the stars in the heavens, of nature's transitory cycles—these have an immediate influence on how someone models the world within his own consciousness. No less important are the physical constants of the human body that assign predetermined relations to the world around it. The dimensions of the human body determine the fact that the world of mechanics, of its laws, appears to a person as "natural," whereas he imagines the world of elementary particles or cosmic spaces only in the abstract, having first committed a certain violence against his own consciousness. The correlation between a person's average weight, the force of earth's gravity, and the body's vertical posture has brought about the opposition of high and low that is universal in all human cultures, with a wide range of substantive interpretations (religious, social, political, moral, or others). One may doubt whether the expression "he reached the summit," which people understand regardless of culture, would be quite so obvious for a thinking fly or a person born in zero-gravity.[i]

"High," "the summit"—these require no explanation. The expression *Qui ne vole au sommet tombe au plus bas degré*[3] (Nicolas Boileau-Despréaux, *Satires*) is just as comprehensible as *La lutte elle-même vers les sommets suffit à remplir un coeur d'homme. Il faut imaginer Sisyphe heureux* (Albert Camus, *Le mythe de Sisyphe*).[4]

Despite the tremendous temporal and spatial distance between Camus and Yan Vyshatich, the commander of the military campaign against the pagans in eleventh-century Rus, they had an identical concept of the semantics of high and low. Before executing their soothsayers (shamans), Yan asked them where their god resides, and (according to the monk-chronicler) he received the following answer: "He rests in the abyss." To which Yan explained authoritatively: "What kind of god rests in an abyss? That is a demon, for God is in the heavens ..."

---

i In his emphasis on underlying unities and his overall binary framework, Lotman's universalism in these pages is close to Lévi-Strauss's structural anthropology, although Lotman advances a more dynamic (and historical) approach, one more sensitive to the variable and fluid cultural interpretations of anthropological constants. The debate in anthropology between universalism and relativism is still not settled, in particular with regard to the question of human rights. There are political pitfalls to both the reduction to universals and the fetishization of difference. The literature on this subject is vast, but for an overview of the issues, see Conrad Phillip Kottak, *Anthropology: The Exploration of Human Diversity*, 14th ed. (New York: McGraw Hill Inc., 2011). For a recent treatment, see *Against Exoticism: Toward the Transcendence of Relativism and Universalism in Anthropology*, ed. Bruce Kapferer and Dimitrios Theodossopoulos (New York: Berghahn, 2016), in particular the introduction. See also Clifford Geertz, "Distinguished Lecture: Anti Anti-Relativism," *American Anthropologists* 86, no. 2 (1984): 263–278.

This turn of phrase delighted the chronicler, and he pressed it into service, in almost the same words, in quoting a pagan priest from near Lake Peipus (Estonia): "Says he [the Novgorodian]: 'Tell me, then, where do your gods live?' Says he [the sorcerer]: 'In abysses. For they are black in appearance, winged, they have tails. And they ascend skyward, obeying your gods. For your gods are in the heavens.'"[5]

The asymmetry of the human body formed the anthropological basis for its semiotization: the semiotics of *right/left* is as universal for all human cultures as the opposition of high/low. Equally primary is the asymmetry of *male/female, living/dead,* that is, moving, warm, breathing, versus immobile, cold, not breathing (the treatment of cold and death as synonyms is affirmed in an enormous number of texts in various cultures, and it is just as common to identify death with petrification, with being turned to stone: consider the numerous legends about the origins of certain mountains or cliffs).

Vladimir Vernadsky remarked that life on earth flows in a special spatial-temporal continuum that it has created for itself:

> ... it is logically appropriate to construct a new scientific hypothesis that when it comes to living matter on Planet Earth we are dealing not with a new geometry, not with one of Riemann's geometries, but with a special manifestation of nature that is as yet peculiar only to living matter, with a manifestation of space-time geometrically incommensurate with space, where time is manifest not as the fourth dimension, but as a change of generations.[6]

Conscious human life—that is, the life of culture—also demands a special "space-time" structure. Culture organizes itself in the form of a defined "space-time" and cannot exist outside of such an organization. This organization is actualized as a semiosphere and, simultaneously, with the help of the semiosphere.

The outer world, in which a person is immersed in order to become a factor of culture, undergoes semiotization: it splits off into a realm of objects that signify, symbolize, indicate something, that is, that have meaning, and objects that represent only themselves. At the same time, the various languages that fill the semiosphere, that hundred-eyed Argus,[ii] mark out different things in

ii In ancient Greek mythology, the all-seeing Argus was a giant who acted as Hera's servant. Using the metaphor of the Argus to describe the semiosphere, Lotman conveys his idea that each language existing within the semiosphere casts its own perspective on the world, resulting in a stereoscopic (or, more accurately, a polyscopic) construction of reality.

external reality. The resulting stereoscopic picture assumes the right to speak in the name of culture as a whole. Simultaneously, for all the diverse substructures of the semiosphere, they are organized within a general system of coordinates: on the temporal axis is the past, present, and future; on the spatial, inner space, outer space, and the boundary between them. Extra-semiotic reality—its space and time—is recoded in this system of coordinates as well, so as to be rendered "semiotizable," capable of becoming the content of a semiotic text. This side of the question will be discussed later.

As has already been mentioned, the extension of metastructural self-description from the culture's center to its entire semiotic space, which, for the historian, unifies a whole synchronic cross-section of the semiosphere, in fact creates merely the appearance of unification. If at the center the meta-structure comes across as its "own" language, then at the periphery it appears as a "foreign" language incapable of adequately reflecting the semiotic praxis underpinning it. It is like the grammar of a foreign language. Consequently, at the center of cultural space, segments of the semiosphere that have been raised to the level of self-description assume a strictly organized character and simultaneously achieve self-regulation. But they simultaneously lose their dynamicity and, having exhausted their reserve of indeterminacy, become inflexible and incapable of evolving. On the periphery—the further from the center, the more pronouncedly—the relationship between semiotic praxis and the normativity imposed upon it becomes ever more fraught. The texts born in accordance with these norms are suspended in air, deprived of a real semiotic environment, while organic creations defined by a real semiotic milieu come into conflict with artificial norms. This is the realm of semiotic dynamics. It is precisely here that the stress field where future languages are produced comes about. Thus, for example, it has long been noted that peripheral genres in art are more revolutionary than those situated at the culture's center, enjoy a higher prestige, and are perceived by their contemporaries as art *par excellence.*[7] In the second half of the twentieth century we have been witness to the violent aggression of marginal cultural forms. One example might be the "career" of the cinematograph, which has transformed from a fairground spectacle, free from theoretical limitations and regulated only by its own technical possibilities, into one of the central arts and, what is more, particularly in recent decades, into one of the most *described* arts. The same can be said about the art of the European avantgarde as a whole. The avantgarde has undergone a period of "periphery in revolt," has become a central phenomenon, dictating its own laws to the era and tending to paint the entire semiosphere in its color and, having effectively congealed, has become an object of intensified theorization on the metacultural level.

The same regularities can appear even within the limits of a single text. Thus, for example, we know that in early Renaissance painting it is on the periphery of the canvas and in the far distances of a landscape that genre scenes and everyday elements are clustered, given the canonicity of the central figures. This process reaches its apex in Piero della Francesca's enigmatic *The Flagellation of Christ* (Ducal Palace, Urbino), where the peripheral figures have stepped boldly into the foreground, while the flagellation scene has been set back, its tones muted, providing a sort of background meaning to the colorful triple portrait up front. Analogous processes can be deployed not in space, but in time, in the movement from draft to final text. There are numerous cases of preliminary versions, in painting as well as in poetry, connected more boldly to the aesthetic of the future than is the "normalized," self-censored, final text. Many examples of shots that directors have removed in the editing process speak to the same point.

An analogous example in another sphere might be the activity of semiotic processes during the European Middle Ages, in those provinces where the Christianization of the "barbarians" did not change pagan popular cultures but sort of draped them in an official mantle, from the remote regions of the Pyrenees and the Alps to the forests and swamps inhabited by the Saxons and Thuringii. It is from precisely this soil that "popular Christianity," heresies, and finally reform movements later emerged.

When such a situation stimulates vigorous semiotic activity, it leads to the accelerated "maturation" of peripheral centers and to their producing their own meta-descriptions, which can in turn appear as pretenders to a universal structure of meta-description for the entire semiosphere. The history of culture provides many examples of such competition. Essentially, the attentive cultural historian detects in each of the culture's synchronous cross-sections not one system of canonizing norms, but a paradigm of competing systems. A typical example might be the simultaneous existence in seventeenth-century Germany, on the one hand, of "language societies" (*Sprachgesellschaften*) and "the Fruitbearing Society" (*Die Fruchtbringende Gesellschaft*), which assigned itself the task of purification, of cleansing the German language of barbarisms, especially of Gallicisms and Latinisms, and grammatically normalizing the language (Justus Georg Schottelius's grammar) and, on the other, of the "Noble Academy of Faithful Ladies" (also called "The Order of the Golden Palm"), which pursued the opposite goal, propagating the French language and a precise style of conduct. One might also point to the rivalry between the Académie Française and the *chambre bleue* salon of the Marquise de Rambouillet. The latter example is especially revealing: both centers work actively and consciously to create their own "language of culture." If *épurer et fixer la langue* was indicated among the principal mandates when the Académie Française was founded (the king signed the charter on January 2, 1635), then for "salon culture" the question of language was likewise the first priority. Paul Tallemant wrote:

> Si le mot de jargon ne signifioit qu'un mauvais langage corrompu d'un bon, comme peut-estre celuy du bas peuple, on ne pourroit gueres bien dire jargon de Precieuse, parce que les Precieuses cherchent le plus poli, mais ce mot signifie aussi langage affecté, et par consequent jargon de Precieuse est une bonne maniere de parler; ce n'est pas la vraye langue que parlent les personnes qu'on appelle Precieuses, ce sont des Phrases recherchées, faites exprés ... .[8] [iii]

This last confession is especially valuable: it points directly to the artificial and normative character of the *langage des Précieuses.* If in satires of ladies' preciosity it seemed that the point was to critique corrupt usage from the position of a higher standard, then from the perspective of the adherents to salon culture themselves the point was to elevate usage to a standard, that is, to create an abstract image of actual usage.[9] [iv]

The controversy in regard to space is equally interesting: Richelieu, who inspired the Académie, envisioned the dissemination of a purified and well-ordered French language within the borders of an ideal, absolutist France, the

iii We have restored the spelling of the original, which Lotman's edition had rendered imperfectly.

iv Lotman's interest in the linguistic debates in seventeenth-century France is augmented by the fact that these debates had an indirect impact on the rise of polite society in eighteenth-century Russia through Vasily Trediakovsky's *Ezda v ostrov liubvi,* his translation of Tallemant's *Voyage de l'isle d'amour.* See Lotman's article "'Ezda v ostrov liubvi Trediakovskogo' i funktsiia perevodnoi literatury v russkoi kul'ture pervoi poloviny XVIII veka,' in *Izbrannye stat'i,* vol. 2 (Tallinn: Aleksandra, 1992–1993), 22–29. Lotman argues that through his translation, Trediakovsky supplies a model of polite behavior that was yet inexistent in Russia, but could be brought into existence by emulating this behavioral "code." For a recent critique of this interpretation, see Igor' Fediukin, "Lost in Translation: Trediakovskii's *Journey to the Island of Love* and its Social Contexts," Basic Research Program, Working Papers, Series: Humanities, https://wp.hse.ru/data/2018/10/08/1157141165/167HUM2018.pdf (accessed 6 July 2019).

scope of his state ambitions. Rambouillet's salon created its own ideal space: the number of documents about "a precious geography" is striking, beginning with Mademoiselle de Scudéry's *Carte de Tendre,* Maulévrier's 1659 *Carte de l'empire des Précieuses,* Gabriel Guéret's 1674 *Carte de la cour,* and Paul Tallemant's 1663 *Voyage de l'isle d'amour.* What comes about is an image of a multi-level space: through a series of conventional renamings, the real Paris transforms into Athens. But on a still higher level what comes about is the ideal space of the "Land of Tenderness" that is identified with the "true" semiosphere. To this one can juxtapose the utopian geography of the Renaissance, in the latter case with its ambition, on the one hand, to create "on top of" reality an image of the ideal city, island, or state, including its geographic and cartographic description (compare Thomas More's *Utopia* and Francis Bacon's *New Atlantis*), and, on the other, to implement the metastructure on a practical level, inventing plans for ideal cities and experiments for realizing such plans. Compare, for example, Luciano Laurana's ingenious drawings of ideal cities (Ducal Palace, Urbino). Works like Caspar Stiblin's *Brief Commentary on the Republic of the Blissful* [*Commentariolus Eudaemonensium republica*] (1555) and Tommaso Campanella's *The City of the Sun* [*La città del Sole,* 1602] paved the way for numerous plans for building ideal cities. At the foundation of Renaissance utopian urban planning were the ideas of Leon Battista Alberti. The urban plans sketched out by Dürer, Leonardo da Vinci, the plan for the city of Sforzinda made by "Filarete," Francesco di Giorgio Martini's map of an ideal city—these represented a direct intrusion of metastructure into reality as they were designed to be realized: "... un succès dont il reste encore aujourd'hui de multiples témoins, depuis Lima (ainsi que Panama et Manille au XVIIe siècle) jusqu'à Zamosc en Pologne, depuis La Valette (à Malte) jusqu'à Nancy, en passant par Livourne, Gattinara (en Piémont), Vallauris, Brouage et Vitry-le-François."[10]

But the "hottest" nodes of semio-formative process are the boundaries of the semiosphere. The concept of boundary is ambiguous. On the one hand, it divides; on the other, it unites. It is always a boundary with something and, consequently, belongs to both bordering cultures—to both adjacent semiospheres—simultaneously. It is a bi- and multilingual boundary. The boundary is a mechanism for translating the texts of a foreign semiotic system into the language of "our" semiotics, the site where the "outer" is transformed into the "inner," it is the filtering membrane that transforms foreign texts so that they fit into the semiosphere's inner semiotics while nevertheless remaining alien. In Kievan Rus there was a term designating those nomads who had settled on the frontiers of the Russian territory, became farmers, and, entering alliances with the Russian princes, campaigned with them against their own fellow tribesmen. They were called "our infidels" (where *poganyi*, "infidel," is simultaneously "pagan" and "foreign," "erroneous" and "non-Christian"). The oxymoron "our infidels" expresses the boundary situation quite well.

In order for Byron to enter Russian culture, his cultural double had to arise, the "Russian Byron" who would be the face of two cultures simultaneously: as a "Russian," he fits organically into the inner processes of Russian literature and speaks in its language (in the broad semiotic sense). What is more, he cannot be excised from Russian literature without leaving a gaping emptiness with nothing to fill it. But at the same time he is also Byron, an organic part of English literature, and in the context of Russian he serves his function only if he is experienced precisely as Byron, that is, as an English poet. It is only in this context that we can understand Lermontov's exclamation, "No, I am no Byron, I am another. ..."[11]

It is not only separate texts or authors, but also entire cultures that, in order for intercultural contact to be possible, ought to have such image-equivalents in "our" culture, similar to bilingual dictionaries.[12] This image's dual role is manifest in the fact that it is simultaneously both a means and a hindrance to communication. Here is a representative example: Pushkin's early Romantic epics, his tumultuous early biography, his exile—in the minds of his readers these created the stereotypical image of the poet-Romantic, the prism through which all his texts were interpreted. In those years Pushkin himself actively participated in shaping "the mythology of his personality," which corresponded to the general system of "Romantic behavior." Yet this image then stood between the writings of the evolving poet and his readership. His austere work, oriented toward truth-to-life and having repudiated Romanticism,[v] was interpreted by his readers as a "fall" and a "betrayal" precisely because the image of the early Pushkin lived on in their minds.

Similar to the way a change in the metalingual structure of the semiosphere sees the emergence of works about "unknown" and "forgotten" agents of culture, with a change in image-stereotypes we find works of the "unknown Dostoevsky" or "Goethe as he really was" variety, suggesting to the reader that what he has known up to this point is the "wrong" Dostoevsky or Goethe, the true understanding of whom is only now at hand.

We observe something analogous when texts of one genre intrude into the space of another. Innovation consists precisely in the fact that the principles

v In the 1830s, when Pushkin developed an interest in fiction and historical narrative.

of one genre are reconstructed according to the laws of another, such that this "other" genre fits organically into the new structure and, at the same time, retains the memory of a different system of coding. Thus when Pushkin inserts the actual text of an eighteenth-century court petition into the fabric of his novella *Dubrovsky* [*Dubrovskii*], or Dostoevsky includes a carefully composed imitation of the actual speech of a prosecutor and an attorney in *The Brothers Karamazov* [*Brat'ia Karamazovy*], these texts stand out simultaneously as the organic fabric of novelistic narrative and as alien document-quotes that fall out of the natural key of artistic narrative.

The notion of a boundary separating the inner space of the semiosphere from the outer space provides only an initial, rough division. In actuality, the entire space of the semiosphere is intersected by boundaries at various levels, boundaries separating languages and even texts, while the inner space of these sub-semiospheres has some semiotic "I" of its own that is realized as the relation of any language, group of texts, or separate text (accounting for the fact that languages and texts are arranged hierarchically at different levels) to some metastructural space that describes them. A multi-level system is created by the semiosphere allowing certain boundaries to run through it. Specific portions of the semiosphere can, on various levels of self-description, form a semiotic whole, an uninterrupted semiotic space bounded by a single boundary, or a group of closed spaces whose discreteness will be marked by the boundaries between them, or, ultimately, a part of a more general space bounded off by a fragment of boundary on one side and left open on the other. Naturally, this is accompanied by a hierarchy of codes: various levels of signification are activated in the single reality of the semiosphere.

An important criterion here is the question of what is interpreted as a subject in a given system, for example, the subject of the law in the juridical texts of a given culture or of "the individual" in the sociocultural coding of one system or another. The idea of the "individual" is identified with the boundaries of a person's physical individuality only under defined cultural and semiotic conditions. It can be collective, include property or not, and relate to a defined social, religious, or moral situation. The boundary of the individual is a semiotic boundary. Thus, for example, one's wife, children, slave-servants, and vassals can, in some systems, be included within the individuality of the landlord, patriarch, husband, patron, or suzerain without having their own independent "individual-ness," while in others they are regarded as separate individuals. Cases of insurrection and rebellion arise from a clash between two ways of coding: when the socio-semiotic structure describes a given individual as a part, yet he recognizes himself as an autonomous unit, a semiotic subject and not an object.

When Ivan the Terrible executed disgraced boyars not only together with their families, but with their servants—and not only their domestic servants, but their peasants and villages (or else the peasants were resettled, the villages renamed, the structures razed to the ground)—this was dictated, despite the tsar's pathological cruelty, not by the danger they posed (as if a serf on a provincial family estate could be a danger to the tsar!) but by the notion that they were all one person, parts of the individual boyar being executed, and they, accordingly, shared responsibility with him. Such a view was evidently not unfamiliar to Stalin, who had the mentality of an Eastern tyrant.

From a European juridical perspective, one reared on the post-Renaissance sense of an individual's right to justice, it seemed incomprehensible that one person would suffer *for someone else.* As late as 1732, Lady Rondeau, the wife of the English envoy in Petersburg (and quite fond of the Russian court, and even inclined to idealize it: in her missives she extols the "sensibility" and "goodness" of Empress Anna Ioannovna, who was as crude as the lady of a provincial estate, and the "nobility" of her cruel favorite, Biron), informing her European correspondent of the Dolgorukov family's exile, wrote: "You will perhaps wonder at the banishing of women and children, but here, when the master of a family is attacked, the whole family is involved in his ruin. ..."[13]

The very same idea of the collective (and, in the given instance, patrimonial) person, rather than the individual, underlies the blood feud, for example, where the killer's entire extended family is seen as a responsible party. The historian S. M. Solovyov drew a convincing connection between the institution of *mestnichestvo*[14]—which in the eyes of eighteenth-century enlighteners, with their pious faith in progress, appeared only as a manifestation of "ignorance"—and the peculiar collective experience of the clan as a single individual:

> One understands that with this strong familial bond, with all family members being responsible one for the other, the import of the separate person necessarily faded before the import of the family. A person was unthinkable without the family. The famous Ivan Petrov was not thought of as one Ivan Petrov, but was thought of only as Ivan Petrov with his brothers and nephews. With such conflation of the person with his family, when the one person was elevated in the service, the entire family was elevated; with the demotion of one member of the family, the entire family was demoted.[15]

Thus, for example, Matvey Pushkin, a boyar and *stol'nik* under Tsar Alexei Mikhailovich (seventeenth century) who belonged to the list of thirty-one families of highest nobility, refused to go on a diplomatic mission as deputy to Nadrin-Nashchokin,[vi] an eminent agent of state and favorite of the tsar, though of lower nobility, preferring to go to prison and steadfastly shouldering the threat that all his property would be confiscated and he would incur the tsar's wrath, responding with dignity, "though you may put me to death, my lord, to me Nashchokin is a young man, and not one of high birth."[16]

The space that appears as a single individual in one coding system can, in another, turn out to be a site of conflict between several semiotic subjects.

For every message circulating within it, the capacity of semiotic space to be intersected by numerous boundaries creates a situation of multifold translations and transformations accompanied by the generation of new information, which assumes an avalanche-like character.

The function of any boundary or film (from the membrane of a living cell to the biosphere as—following Vernadsky—a film enveloping our planet, to the boundary of the semiosphere itself) amounts to limiting penetration, to the filtration and adaptive reworking of what is external into the internal. This invariant function is realized in diverse ways on different levels. On the level of the semiosphere, it signifies the separation of the self from the other, the filtration of the external, which is assigned the status of text in a foreign language, and the translation of that text into one's own language. In this way, external space acquires some structure.

In cases where the semiosphere includes real-territorial features, the boundary assumes a spatial meaning in the direct sense. The isomorphism between different kinds of settlement—from ancient settlements to the ideal cities of the Renaissance and the Enlightenment—and notions about the structure of the cosmos has been frequently noted. Connected to this is how the center of construction gravitates around the most important religious and administrative buildings. It is on the periphery that the least valued social groups are settled. Those who are situated beneath the line of social value are distributed along the boundary of the outskirts; the very etymology of the Russian word *predmest'e*, "outskirts," signifies *pered mestom,* that is, "before the city," at its boundary line. Along a vertical orientation, this will be attics and basements and, in the modern city, the subway. If, however, the center of "normal" habitation is the apartment,

vi Lotman refers here to A. L. Ordin-Nashchokin (1605–1680), who was the head of the Posolsky prikaz (that is, Foreign Office) under Alexei Mikhailovich.

then it is the stairwell or entryway that becomes the boundary space between "home" and "outside of home." It is no accident that it is precisely these spaces that become "one's own" for "boundary" groups—the marginalized—within society: the homeless, the addicted, the youth. Urban public space, stadiums, and cemeteries are among the boundary places. No less revealing, too, is the change in norms of acceptable behavior as one moves from the boundary of such a space toward its center.

There are specific elements, however, that are generally situated *outside*. If the inner world recalls the cosmos, beyond its boundary we find chaos, the anti-world, an iconic space beyond structure that is inhabited by monsters, infernal forces, or the people connected to them. In the village, beyond the line of settlement is where the sorcerer, the miller, and (sometimes) the smith have to live, and, in the medieval city, the hangman. "Normal" space has not only spatial boundaries, but temporal ones as well. Beyond its line we find nighttime. When he is needed, people go to see the sorcerer at night. It is in anti-space that the bandit lives: his home is the forest (an anti-home), his sun is the moon ("the thief's sunshine," as the Russian saying goes), he speaks an anti-language, he demonstrates anti-behavior (he whistles loudly, curses indecently), he sleeps when people are working, and he robs while they're asleep, and so forth.[vii]

The "night world" of the city is likewise situated on the border of cultural space or beyond its line. This travestied world is oriented toward anti-behavior.

We have already paid attention to the process by which a culture's periphery is shifted to its center and its center removed to the periphery. Even more pronounced is the movement of these contradirectional flows between the center and the "periphery of the periphery"—the boundary zone of culture. Thus, following the October Revolution of 1917 in Russia, this process received a manifold, non-metaphorical realization: the poor from the suburbs moved *en masse* into "bourgeois apartments," from which they evicted their former occupants or "consolidated" their space. Of course, taking the highly artistic, wrought-iron barrier that had surrounded the royal garden around the Winter Palace in Petrograd up until the Revolution and removing it to a working-class district, where it enclosed a suburban square, with the royal garden remaining entirely without a fence—"open"—this had a symbolic meaning. In the utopian

vii The notion of anti-behavior, the inversion of normative behavior, was developed extensively in the works of Lotman's coauthor B. A. Uspensky. See, in this collection, their joint article, "The Role of Dual Models in the Dynamics of Russian Culture (until the End of the Eighteenth Century)."

plans for the socialist city of the future, which were created in abundance in the early 1920s, one often finds the notion that in the center of such a city—"where the palace and church had been"—there will be an enormous factory.

It is in this sense that Peter I's transferring the capital to Petersburg—to the border—was telling. Transferring the political-administrative center to a *geographic* boundary was simultaneously shifting the boundary into the state's administrative-political center. And the Pan-Slavists' subsequent plans to transfer the capital to Constantinople even shifted the center beyond all actual borders.

In the same way, we can observe a shift in norms of behavior, language, style of dress, and so on, from the sphere of the boundary and into the center. Jeans can serve as an example: work clothes designed for physical labor, they became something youthful, insofar as the youth, having rejected the core culture of the twentieth century, saw its ideal in peripheral culture, whereupon jeans, having been spread across the entire sphere of culture, became a neutral—that is, "common"—article of clothing, the most important mark of core semiotic systems. The periphery is brightly hued, it stands out: the core is "normal," that is, it has no color, no smell, it "just is." This is why the triumph of one or another semiotic system is its shift into the center and its inevitable "de-coloration." One can juxtapose this to the "usual" aging cycle: with the years, rebellious young people become "normal," respectable gentlemen, at the same time performing an evolution from "colorfulness" toward "decoloration."

The intensification of semiotic processes within the boundary zone of the semiosphere is connected to the fact that this is where constant intrusions from outside are taking place. The boundary, as we have already said, is double-sided, and one side of it is always turned toward the outside space. Furthermore, the boundary is a realm of pronounced bilingualism. This usually finds direct expression in the language practice of the population on the border between cultural spheres. Insofar as the boundary is an indispensable part of the semiosphere, and there can be no "we" in the absence of a "they," culture creates not only its own kind of inner organization, but also its own kind of outer "disorganization." In this sense one can say that the "barbarian" is a creation of civilization, and he needs it just as much as it needs him. The space beyond the outer limits of the semiosphere is a place of uninterrupted dialogue. Regardless of whether a given culture sees the "barbarian" as a savior or an enemy, the bearer of healthy moral qualities or a depraved cannibal, it is dealing with a construct built as its very own reverse image. Thus, in the thoroughly rational, Positivist society of nineteenth-century Europe, images will necessarily appear of the "pre-logical savage" or of the irrational unconscious, of an anti-sphere beyond the rational space of culture.

Insofar as no semiosphere is actually immersed in an amorphous, wild space, but is contiguous with other semiospheres that possess their own organization (from the perspective of the first, they can seem unorganized), what comes about here is a constant exchange, the production of a common language, of a koine, the formation of creolized semiotic systems. Even in order to wage war, one must have a common language. We know that if, on the one hand, barbarian soldiers during the last period of the Roman Empire elevated the emperors of Rome to the throne, then, on the other, many "barbarian'" military leaders did their "training" in the Roman legions.[17] At the borders of China, the Roman Empire, and Byzantium, we observe the very same picture: the technical achievements of settled civilizations pass to the nomads, who turn them against those from whom they were received. These struggles, however, inevitably lead to a levelling of cultures and the creation of some new, higher-order semiosphere that includes both sides, now as equals.

CHAPTER 2

From *The Structure of the Artistic Text*

This chapter originates from The Structure of the Artistic Text, *first published in 1970. We translated it from Iu. M. Lotman, "'Shum' i khudozhestvennaia informatsiia," in* Struktura khudozhestvennogo teksta, Ob iskusstve *(St. Petersburg: Iskusstvo-SPB, 1998), 84–87. While it goes back to a period of Lotman's intellectual development often characterized as "structuralist," this section shows that, already then, Lotman's thinking about the behavior of semiotic systems demonstrated a keen sense of the contextual and historical embedding of systems and of their dependency from, and openness to, surrounding systems and historical contingencies.*

"NOISE" AND ARTISTIC INFORMATION

From the perspective of information theory, noise is what we call an intrusion of disorder, entropy, or disorganization into the sphere of structure and information. Noise muffles information. All kinds of destruction—stifling a voice through acoustic interference, the loss of books to physical deterioration, the deformation of the structure of an author's text as a result of the censor's meddling—all of this is noise within the channel of communication. Any communication channel (from a telephone line to the centuries separating us from Shakespeare) entails, according to a well-known law, noise that swallows up information. If the magnitude of the noise is equal to that of the information, the message will be nullified. Entropy's destructive action is constantly felt by man. One of the basic functions of culture is to oppose the onset of entropy.

Art is allotted a particular role in this affair. From the perspective of non-artistic information, there is no difference between a non-systemic fact and a fact that belongs to another system. For a Russian-speaker who does not speak French, a French-language conversation will pose as much obstruction as physical noise does.

Art—and in this we see its structural kinship with life in nature—has the capacity to transform noise into information; it complicates its own structure by virtue of correlating it to the outside (in all other systems, any conflict with the outside can only lead to information decay).

This peculiarity is connected, as we have seen, with the structural principle that defines the polysemy of artistic elements. In entering the text or the extra-textual background of the work of art, new structures do not cancel out old meanings, but join into semantic relations with them. The difference between the structure that enriches a text's informational content and a destructive, heterogenous structure evidently consists precisely in the fact that anything alien that correlates in one way or another to the structure of the authorial text stops being noise. A statue tossed into the grass can create a new artistic effect due to the appearance of a *relation* between grass and marble. A statue tossed into a garbage heap creates no such effect for the contemporary viewer: his consciousness cannot produce a structure that would unite these two entities within a mutually correlative and mutually conceptualizing whole. But this still does not mean that such unification is theoretically impossible. Consequently, the question of whether "noise" is transformed into artistic information always implies a description of the type of culture that we assume as its audience.

Up to this point, we have been discussing the fact that an alien system (a "non-systemic system," from the point of view of a given text) manifests itself through the specific recurrence of its elements, which forces the listener[1] to detect in them not accident, but a different regularity. This question, however, becomes even more complicated in an artistic text. We can point to several instances in which the singular, the accidental, by invading the text leads, if only partially, to the destruction of its semantics, which itself generates several new meanings. The missing arms of Venus de Milo, as well as every instance of a canvas darkening over time, of a historical monument falling to ruin—these are, from the perspective of non-artistic information, trivial instances of noise, entropy encroaching on structure. In art, however, things are more complicated, and an overly determined "restoration" executed without the necessary care and tact, powerless to rehabilitate that unknown appearance with which the monument struck the eyes of its creator and contemporaries, strips it of all subsequent cultural contexts and often comes off as a much greater entropy than that of the blows inflicted upon the monument by time (one cannot say this, of course, of an absolutely necessary conservation or a thought-out, tactful, and scientifically based restoration).

Here, however, we are interested in something else. Let us consider two examples. The first is the artist Mikhailov in *Anna Karenina*, who cannot find the necessary pose for a figure in a drawing until he is assisted by an accidental blotch of stearin: "Suddenly he smiled and waved his hands delightedly. 'Yes, yes,' he pronounced, and having taken up his pencil he immediately began to draw quickly. The blotch of stearin was giving the person a new pose."[i]

The second is from Anna Akhmatova's "Poem without a Hero" [Poema bez geroia]:

> ... and since I didn't have sufficient paper,
> I'm writing now in your old copy book.
> And here another's word is shining through. ...[ii]
>
> ... а так как мне бумаги не хватило,
> Я на твоем пишу черновике.
> И вот чужое слово проступает. ...

A blotch of stearin, another's word: in both cases we are dealing with a one-time, non-systemic interference that does not offer us a series of recurrences. And yet, there is a complication of structure nonetheless. It is caused by our placing this fact alongside others held in our consciousness, making it part of an extratextual order that runs up against the text itself (the order that corresponds to the arms of Venus de Milo may include "the ancient," "authenticity," "the ineffable," and so forth). And, once again, a separate fact, a part of the text's material, physical appearance, turns out to be an artistic reality because it emerges at the intersection between two regularities.[iii]

So, we are forced to conclude that a relational structure is not the sum of substantive details but the set of relations that is primary within the work of art and forms its basis, its reality. But this set is constructed not as a multi-level hierarchy having no internal intersections, but as a complex structure of mutually intersecting substructures, wherein one and the same element enters various constructive contexts multiple times.[iv] And these intersections also make

---

i Leo Tolstoy, *Anna Karenina*, part 5, ch. 10.

ii Anna Akhmatova, "Poem without Hero" [Poema bez geroia], from the First Dedication, *Sochineniia* (Munich: Inter-Language Literary Associates, 1968), 101.

iii One can see in this interest for the productive intersections between two systems with their differing regularities the seeds of Lotman's later theory of the two channels of communication, the I–HE and I–I channels.

iv Lotman's premise that semiotic systems are sets of relations goes back to Saussurean epistemology, in particular the idea that elements in a system derive their meaning from their

up the "physicality" of the artistic text, its material diversity, which reflects the fantastic asystematicity of the surrounding world with such credibility that the inattentive viewer comes to trust that this accidental, unrepeated individuality of the artistic text can be identified with the properties of the reality it reflects.

The law of the artistic text: the more regularities intersect at a given structural point, the more individual it seems. It is for precisely this reason that a study of what is unique in the work of art can be accomplished only by exposing what is regular, with an inevitable sense of the regular's inexhaustible richness.

This is where we can derive a response to the question of whether exact knowledge kills the work of art. The way toward knowing the diversity of the artistic text—ever an approximate knowledge—moves not through lyrical discussions about uniqueness, but through the study of uniqueness as a function of specific recurrences, of the individual as a function of the regular.

As always in genuine science, one can only ever walk this path. One cannot reach its end. But this is a shortcoming only in the eyes of those who do not understand what knowledge is.

THE PROBLEM OF PLOT

This chapter likewise comes from The Structure of the Artistic Text *(Iu. M. Lotman, "Problema siuzheta," in* Struktura khudozhestvennogo teksta, Ob iskusstve, *221–229). Lotman's definition of the event has had a noticeable impact on narrative theory, as it provides a relational framework to capture the variability of what counts as an event in a narrative. For a discussion of narratological extensions of Lotman's concept of event, see "Event and Eventfulness," in* The Living Handbook of Narratology, *https://www.lhn.uni-hamburg.de/node/39.html, accessed 14 July 2019. Lotman's chapter also can serve as an example of the productive intersection between systems of different orders in an artistic work. Here the relational system that gives meaning to space, an element of the setting, exerts a defining impact on the eventfulness of an occurrence on the level of the plot.*

We have concluded that setting is not only descriptions of landscapes or of a decorative background. The entire spatial continuum of the text where the

reciprocal interrelationships, rather than from any reference to extra-semiotic reality. However, in his emphasis on mutually intersecting substructures from different levels, Lotman confers to artistic systems a much higher degree of complexity, fluidity, and openness, which lends them the appearance of asystematicity.

world of the object is reflected coalesces into some topos. This topos is always endowed with some object-ness, insofar as space is always given to a person in the form of its being somehow concretely filled in. In this sense, it is immaterial that sometimes (as, for example, in nineteenth-century art) this filling-in strives for a maximal approximation of the everyday surroundings of the author and his audience, whereas in other instances (for example, in Romanticism's exotic descriptions, or else in modern "cosmic" science fiction) it distances itself by definition from the usual "material" reality.[1]

But the important thing is that beyond the representation of the things and objects among which the text's characters act, there arises a system of spatial relations, the structure of the topos. In so doing, serving as the principle for the organization and arrangement of the characters in the artistic continuum, the structure of the topos functions as a language for expressing the text's other, non-spatial relations. This is connected to the peculiar modeling role of artistic space within the text.

Closely connected with the idea of artistic space is the idea of plot.

At the heart of the idea of plot lies the notion of *event*. Thus, in his *Theory of Literature* [*Teoriia literatury*], whose precise formulations have made it a classic, Boris Tomashevsky writes:

> Story is what we call the aggregate of interconnected events communicated in the work. ... To the story we oppose the plot: those same events, but as they are told, in the order they are communicated in the work, in the connection between messages communicating about them in the work.[2]

An event is taken to be the smallest indivisible unit of plot construction, what Alexander Veselovsky defined as "motif."[i] In searching for the motif's fundamental marker, he turned toward the semantic aspect: a motif is the elementary, indivisible unit of narrative that corresponds to a generic integral event in the external world (that of everyday life): "By 'motif,' I mean a formula that for

---

i Alexander Veselovsky (1838–1906) was a prominent literary comparativist, known for his critique of the then mainstream "mythological school," a theory which imputed similarities in European folklore to its shared roots in a common, Indo-European, pre-historical, totalizing mythology. In contrast, Veselovsky held that literature, folklore, and mythology were all composed of "motifs," that is, a shared repertoire of units of plot construction, based on life experience, which predate the development of mythology and are reactualized in various historical situations. See A. L. Toporkov, *Teoriia mifa v russkoi filologicheskoi nauke XIX veka* (Moscow: Indrik, 1997), 315–380.

the general public has given an initial response to the questions posed to mankind everywhere by nature, or that has solidified especially glaring, seemingly important, or repeated impressions of reality. The marker of a motif is its figurative, monomial schematism."[3]

Let us remark the indisputable profundity of this definition. Having singled out the bipartite nature of the motif—the literary expression and the conceptual-experiential content—and having pointed to its recurrence, Veselovsky has clearly come close to a definition of the semiotic nature of the concept he has introduced.[ii] However, attempts at applying a model of the motif so construed to further work in textual analysis immediately encounter difficulties: we will later come to the realization that one and the same lived reality may or may not, in various texts, assume the quality of an event.

Viktor Shklovsky proclaimed a different way of singling out the unit of plot from Veselovsky's, a purely syntagmatic one: "The fairy tale, the novella, the novel: these are combinations of motifs; a song is a combination of stylistic motifs; this is why plot and plot-ness are as much form as rhythm is."[4] True, Shklovsky himself did not abide by this principle as consistently as Vladimir Propp did in his *Morphology of the Folktale* [*Morfologiia skazki*]: the actual basis of his analysis is not the syntagmatics of motifs, but the composition of devices. But a device is conceived according to the general notion of "slow perception" and the de-automatization of form, as the relation between expectation and the text.[iii] In this way, the "device" in Shklovsky is the relation of an element of one syntagmatic structure toward another and, consequently, includes the semantic dimension. Therefore, when Shklovsky asserts, "In analyzing a work of art, one has no need, from the perspective of plot-ness, for the idea of 'content,'" this is

---

ii In his interpretation of Veselovsky's ideas, Lotman emphasises the intersection between what we could call two systems of coordinates: the narrative expression (which alone enables one to define what the "smallest, indivisible unit" of plot construction would be) and a certain conventional understanding of reality, which he called "solidified, glaring … impressions of reality."

iii Shklovsky's concept of the device goes back to his seminal article "Art as Device" (1917), in which he rejects the notion that art is a way of thinking in images and defines instead the purpose of art as restoring a de-automatized sensation of things by way of devices that make the perception of language difficult or strange. This "defamiliarizing" effect of devices undermines the shortcuts of habitual perception, which substitute recognition for vision. See Svetlana Boym, "Poetics and Politics of Estrangement: Victor Shklovsky and Hannah Arendt," *Poetics Today* 26, no. 4 (2005): 581–611. Lotman argues that because a device operates against an "automatized" representation of reality, it necessarily contains a semantic aspect, provocatively drawing out the parallels between Veselovsky and Shklovsky, despite their initial opposing starting points.

a polemical stab and not an exact articulation of the author's own position.[5] At the heart of Shklovsky's position is the effort to understand the mystery of why all the automatic elements of a text become content-bearing in art. Here one cannot help but see a stab against that academic school that, in Veselovsky's words, accused Edwin Rohde of the following: "He relates to poetic works only as poetic works." And further: "A poetic work is as much a historical monument as any other, and I do not see a particular need for a mass of archeological and other supports and proofs to confirm its innate title."[iv] The following naïve argument is also typical: "After all, none of the troubadours' contemporaries denounced them as being untrue to life."[6] None of the listeners, whose experience of the fairytale is aesthetic, condemns the storyteller for not being true to life: does that mean that Baba Yaga and Zmei Gorynych belong to lived reality? For it is precisely because the correct thesis, that the work of art represents a historical monument, has been replaced by the position that it is a monument "like any other," that there are continued efforts in pseudoscientific literature to see fossilized dinosaurs in mythological monsters, and recollections of an atomic explosion and space travel in the legend of Sodom and Gomorra.[7] Veselovsky's profound premises were not fully realized in his works. Yet Veselovsky's ideas about the sign-motif as a fundamental element of plot, together with Vladimir Propp's syntagmatic analysis and Viktor Shklovsky's syntagmatic-functional one, have blazed multiple paths toward a contemporary resolution of this question.

What, then, is the event as a unit of plot construction?

An event in a text is a character's movement across the boundary of the semantic field. From this it follows that no one description of some fact or action relative to its real denotation or the semantic system of natural language can be defined as an event or nonevent so long as we have no resolution of the question of its place in the secondary structural semantic field defined by the kind of culture. But this isn't yet an ultimate solution, either: within the bounds of one and

iv Erwin Rohde (1845–1898) was a major German classicist, the author of a noted study of the Greek novel, *Der Griechische Roman und seine Vorläufer* [*The Greek Novel and Its Precursors*] (1876), which drew the attention of Mikhail Bakhtin and others. Rohde approaches the Greek novel genetically as an outgrowth of Hellenistic erotic poetry, itself a manifestation of the demise of collective religious feeling and the rise of individualism. In an extensive review of Rohde's study, Veselovsky takes him to task for claiming that the Greek novel only contains idealised images of life and therefore cannot be drawn upon to flesh out our knowledge of everyday life in Greek society. See A. N. Veselovskii, "Grecheskii roman," in *Izbrannye stat'i* (Leningrad: Khudozhestvennaia literatura, 1939), 23–45.

the same cultural framework, the very same episode, when placed at different structural levels, may or may not become an event. But insofar as there are local orderings of the text, each of which has its own conceptual boundary, alongside the general semantic ordering, the event can be realized as a hierarchy of events of more particular levels, as a chain of events—a plot. In this sense, what represents a *single* event on the level of the text of culture can be unfolded into a *plot* in one or another actual text. And so one and the same invariant construct of the event can be unfolded into any number of plots at different levels. Representing one plot segment at the highest level, it can vary the number of segments, depending on the level of its textual unfolding.

The plot, so construed, does not represent something independent, plucked out of everyday life or passively received from tradition. Plot is organically connected with the world picture, which provides the scale for determining what is an event and what is a variant that provides no new information.

Let's imagine that a married couple has had an argument over their divergent assessments of abstract art and have turned to law enforcement to write up a report. Ascertaining that there has been neither an assault, nor any other violation of civil or criminal law, the commanding officer will refuse to take a report, seeing as there has been no event. From his perspective, nothing has happened. But for the psychologist, the moralist, the historian of everyday life or, for example, the historian of painting, the reported fact will represent an event. Repeated arguments about the relative merit of these or other plots occurring over the course of the entire history of art are connected to the fact that one and the same event is presented as significant from some positions, insignificant from others, and from still others as completely nonexistent.

This applies not only to artistic texts. It would be instructive in this regard to examine the "Incidents" section of newspapers in different eras. An incident is a meaningful deviation from the norm (that is, an "event," insofar as satisfying a norm is not an "event"); it depends on the idea of the norm. From what has been said about the event as a revolutionary element standing in opposition to an accepted classification, it follows that there is some logic in the disappearance of the incidents section from newspapers during reactionary eras (for example, during the "seven dark years" [*mrachnoe semilet'e*] at the end of Nicholas I's reign). Insofar as the only things that happen are the events that have been anticipated, plot-ness disappears from newspaper accounts. When, in a personal letter (November 1840), Alexander Herzen gave his father information about what was going on in the city (a policeman had murdered and robbed a merchant), he was quickly sent away from Petersburg by order of the emperor, "for disseminating baseless rumors." Typical here is both the fear of "incidents" and the belief that a murder committed by a policeman is an event and that, consequently, one cannot admit to its existence, whereas agents of state reading private letters is not an event (it is the norm, and not an incident) and, consequently, is completely permissible. Let us recall the indignation this caused Pushkin, for whom state interference in one's private life was an outrageous anomaly, and thus an event: "... what profound immorality there is in the habits of our government! The police break the seals on a husband's letters to his wife and take them to be read by the tsar (a well-bred and honorable man), and the tsar is not ashamed to admit it."[8] What we have before us is a stark example of how a fact's qualification as an event depends on the system of concepts (in the given instance, a moral system), and those of Pushkin and Nicholas I do not agree.

In historical texts, too, the relationship between this or that fact and events is dependent upon the general world picture. This can be easily traced by juxtaposing various kinds of memoirs and various historical studies written on the basis of the very same documents.

This is all the more fitting for the structure of artistic texts. In a thirteenth-century Novgorodian Chronicle, an earthquake is described as follows: "The earth shook ... at dinner, but others had finished dinner." Here, an earthquake and dinner are treated equally as events. Clearly, for a Kievan chronicle this would not be possible. One could point to many cases where a character's death is a non-event.

In Marguerite of Navarre's *Heptaméron,* the brilliant company, separated by a dangerous journey through flood-prone highlands, gathers again safely in a monastery. The fact that their servants have perished in the process (drowned in a river, eaten by bears, or otherwise) is a nonevent. It is merely a circumstance, a version of an event. In "Lucerne" [Liutsern], Leo Tolstoy defined a historical event as follows: "On the seventh of July 1857, in Lucerne, in front of the Hotel Schweizerhof, where the very wealthiest stay, a destitute wandering singer sang songs and played the guitar for half an hour. About a hundred people listened. The singer thrice asked everyone to give him something. Not one person gave him anything, and many laughed at him. ... *This is an event* that historians of our times should record in fiery, indelible letters. It is an event more significant, more serious, and one with more profound a meaning than the facts recorded in newspapers and histories."[9] Love is an event from the perspective of a novel, but it is not an event from the perspective of a chronicle, which registers weddings that are important to the state but never notes the facts of familial life (unless they are woven into the fabric of political events).

The chivalric romance does not register changes in the hero's material wellbeing—from its perspective, this is not an event—whereas the Gogolian school stops registering love. Love as a "nonevent" becomes the basis for an entire scene in *The Inspector General* [*Revizor*]:

> Maria Antonovna *(looking out the window):* What is that, that would fly off? A magpie, or some other bird?
> Khlestakov *(kisses her on the shoulder and looks out the window):* It's a magpie.[10]

What turns out to be an event is not love, but actions whose goal is "rank, capital, a favorable marriage." Even the death of the hero is not presented as an event in all texts. In chivalric texts of the Middle Ages, death is an event if it is bound up with fame or infamy. In this case, it is also correspondingly evaluated, positively or negatively, as a good or bad event. Yet it is not considered in and of itself "the glaring impression of reality."[v] "Is it so strange that a man should die on the field?" wrote Vladimir Monomakh. "Better that our families die out." His son was of the same opinion: "If you were to kill my brother, that is not strange, for in wars both tsars and men perish."[11] The notion that it is not death, but fame that is the event is expressed vividly by Daniil of Galicia in a speech before his forces: "Why do you fear? Do you not know that there is no war without those who have fallen dead? Do you not know that it falls to you men to be warriors, and not to women? If a man is killed in battle, what is there to wonder? Others die at home without fame, while we die with it."[12]

This last example leads us to the heart of the question. An event is conceived as that which has happened, though it might not have. The less likelihood that a given incident can take place (that is, the more information a message about it contains), the more highly positioned it is on the scale of plot-ness. For example, when the hero dies in a modern novel, one presumes that he might not die and could, say, get married. The author of a medieval chronicle, however, starts from the notion that everyone dies, and an account of a death therefore conveys no information. But some die with fame, others "at home"—this is what is worthy of note. In this way, an event is always the violation of some prohibition, a fact that has taken place even though it wasn't supposed to. For a person thinking in the categories of a criminal code, breaking traffic rules—jaywalking—will be an event.

---

v Lotman here refers back to the quotation from Veselovsky he discussed above, that is, to the notion of motif.

If we examine texts from this perspective, it will be easy to divide them into two groups: those with a plot, and those without one.

Plotless texts have a distinct classificatory nature: they affirm some world and how it is arranged. Examples of plotless texts might include a calendar, telephone book, or a plotless lyric poem. Taking the example of the telephone book, let us consider some of the characteristic features of this kind of text. First of all, these texts have a world of their own. On the abstract linguistic level, these texts will affirm a world of denotations as a universe. The list of names will aspire to function as universal description. The world of the telephone book consists of the surnames of those with telephone lines. Everything else simply does not exist. In this sense, a significant feature of the text is what, from its perspective, *does not exist.* The world that is excluded from its representation is one of the fundamental typological indicators of the text as a model of the universe.

Thus, from the perspective of the literature of specific periods, there is no lowly reality (Romanticism), or else there is no sublime, poetic reality (Futurism).

Another important property of the plotless text will be the establishment of a specific *order* for this world's internal organization. The text is constructed in some specific way, and one is not allowed to shuffle its elements in a way that disturbs the established order. For example, the surnames of the people in the telephone book are listed in alphabetical order (in the given instance, the order is conditioned by ease of use; there can be any number of other organizational principles). Shuffling any surnames to disturb the established order is not allowed.

If you pick up not the telephone book, but some artistic or mythological text instead, it is not difficult to prove that the basis of the inner organization of the text's elements is, as a rule, the principle of binary semantic opposition: the world will break down into rich and poor, native and foreign, orthodox and heretical, enlightened and unenlightened, people of Nature and people of Society, enemies and friends. In the text, as we have already said, these worlds almost always receive a spatial realization: the world of the poor is realized as "outskirts," "slums," "the attic apartment"; the world of the rich is "main street," "palaces," "the second floor." Ideas arise about sinful lands and righteous ones, the antithesis of the city and the country, of civilized Europe and the desert island, of the Bohemian woods and the castle of one's fathers. The classificatory boundary between opposing worlds is marked by a spatial line—of the Lethe dividing the living from the dead, of the Gates of Hell with the inscription destroying all hope of return, the rejection stamp that worn soles place on the pauper, prohibiting him from penetrating the space of the rich, Olenin's long fingernails and white hands, which prevent him from blending with the world of the Cossacks.[vi]

The plotless text affirms the stability of these boundaries.

The plotted text is constructed on the basis of the plotless one as its negation. The world is divided into the living and the dead and is split into two parts by an insurmountable line: while one is living, one cannot approach the dead, and being dead, one cannot visit the living. The plotted text, while maintaining this prohibition for all characters, introduces a single person (or a group) who liberates himself from it: Aeneas, Telemachus, or Dante descend into the empire of shadows; in Vasily Zhukovsky or Alexander Blok, the folkloric dead man visits the living. In this way, two groups of characters stand out: the mobile and the immobile.[13] The immobile obey the basic, plotless type of structure. They belong to a classification and affirm it in their own person. They are forbidden to pass across boundaries. The mobile character is an individual with a right to cut across boundaries. This is Eugène de Rastignac moving from the bottom to the top,[vii] Romeo and Juliet stepping over the line separating their inimical "houses," the hero who breaks free from the house of his fathers in order to join a monastery and become a saint, or the hero who breaks free of his social milieu and goes out to the people, to the revolution. Plot movement, *the event*—this is the crossing of that prohibitive boundary that a plotless structure establishes. The hero's movement *within* the space allotted to him is not an event. This lays bare the dependence of the concept of an event on the spatial structure adopted within the text, on its classificatory dimension. Plot can therefore always be reduced to a basic episode—the crossing of a basic topological boundary within its spatial structure. At the same time, insofar as a layered system of semantic boundaries is created at the heart of a hierarchy of binary oppositions (and, beyond that, specific orderings can arise that are sufficiently autonomous from the basic one), we find the potential for specific crossings of prohibitive lines, subordinate episodes being deployed within the hierarchy of plot movement.

In this way, the plotless system is primary and can be incarnated in a self-standing text. The plotted system, however, is secondary and always serves

vi Lotman refers to Leo Tolstoy's novella *The Cossacks*, in which a world-weary young aristocrat, Dmitry Olenin, heads for the Caucasus in pursuit of authentic life among the Cossacks, only to be rejected by them for his inability to adjust to their ways.

vii This is a reference to Balzac's novel *Le Père Goriot*, in which Rastignac is the main protagonist, and some other novels in his series *La comédie humaine*. Rastignac is a poor provincial noble who comes to Paris to make a rapid social ascent, mostly by way of deploying his charms on wealthy women who introduce him to society.

as a stratum superimposed on the basic plotless structure. Meanwhile, the relationship between both strata is always conflicted: plot content consists precisely of that whose impossibility is affirmed by the plotless structure. Relative to the "world picture," plot is a "revolutionary element."

If we interpret plot as an event's unfolding, a movement across a semantic frontier, then the reversibility of plots becomes obvious: the overcoming of one and the same boundary within the limits of one and the same semantic field can be developed into plot chains moving in opposite directions. Thus, for example, the world picture implied by the division into people (the living) and non-people (gods, beasts, the dead), or into "us" and "them," implies two kinds of plot: a person overcomes a boundary (the forest, the sea), visits the gods (beasts, the dead), and returns, having grabbed something, or else a god (beast, dead man) overcomes the boundary (forest, sea), visits people, and returns home, having grabbed something. Or else: one of "us," having overcome a boundary (crawling over a wall; walking across a border; dressing up "their own way"; starting to speak "not like us"; "shouting Mohammed," as Afanasy Nikitin advises;[viii] dressing up like a Frenchman, as Dolokhov does[ix]), gets through to "them," or else one of "them" gets through to us.

An event that is invariant relative to plot development can be regarded as a language, and the plot as a certain message in that language. But as a certain text—a construct—in its own right, the plot functions as a kind of language relative to texts at lower levels. Even within the limits of a given level, plot affords the text only a standard resolution: for a given world picture and a given structural level, there is but one plot. But in an actual text this plot is manifest only as some structural expectation that might be fulfilled, or might not be.

---

viii The reference is to Afanasy Nikitin, *The Journey Beyond Three Seas* [*Khozhenie za tri moria*]. Afanasy Nikitin (presumed to have died around 1475) was a merchant who took a trading trip to Persia and India in the years 1468–1474, before attempting to return to Russia. He left an interesting account of his journey, which was unearthed in the early nineteenth century. A polemic arose among scholars as to whether he might have converted to Islam during his journey. His notes are peppered with regrets at the difficulties of celebrating the Christian rites while living among "infidels." Analyzing Afanasy's behavior during his journey, B. A. Uspensky describes it as a typical example of "anti-behavior" induced by what amounts to a pilgrimage into "unclean" lands, that is, an anti-pilgrimage. See B. A. Uspenskii, "Dualisticheskii kharakter russkoi srednevekovoi kul'tury (na materiale *Khozheniia za tri moria* Afanasiia Nikitina)," in *Izbrannye Trudy*, vol. 1: *Semiotika istorii. Semiotika kul'tury* (Moscow: Gnozis, 1994), 254–297.

ix Fyodor Dolokhov is a character from Leo Tolstoy's *War and Peace* who epitomizes the behavior of Europeanized officers at the time of the campaign of 1812. He fights a duel with Pierre Bezukhov, during which he is nearly killed by a bungling Pierre.

CHAPTER 3

From *Culture and Explosion*

Culture and Explosion *is Lotman's last monograph, in which he returns to the notion of the heterogeneity at the heart of dynamic semiotic systems. Yet now his focus is on the temporal axis, on how culture as a complex semiotic system changes and how these changes contribute in fundamental ways to the creation of new information. Semiotic systems change at different speeds, and their changes assume different modes, gradual or explosive. And this complexity is itself an inherent property that is conducive to the meaning- and innovation-producing capacity of culture as a set of interlocking semiotic systems.* Culture and Explosion *also represents a meditation on the role of random occurrences in historical evolution, one stimulated, if not initiated, by the encounter with the thoughts of Ilya Prigogine. True to Lotman, this volume also contains some fascinating analyses of specific cultural phenomena, from Ivan the Terrible's tyranny to Charlie Chaplin. Regrettably, it has not been possible to include these sections in this anthology, but they are available in English in Juri Lotman,* Culture and Explosion, *ed. Marina Grishakova and trans. Wilma Clark (Berlin, 2009). For a good analysis of the place of* Culture and Explosion *in Lotman's scholarly career, see Marina Grishakova, "Afterword. Around* Culture and Explosion: *J. Lotman and the Tartu-Moscow School in the 1980–90s," in Lotman,* Culture and Explosion, *175–187.*

THE INTERRUPTED AND THE UNINTERRUPTED[i]

Up to this point we have turned our attention to the correlation between instances of explosion and of gradual development as two stages, one alternating with the other.[ii] Yet, their relationship unfolds in synchronous space as well.

i For our translation, we have used Iu. M. Lotman, "Preryvnoe i nepreryvnoe," in *Kul'tura i vzryv, Semiosfera* (St. Petersburg: Iskusstvo-SPB, 2000), 21–26.

ii In the previous section, entitled "Gradual Progress," Lotman had defined continuous movement as "reasoned predictability," of which the antithesis is "unpredictability, change realized in the form of an explosion." He explains these two modalities of change through a metaphor: "A minefield with unpredictable zones of explosion and a river in spring, carrying

In the dynamics of cultural development they are correlated not only by their sequence, but by their existing within a single, simultaneously operative mechanism. As a complex whole, culture consists of layers of varying speeds of development, such that any of its cross-sections reveals the simultaneous presence of its diverse phases. Explosions in some layers may be intermingled with gradual development in others. This, however, does not exclude these layers' interaction.

For example, the dynamics of processes in the sphere of language and politics, morality, and fashion demonstrates the diverse speeds by which these processes progress. And while the faster processes can exert an accelerating influence on the slower ones, and while the slower processes can assume the autonym of the faster ones, thereby accelerating their own development, their dynamics is not synchronous.

Even more essential is the simultaneous combination of abrupt and gradual processes in different cultural spheres. This question is complicated by the fact that they assume inadequate autonyms. This often mystifies researchers. It is their habit to reduce synchrony to structural unity and to interpret the aggression of any given autonym as establishing structural unity. First there is a wave of autonyms, and then a second wave, that of scholarly terminology, artificially unifies the picture of the process, smoothing out the structures' contradictions. Meanwhile, it is precisely these contradictions that generate the mechanisms of dynamic change.

Both gradual and explosive processes serve important functions in a synchronously operative structure: some foster innovation, others continuity. In the self-assessment of contemporaries, these tendencies are experienced as antagonistic, and the struggle between them is conceived through the categories of an all-out military battle. In fact, these are two sides of a single, integrated mechanism, of its synchronous structure, and the aggressiveness of one does not deaden the development of its counterpart, but stimulates it.

Thus, for example, the aggressiveness of the Karamzin-Zhukovsky school at the dawn of the nineteenth century stimulated the aggressiveness and development of the school of Shishkov, Katenin, and Griboedov.[iii] The

---

its powerful, but directed current—those are the two visual images, which arise in the mind of the historian studying dynamic (explosive) and gradual processes." Explosion is thus tightly connected to the notion of unpredictability.

iii The reference is to two different models for the evolution of the Russian literary language, one based on widespread lexical borrowings from French (Nikolay Karamzin's practice in the early stages of his writerly career) and the other on coining neologisms based on Old-Church Slavonic roots (which Alexander Shishkov had promoted in a series of articles). To this are

triumphant procession of "anti-Romanticism" from Balzac to Flaubert was synchronously intertwined with the blossoming of Hugo's Romanticism.

The intersection of various structural organizations becomes a source of dynamics. An artistic text, so long as it maintains its potency for an audience, constitutes a dynamic system.

Traditional structuralism originated in a principle already formulated by the Russian Formalists: the text is approached as a closed, self-sufficient, synchronously organized system. It is isolated not only temporally, from the past and future, but also spatially, from the audience and from everything else located outside it.

Contemporary structural-semiotic analysis has complicated these principles. Temporally, the text is interpreted as a kind of freeze-frame, an instant artificially "fixed" between past and future. The relationship between past and future is not symmetrical. The past is given in its two manifestations, one internal—as the intrinsic memory of a text embodied in its structure, in that structure's inevitable contradictions, its immanent struggle with its own internal synchrony—and the other external, as a correlation with extratextual memory.

Having placed himself mentally in the "present" that is realized in the text (for example, in the *given* painting, at the moment when I am looking at it), the spectator seems to turn his gaze toward the past, which comes together like a cone whose top touches the present. Turning toward the future, the audience is plunged into a bundle of possibilities that are yet to achieve their potential selection. Not knowing the future allows one to ascribe significance to everything. Chekhov's infamous gun, which, according to the author, must necessarily fire at the end of any play when it has appeared at the beginning, quite often does not fire. Chekhov's rule made sense only within the framework of a specific genre that has furthermore ossified in fixed forms. In fact, it is our ignorance of whether the gun will fire or not, of whether the shot will turn out to cause a mortal wound or be nothing more than a sound effect, which lends the moment its plot significance.

The future's uncertainty, however, has limits of its own, fuzzy as they are. Locked out of the future are those things that, within the bounds of a given system, by definition cannot enter it. The future appears as a space of potential

---

tied important considerations as to the relationship between written literature and oral usage. See B. A. Uspenskii, *Iz istorii russkogo literaturnogo iazyka XVIII–nachala XIX veka (Iazykovaia programma Karamzina i ee istoricheskie korni)* (Moscow: Izdatel'stvo MGU, 1985).

states. The relationship of past to future is shaped as follows: the present is the spark of an as-yet undeveloped semantic space. It potentially contains all possible future paths of development. It is important to emphasize that the selection of any one of them is determined neither by the laws of causality, nor by probability: at the instant of explosion, these mechanisms shut down completely. The selection of the future is realized as chance. It therefore possesses a high informational capacity. At the same time, the instant of selection is both the foreclosure of those paths condemned to remain merely potential possibilities and the instant when the laws of causality are restored to power.

The instant of explosion is simultaneously the place where there is a surge in the entire system's informational capacity. Here, the developmental trajectory leaps onto a completely new, unpredictable, and more complicated path. The dominant position that emerges as a result of the explosion and that determines its future course can be assumed by any element of the system or even by an element from a different system that the explosion happens to have pulled into the tangle of potential future courses. At the next stage, however, it already creates a predictable chain of events.

The loss of a soldier to shrapnel that just happens to intersect with him cuts off an entire sequence of potentially realizable future events. The older of the Turgenev brothers died of a random illness at the very beginning of his creative life.[iv] This young genius, according to Wilhelm Küchelbecker, could have rivaled Pushkin's talent and would have left a great mark on Russian literature. Here we may recall what Pushkin wrote of Lensky:[v]

> His lyre, gone silent now, could raise
> A ring uninterrupted, roaring
> Across the ages (VI, 133).
>
> Его умолкнувшая лира
> Гремучий, непрерывный звон
> В веках поднять могла.

Striking the feature of unpredictability from the historical process, we render it utterly pointless. From the position of a bearer of Reason, who assumes an

---

iv The reference is to Andrey Turgenev (1783–1803), a poet, translator, and author of interesting memoirs. He died of typhoid fever.

v In Pushkin's *Eugene Onegin*, Vladimir Lensky is a romantic poet unexpectedly killed by his friend Onegin in a duel over a trifling matter.

external point of view relative to the process (this could be God, Hegel, or any given philosopher who has mastered "the one and only scientific method"), this course is devoid of informativity. Meanwhile, every attempt at prognosticating the future in its dramatically ruptive instants demonstrates the impossibility of an unambiguous foretelling of history's sharp turning points. The historical process can be compared to an experiment. This is not, however, the vivid demonstration that the physics teacher offers to his audience with precise foreknowledge of the outcome. It is an experiment that the scientist assigns himself in order to reveal patterns that he does not yet know. From our point of view, the Principal Investigator is not the pedagogue demonstrating his knowledge, but the researcher uncovering spontaneous information from his own experiment.

The turning point in the process is the instant when the explosion exhausts itself. In the sphere of history, this is not only the initial point of future development, but also the locus of self-knowledge: it triggers those mechanisms of history that ought to explain to history itself that which has happened.

Further development returns us—now consciously, as it were—to the explosion's starting point. What has occurred is granted new life, one that is reflected in the notions of the observer. At the same time, there is a radical transformation of the event: that which happened randomly, as we have seen, now appears as the only possible course. In the observer's consciousness, unpredictability is replaced by regularity. From his point of view, the choice had been fictive: "objectively," it had been predetermined by the entire causal chain of the events preceding it.

It is precisely this kind of process that occurs when the complex interweaving of causally conditioned and random events, which we call "history," is turned into the object of description, first by contemporaries, then by historians. This double layering of description is intended to remove randomness from the events. This kind of substitution is easily carried out in those historical spheres where gradual processes prevail and there is a minimal role for abrupt turns of events. These are the strata of history wherein, firstly, action is slowest to develop, and secondly, the individual personality plays a lesser role.

Thus the way researchers of the French *La nouvelle histoire* school describe history provides the most convincing results in their examination of slow and gradual processes. It is just as natural that the era perceives the history of technology as anonymous. A painting is remembered by the name of the artist, but brands of automobile by makes and models.

In Chekhov's story "A First-Class Passenger" [Passazhir pervogo klassa], the hero, a prominent engineer who has built many bridges in his lifetime and made a series of technical discoveries, is indignant at the fact that his name is unknown to the pubic:

> In my life I have built a couple dozen magnificent bridges in old Mother Russia, I have furnished three cities with running water, I have worked in Russia, England, and Belgium ... Secondly, I have written many specialized articles in my field ..., I have discovered methods for deriving several organic acids, so that you will find my name in all the chemistry textbooks abroad. ... I won't abuse your attention by enumerating my works and the services I have rendered; I will say only that I have done a great deal more than certain famous people. And so what? Here I am already old, I'm getting ready to kick off, one could say, and I'm about as famous as that black dog running there along the embankment.

The story's hero is furthermore indignant at the fact that his lover, an untalented provincial songstress, enjoys widespread fame, and her name has been printed more than once in the newspapers: "The girl is shallow, capricious, greedy, and a fool besides." The hero, in a fit of pique, narrates the following episode: "As I now recall, we were taking part in a ceremonial opening to traffic along a newly built bridge. ... 'Well,' I thought, 'now all eyes will be upon me. Where is there to hide?' But my concern, my dear sir, was in vain." The hero had not drawn the audience's attention: "The audience suddenly began to stir: *shhh* ... Faces started to smile, shoulders to move. 'They must have seen me,' I thought. Fat chance!"[1] The audience had been brought to life by the appearance of the very same songstress of whom he had spoken so ironically.

The hero of the story faults the audience's ignorance and lack of culture. True, he immediately falls into a comic situation, insofar as he has never heard anything about his interlocutor, who turns out to be a prominent scientist. The storyteller complains of injustice. Yet the roots of the phenomenon that Chekhov has grasped run deeper. It is not just society's superficiality and lack of culture that are the cause of the injustice that Chekhov has noted. The point is that even a bad songstress's artistic production is, by its very nature, personal, whereas what even a good engineer produces seems to dissipate into the generalized, anonymous technological progress. Should the bridge collapse, the engineer's name would likely be remembered because the event would be remarkable. No one notices the merits of a bridge unless they are extraordinary. Technological development is, in broad outline, predictable, and this is demonstrated, for example, in the most successful works from the field of science fiction. Unless this or that discovery is incorporated into the normal process of sequential development, it finds no technological application.

And so the instant of explosion marks the beginning of another stage. In processes that are realized through the active participation of the mechanisms of self-consciousness, this is a pivotal moment. Consciousness moves, as it were, in reverse, to the moment preceding explosion, and interprets everything that has occurred retrospectively. The process that has actually taken place is replaced by its model, born from the consciousness of a participant in the act. A retrospective transformation occurs. What has happened appears as the only possibility—as something "fundamental, historically predetermined." What has not happened is interpreted as something impossible. The weight of the regular and inevitable is ascribed to the random.

In such a way are events transferred into the memory of the historian. He receives them as already having been transformed, influenced by memory's initial selection. It is especially important that all accidents in the material are isolated, and that the explosion has been transformed into a regular, linear development. If any discussion of explosion is permitted, then the whole notion's meaning is decisively altered: it includes a sense of the energy and speed of the event, its overcoming the resistance of opposing forces, but it categorically excludes the notion that the choice of one among many possibilities is unpredictable. As a result, the concept of "explosion" no longer entails informativity, which yields its place to fatalism.

The historian's gaze is a secondary process of retrospective transformation. The historian looks at the event through a gaze that looks from the position of the present toward the past. This gaze, by its very nature, transforms the object of description. Once the historian has had his hands on it, the portrait of events, though chaotic to the simple observer, has acquired another layer of organization. It is typical of the historian to start from the assumption that what has happened was inevitable. But his creative activity manifests itself elsewhere: from the accumulation of facts retained in memory, he constructs the contiguous line that leads most reliably to this conclusive point. Under the historian's pen, this convergence, with accident as its foundation, with chance concealed under a whole layer of arbitrary assumptions and quasi-convincing causal connections, attains an almost mystical character. In it one can see the triumph of divine or historical predestinations, the bearer of meaning for the entire process that came before. The concept of an endpoint, objectively alien to history, is imposed on it.

Ignatius of Loyola once made so bold as to say that the end justifies the means, but this principle was widely known before the Jesuits appeared, and it has guided people who have never heard or thought about the Jesuits. It is the basis by which history is justified and infused with Higher Meaning. It is, however, a fact of history, and not the instrument of its knowledge. And it is no accident that every similar event—"the salt of the salt of history"—is canceled by a subsequent explosion and lapses into to oblivion. But reality consists of other stuff.

At the moment of explosion, such eschatological ideas as the assertion that the Day of Judgement is nigh, of worldwide revolution, independent of whether it begins in Paris or Petersburg, and other analogous historical facts, are imbued with significance not by their giving rise to the "last and final battle," which is supposed to be followed by the Kingdom of God on earth, but by their provoking an unprecedented straining of national forces and introducing dynamism into what would seem to be stable layers of history. It is natural to humans to evaluate these moments through the categories inherent to us, positive and negative. To the historian, it suffices to point them out and to make them objects of study with as much objectivity as he or she can muster.

PERSPECTIVES[i]

And so, explosions are an inescapable feature of a linear, dynamic process. I have already said that in binary structures these dynamics are marked by their stark peculiarity. But what does this peculiarity consist of?

In ternary social structures the explosions that are most powerful and deep do not encompass the whole complex richness of various social layers.[ii] The central structure might experience an explosion so powerful and catastrophic that its rumbling undoubtedly echoes across the entire depth of the culture. And yet under the conditions of a ternary structure the assertions of contemporaries, and after them also of historians, regarding the complete ruination of the old system's order are a blend of self-delusion and tactical sloganeering. And it is not just that the absolute destruction of the old is as impossible in ternary structures as it is in binary ones, but a deeper process is taking place:

---

i Translation is from Iu. M. Lotman, "Perspektivy," in *Kul'tura i vzryv, Semiosfera*, 141–146.

ii For the difference between binary and ternary structures, see "The Role of Dual Models in the Dynamics of Russian Culture (until the End of the Eighteenth Century)" in this anthology.

ternary structures retain specific values from the preceding period, transferring them from the system's periphery to its center. Against this, the ideal of binary systems is the complete destruction of all that has come before as tainted by irremediable defects. The ternary system strives to adapt the ideal to reality, the binary to realize an unrealizable ideal in practice. In binary systems the explosion encompasses all strata of everyday life. The ruthlessness of this experiment will not reveal itself all at once. Initially, it uses the poetry of instantaneously constructing "a new earth and a new heaven"—that is, its own radicalism—to draw in society's most maximalist layers.

The price one must pay for utopias is revealed only at the next stage. A characteristic aspect of moments of explosion in binary systems is that they are experienced as a unique moment incomparable with anything else in the whole history of mankind. What is declared to have been vanquished is not any concrete layer of historical development, but the very existence of history. In the ideal, this is the apocalyptic "there should be time no longer" (Revelation 10:6), but in its practical realization it leads to the words with which Mikhail Saltykov-Shchedrin closes his *The History of a Town* [*Istoriia odnogo goroda*]: "History halted its own flow."[1]

No less characteristic of binary systems is the aspiration to replace jurisprudence with moral or religious principles.

In *The Captain's Daughter* [*Kapitanskaia dochka*] there is a passage that draws our attention in this regard: Masha Mironova travels to the capital to rescue Grinev, who has gotten himself into trouble. A remarkable conversation occurs between her and Catherine the Great, who thinks as a sovereign: "You are an orphan: most likely you're here to complain of injustice and injury?" An unexpected answer follows: "Not at all, my lady. I came to ask for mercy, not justice" (VIII, 372).[iii]

This theme, which Boris Pasternak, in *Doctor Zhivago,* calls "the unscrupulousness of the heart," perturbed Pushkin in the 1830s, and he would revisit it more than once. The hero of "Angelo" [Andzhelo], a strict moralist who has fallen into sin, does, upon recognizing his own fall, subject himself to the very same inhuman adherence to principles that had guided him in judging transgressors:

---

iii *The Captain's Daughter* is a historical novel by Pushkin. The plot centers around Pyotr Grinev's attempts to serve his country as officer while also aiming to protect and save his beloved Masha Mironova. This situation forces him into contacts with the enemy, which earns him a charge of treason. Here and elsewhere Lotman uses the following edition: A. S. Pushkin, *Polnoe sobranie sochinenii* (Leningrad: Izdatel'stvo ANSSSR, 1937–1959).

> … So said the Duke, "Now, Angelo, tell me
> What you deserve?" With neither pleading, nor confusion,
> He answered firm, if sulkily: "Execution. …"[2]

> Дук тогда: «Что, Анджело, скажи,
> Чего достоин ты?» Без слез и без боязни,
> С угрюмой твердостью тот отвечает: «Казни. …»

What triumphs, however, is not justice, but mercy:

> Isabella, with all her soul,
> Showed pity, like an angel, for the sinner bound for Hell …

> Изабела
> Душой о грешнике, как ангел, пожалела …

And the whole point of the poem is compressed into the closing line, graphically separated from the rest:

> And the Duke offered him his pardon (V, 129).

> И Дук его простил.

Finally, in the very same sequence of calls for mercy, Pushkin's concluding verse rings out:

> And he urged mercy for the fallen (III, 424).

> И милость к падшим призывал.[iv]

Mercy stands against the Law, which had been the "hero" of the early ode "Liberty" [Vol′nost′].[3]

In the antithesis of mercy and justice, the Russian idea, rooted in binarity, stands against Latin rules, which are suffused with the spirit of the law: *Fiat Justitia—pereat mundus*, and *Dura lex, sed lex.*[4] [v]

---

iv This line is from Pushkin's famous poem "I've raised myself a monument" ["Ia pamiatnik sebe vozdvig"], a reworking of Horace's ode "Exegi monumentum."

v An extended discussion of Pushkin's thoughts around the opposition between justice and mercy can be found in Ju. M. Lotman, "'Agreement' and 'Self-Giving' as Archetypal

All the more momentous is Russian literature's steadfast tendency to see in the law a dry and inhuman principle, as opposed to such informal concepts as mercy, sacrifice, love. Behind this one discerns the antithesis of state law and personal virtue, politics and sanctity.

The tradition of opposing the law of the state to human morality begins with Gogol, particularly with his *Selected Passages from Correspondence with Friends* [*Vybrannye mesta iz perepiski s druz'iami*]. Although the Gogolian advice for setting a drunken peasant right with such exhortations as "Oh, you filthy mug, you!" met with general disapproval, even among the Slavophiles,[vi] the very notion of building a non-juridical society of some kind is proclaimed throughout the second half of the nineteenth century.[5] The lawyer is invariably a negative figure in both Tolstoy and Dostoevsky.

Court reform was indisputably the most thoroughly considered fruit of the era of reforms, and yet it was subject to the most vicious attacks from both the right and the left. Political liberalism stood in opposition to utopia. Through Sonia's lips, Dostoevsky summoned Raskolnikov to kneel in the middle of the square and repent before the people.[vii] In *The Power of Darkness* [*Vlast' t'my*], Tolstoy—together with Akim, who is tongue-tied, but who because of this articulates the truth that has been hidden "from the scribes and Pharisees"—proclaims the supremacy of conscience over the law and of penitence over judgement:[viii]

Models of Culture," in Ju. M. Lotman and B. A. Uspenskij, *The Semiotics of Russian Culture*, ed. Ann Shukman (Michigan Slavic Contributions, vol. 11) (Ann Arbor: The University of Michigan, 1984), 125–140. See also Caryl Emerson, "Pushkin's 'Andzhelo,' Lotman's Insight into It, and the Proper Measure of Politics and Grace," in *Lotman and Cultural Studies: Encounters and Extensions*, ed. Andreas Schönle (Madison: Wisconsin University Press, 2006), 84–111.

vi In letter 22, entitled "The Russian Estate Owner," of his *Selected Passages from Correspondence with Friends*, Gogol gives advice on how a landowner should manage his serfs, namely by resting his authority on divine dispensation and instilling in them the fear of God, while responding to signs of disrespect with streams of invectives. *Selected Passages*, Gogol's last and highly controversial work, sketches out the vision of a somewhat idiosyncratic Slavophile theocracy.

vii In Fyodor Dostoevsky's *Crime and Punishment*, Sonya is a young woman who has to prostitute herself to feed her parents and siblings. She is instrumental in prodding Raskolnikov to confess his crime to the people and embark on the path of spiritual redemption. The novel draws a sharp line between the state administration of justice and moral rebirth.

viii *The Power of Darkness* is a play by Leo Tolstoy, written in 1886 and depicting a series of sordid murders in a peasant family. The quoted scene is from the end of the play, when Nikita confesses to murdering the husband of his lover Anisya and subsequently the child he had with

The people approach, wanting to seize him [Nikita].

AKIM (*pushing them away*): Stop! Lads! Stay where you are, I say!

NIKITA: I have poisoned him, Akulina. In Christ's name, forgive me. [...]

AKIM: O Lord! Such a sin, such a sin.

CONSTABLE: Seize him! And send for the mayor and for witnesses. An indictment must be drawn up. Stand up, come here.

AKIM (*to the Constable*): And you, I, um, those, the bright buttons, um, I, well look. Let him, um, you know, speak.

CONSTABLE (*to Akim*): Look here, old man, stay out of it. It's my duty to draw up an indictment.

AKIM: Oh, um, my. Let him, I say. Forget it, um, the *in-dit-mint,* I mean. This, uh, this here is God's work ... a person repenting, I mean, and you about *in-dit-mint.*[6]

The binary system breaks evolution into fragments ("nature is all in fracture," after the words that Mandelstam ascribed to Lamarck).[7][ix] In Western-style civilizations, as I have already said, an explosion disrupts only a portion of the layers of the culture, even perhaps a very significant portion, though as it does so the historical continuity is not interrupted. In binary structures, moments of rupture disrupt the chain of uninterrupted contiguity that inevitably leads not only to deep crises, but also to radical renewal.

Thus the reforms taking place in Russia in the last third of the nineteenth century were halted by the simultaneous shift toward methods of terror by both the administration and the democrats alike. The desire to bring an end to history clashed against the ambition to make it leap. The warring sides converged on one point: their dislike for "gradualists." Besides, the high morality of certain actors among the warring parties turned out to be not entirely stainless when it came to the interests of a cohesive structure.

A cohesive structure is aimed at levelling and survival, its mechanism juridical. Partisanship is directed toward the truth (always its own truth)—at any cost. The extreme embodiment of the former is compromise, of the latter—war

---

his step-daughter, Anisya's daughter. Akim is Nikita's father, a pious man who encourages his son's confession.

ix In Mandelstam's poem "Lamarck."

to absolute victory and the complete destruction of one's enemy. Accordingly, victory ought to be preceded by a bloody battle, where defeat is a possibility. But then victory is presented as "the last and decisive battle"—the establishment of the kingdom of God on earth.

When the Virgin Mary appeared to Girolamo Savonarola, promising to intercede in the fulfillment of his ideas, she forewarned him: "But, as you well know, the renewal and comforting of the church cannot proceed without tremendous discord and bloody conflict, especially in Italy. It is the latter that is the cause of all these evils, on account of the opulence, pride, and innumerable other unspeakable sins of its supreme leaders." The Madonna showed Savonarola the spectacle of Florence and all of Italy engulfed in mutinies and wars. But then the Madonna showed Savonarola a different globe:[8] "When I opened this sphere, I saw Florence all in lilies woven into the undulations of the walls and stretching from everywhere on long stalks. And the angels, soaring above the walls surrounding the city, looked down upon them."[9] The miraculous utopian reincarnation of mankind always begins in theory with a redemptive sacrifice, with the spilling of blood. In practice, it is doomed to drown in blood.

Among the brilliant pleiad of Russian writers of the last [nineteenth] century who have won worldwide recognition, our gaze somehow always glides past the lonely and enigmatic figure of Ivan Krylov. Acknowledged by readers from every layer of society, he is completely alone in the literary struggle of his era. He had no need to idealize the people, since he himself *is* the people. He is free of illusions. His sober mind is not untouched by skepticism, but his principal emotion is sobriety. He does not believe in miracles, no matter who created them, whether the tsar or the people. He does not beautify the peasant, though in the deep foundations of his consciousness he is, of course, a democrat. Sometimes he raises himself almost to the point of prophecy. In a version of his fable "Parnassus" [Parnas] that was not intended for print, Krylov wrote:

> As the gods in Greece were facing a frightful juncture
>   Which set to sway their throne,
> Or, one might say, striking a simpler tone,
> As fashion cast the gods out of their home,
> Against the gods the people applied pressure. ...
>   The many pranks on gods were callous:
>   Their life is harder every year!
>   And finally, with equal malice,
>   They had one day to quit Greece clear.

No matter that they were obstinate,
It was time to clean the temples out;
But that is not the end: everything the gods took in,
It's time we beat it out of them.
May God forbid a god's made undivine!

Как в Греции богам пришли минуты грозны
И стал их колебаться трон;
Иль, так сказать, простее взявши тон,
Как боги выходить из моды стали вон.
То начали богам прижимки делать розны. …
Богам худые шутки:
Житье теснее каждый год!
И наконец им сказан в сутки
Совсем из Греции поход.
Как ни были они упрямы,
Пришло очистить храмы:
Но это не конец: давай с богов лупить
Всё, что они успели накопить.
Не дай бог из богов разжаловану быть!

True, the exile of the gods led to the fact that a new master, for whom they had cordoned off Parnassus, "started grazing his Asses upon it."[10] Neither the old, nor the new summoned illusions in Krylov. What drives Krylov is sound reason, liberation from illusions, from the power of words and slogans. But Krylov is powerful not only as a destroyer of illusions: it may be that in the whole history of Russian culture no one has succeeded in creating so organic a unity between the unadulterated spirit of the people and the very highest European culture.

Krylov is, of course, not the sole representative—though he is the most brilliant—of this tendency in Russian culture, alien to both Slavophilism and Westernism, alien to the very principle of "Whoever is not with us is against us," the guiding principle of binary systems. In this regard one ought also to cite Alexander Ostrovsky and especially Chekhov.

This discussion has an immediate bearing on events now taking place in the former territory of the Soviet Union.[x] From the perspective of the questions

x Lotman wrote *Culture and Explosion* in early 1992 during the period of "shock therapy," the radical, if incomplete program of liberalization embarked upon by Boris Yeltsin's government after the collapse of the Soviet Union in 1991.

we have been investigating, the process we are witnessing can be described as a switch from a binary system to a ternary one. Yet one cannot help but notice the moment's peculiarity: the shift is itself conceived through the traditional concepts of binarism. In fact, two potential paths come into play here. One, which led to Gorbachev's loss of power, consisted of replacing reform with declarations and plans and brought the country to an impasse fraught with the gloomiest prognoses. The other, expressed in myriad plans of the "500 days" variety and in other projects for rapid economic transformation, fights fire with fire, explosion with explosion.

The shift from thinking oriented around explosions and toward an evolutionary concept now assumes a special meaning, insofar as all earlier culture familiar to us was drawn to polarism and maximalism. Yet the self-concept does not match reality. In the sphere of reality, explosions cannot disappear; we are speaking only of overcoming the fatal choice between stasis and catastrophe. Besides, ethical maximalism rooted itself so deeply in the very foundations of Russian culture that it is hardly possible to speak of the "danger" of an absolute imposition of the golden mean, let alone being concerned that reconciling the contradictions would halt the creative processes of explosion. If progress—and the alternative would only be catastrophe, the limits of which are difficult to predict—will nevertheless cross the line we find ourselves on now, then the emergent order will hardly be a simple copy of the West. History does not know repetition. It loves new and unpredictable paths.

INSTEAD OF CONCLUSIONS[i]

The notion that the point of departure for any semiotic system is not the separate, isolated sign (word) but the relationship between at least two signs forces us to look differently at the fundamental bases of semiosis. The point of departure is not a singular model, but semiotic space. This space is filled with an agglomeration of elements entertaining the most varied relationships with one another: they can appear in the form of conflicting meanings wavering in the space between being completely identical and absolutely non-contiguous. These multilingual texts feature both possibilities simultaneously—that is, one and the same text can have zero overlap with a given semantic field while being identical with another. This diversity of potential connections between elements of meaning creates a capacious meaning that is fully grasped only in

i Translation is from Iu. M. Lotman, "Vmesto vyvodov," in *Kul'tura i vzryv, Semiosfera*, 146–148.

the relationship between all the elements, of each to the others and of each to the whole. Beyond that, one ought to bear in mind that the system retains the memory of all its preceding conditions and a potential "premonition" of the future. In this way, the signifying space is multidimensional, both in synchronic and diachronic relations. It possesses blurry boundaries and the capacity to be included in the processes of explosion.

A system that has passed through the stage of self-description undergoes changes: it assigns itself sharp boundaries and a significantly higher degree of unification. Separating self-description from the condition that had preceded it, however, can only ever be done theoretically. In actuality, both levels are constantly influencing one another.

Thus a culture's self-description turns a boundary into an element of its self-consciousness. Self-consciousness crystalizes the boundaries of cultures, while including national-political considerations in this process has not infrequently lent it a dramatic character. One can juxtapose this with the blurry boundaries of languages on the map of their actual distribution and their distinct separation on, for example, a political map.

We were speaking earlier of binary and ternary cultural systems. They cross the critical line of explosion differently. The processes of explosion in a tripartite system rarely encompass the whole depth of culture. As a rule, what occurs here is a simultaneity of explosion in some cultural spheres and gradual development in others. Thus, for example, the collapse of the Napoleonic Empire, which witnessed a total explosion in politics, state structure, and culture writ large, had no effect on ownership rights to land that had been sold off in the years of the Revolution (*biens nationaux*). One could just as well point to the way the Roman structure of municipal authority grew doggedly throughout the numerous upheavals of the barbarian invasions and, when all was done, having transformed beyond recognition, has maintained an uninterrupted continuity up to our own time.

This capacity of a culture that grew out of the Roman Empire to preserve its sameness amidst change, and to turn the unchanging into a form of change, placed its seal on the fundamental characteristics of Western European culture. Even such attempts at an absolute reordering of the whole living space as Cromwell's socio-religious utopia or the explosion of the Jacobine dictatorship, when it comes down it, encompassed only rather limited spheres of life. Already Nikolay Karamzin remarked that at the same time as passions were boiling in the National Assembly and the theater, the streets of Paris near the Palais-Royal were living a happy life quite far from politics.

For Russian culture, with its binary structure, a completely different self-appraisal is typical. Even where an empirical examination reveals manifold and gradual processes, on the level of self-consciousness we are dealing with the idea of the complete and unconditional destruction of the preceding development and the apocalyptic birth of the new.

The theoreticians of Marxism wrote that the transition from capitalism to socialism would inevitably assume the character of an explosion.[ii] This was grounded in the fact that all other formations have been conceived within the framework of the preceding stages, whereas socialism initiates an entirely new period, and its conception is possible only on the ruins, and not in the lap of the preceding history. At the same time, they pointed out how both the feudal and bourgeois orders first arose in the field of economics and only then received state-legislative formalization. What occurred, however, was a curious holdover: examples of a new structure maturing within the deep soil of the old one were drawn from the history of the Roman Empire and its cultural descendants, but the theory of socialism "in one country taken separately" was argued through the facts of Russian history in the present century, that is, a history with a distinctly binary self-consciousness.

Here one ought first to note that the idea that socialism cannot possibly grow out of capitalism diverged from the ideas of Western social democracy while distinctly recalling notions that had periodically circulated in Russian history. Apocalyptic words about the "new heaven" and the "new earth" have captivated numerous socio-religious movements throughout history. But in the West these have been, as a rule, peripheral religious movements that have periodically bubbled to the surface without ever becoming dominant forces in the great historical cultures for any length of time. Russian culture conceives of itself in the categories of explosion.

Perhaps the most interesting moment in this regard is the one we are now living through. Theoretically, it is understood as the victory of the real,

---

ii The term Marx and his followers used was, of course, revolution, but this passage raises the interesting question of Lotman's relationship to Marxist thought. See M. L. Gasparov, "Lotman i marksizm," *Novoe literaturnoe obozrenie* 19 (1996): 7–13. Gasparov somewhat facetiously argues that in its method Lotman's structuralism was more genuinely Marxist than the scholarship of his Communist contemporaries. B. F. Egorov writes more narrowly of the endurance of basic Hegelian and early Marxian premises, but accompanied by a rejection of the primacy of class consciousness and a greater sense of the complexity of cultural phenomena. See B. F. Egorov, *Zhizn' i tvorchestvo Iu. M. Lotmana* (Moscow: Novoe literaturnoe obozrenie, 1999), 87–92.

of "natural" development over an unsuccessful historical experiment. A most fitting slogan for this era might be the old rule of the Physiocrats, *Laissez faire laissez passer.*[1]

The notion of autonomous economic development in Western Europe was organically bound to gradual development in time, with a rejection of the "flogging of history." In our context, this very same slogan is weighed down by the idea of state interference and the instantaneous overcoming of the space of history in the shortest possible timeframe, whether in 500 days or in whatever other time dictated to history from the outset. Psychologically, what we see here is the same principle as in the Petrine idea of "catching up to and overtaking Europe" (in the period between the Battle of Narva and the Treaty of Nystad)[iii] or the more memorable "five-year plan in four years."[iv] We even want to realize a gradual development through the technics of explosion. This is not the result of someone's intellectual incompetence, however, but the strict dictate of a binary historical structure.

The fundamental change in relations between Eastern and Western Europe now taking place before our eyes may offer the possibility of shifting to a pan-European, ternary system and rejecting the ideal of razing "the old world to its foundations, and then" building a new one upon its ruins. Missing this opportunity would be a historical catastrophe.

---

iii The Russian defeat at Narva against the army of Charles XII of Sweden in 1700 signalled the need for fundamental reforms to modernize Russia's army. The battle inaugurated the Great Northern War, the war against Sweden, which was concluded in 1721 with the Treaty of Nystad.

iv The Soviet practice of adopting "Five-year plans," an instrument of central industrial planning, was started in 1928. Several of them took only four years to complete.

CHAPTER 4

Memory in a Culturological Light

Translation is from Iu. M. Lotman, "Pamiat' v kul'turologicheskom osveshchenii," in Kul'tura i vzryv, Semiosfera *(St. Petersburg: Iskusstvo-SPB, 2000), 673–676, which was first published in 1985. Lotman's idea of cultural memory as a creative and meaning-generating process resonates with the vast literature on collective memory. One central insight here is the distinction between memory as texts preserved for their informational value and the memory inscribed in art, which undergoes much more creative transformations. Lotman strongly emphasizes the variability of memory over time, as cultural texts can go through phases of latency, that is, temporary oblivion, before resurfacing. Yet even then, in a new semiotic environment, these texts acquire new meanings. Lotman's description of the tension between shared memory and its individuation, inscribed in local "dialects of memory," can provide a useful corrective to approaches that emphasize too strongly the homogeneity of collective memory or conceive of the relation between collective and individual memory in overly stark binary terms.*

1. From the perspective of semiotics, culture presents itself as collective intellect and collective memory, that is, a supra-individual mechanism for preserving and transmitting certain messages (texts) and producing new ones. In this sense, the space of culture can be defined as the space of a certain common memory, that is, a space within whose boundaries certain common texts can be preserved and actualized. Their actualization occurs within the bounds of a certain semantic invariant, which allows us to say that in the context of a new era the text retains, despite all the variability of its interpretations, an identity with itself. So the memory that is common within the space of a given culture is preserved, first of all, by the availability of certain textual constants and, secondly, by the codes' uniformity, their invariability, or else the continuity and rule-bound character of their transformations.

2. Culture's memory is not merely unitary, but also internally variegated. This means that its unity exists only on a certain level and implies the availability

of particular "dialects of memory" corresponding to the internal organization of the collectives that constitute the world of a given culture. The tendency toward the individuation of memory constitutes the second pole of its dynamic structure. The availability of cultural substructures of diverse composition and mnemonic capacity leads to varying degrees of ellipticism in a text circulating within cultural subgroups and to the emergence of "local semantics." In crossing the boundaries of a given subgroup, the elliptical texts are supplemented so as to become comprehensible. A similar role is played by various commentaries. When, at the end of his life, Gavrila Derzhavin was compelled to write an extensive commentary on his own odes, this was called for, on the one hand, by a sense of the flow of the "river of time,"[i] by his clear awareness of the fact that the cultural collective of his audience in the time of Catherine the Great had collapsed, and that the text could become entirely incomprehensible to the posterity that Derzhavin regarded as his actual audience. On the other hand, Derzhavin was acutely aware of the collapse of the ode as a genre and of eighteenth-century poetics in general (a collapse he himself had actively fostered). Had literary tradition remained unchanged, the "genre memory" (Mikhail Bakhtin) would have retained the comprehensibility of the text regardless of the change in collectives. The appearance of commentaries and glossaries, as well as the process of filling in the elliptical omissions in the text, bears witness to its passing into the sphere of a collective with different mnemonic baggage.

3. If I permit myself a certain degree of simplification and identify memory with the preservation of texts, it will be possible to distinguish between "informative memory" and "creative (generative) memory." To the former we can ascribe the mechanisms by which the results of a given cognitive activity are retained. Thus, for example, in storing technical information, its ultimate (chronologically, as a rule, final) version will be the most relevant. A person interested in the history of a technique is certainly not someone intent on making practical use of its results. This interest can arise in someone who seeks to *invent* something new. But from the point of view of information *preservation*, in this case it is only that result, the final text, that is active. Memory of this kind has a character that is flat, situated in a single temporal dimension, and subject to the law of chronology. It develops in the same direction as the flow of time itself and is consistent with it.

---

i "The River of Time in Its Coursing" (1816) is one of Derzhavin's most famous poems, and his last. It is about the supreme equality with which "the river of time" destroys the works of people.

The memory of art in particular is an example of creative memory. Here an entire stratum of texts turns out to be potentially active. Actualizing certain texts or others is subject to the complicated laws of wider cultural movement and cannot be reduced to the formula that "the newest is the best." In its simplest form, the line of alternation between a culture's "forgetting" and "remembering" assumes a sinusoidal character (for example, the decline in Pushkin's actuality for the Russian reader from the 1840s to the 1860s, its rise from the 1880s to the 1900s, its fall in the 1910s and 1920s and rise in the 1930s and the years following, the shift between being "jettisoned from the ship of modernity"[ii] and being "raised on a pedestal"). The general actualization of all forms of ancient art, not only of the Middle Ages, but the Neolithic as well, has become a characteristic feature of European cultural memory in the second half of the twentieth century. Simultaneously, de-actualization ("quasi-oblivion") has enveloped the cultural paradigm that includes classical and Renaissance art. Hence this aspect of cultural memory has a panchronic, continuous-spatial character. Memory sheds light on current, relevant texts, while non-actual ones do not disappear, but sort of die down, transitioning into potential. This arrangement of texts has a character that is not syntagmatic, but continuous, and in its integrity it constitutes a text that one ought to associate not with the library or with machine memory in the forms that technology makes available at present, but with the film reel in the manner of Andrey Tarkovsky's *The Mirror* or Miklós Jancsó's *Agnus Dei*.

As a creative mechanism, cultural memory is not only panchronic, but stands in opposition to time. It preserves the past as what endures. From the perspective of memory as a mechanism operating within its entire depth, the past has not passed. This is why historicism in the study of literature, in the way in which it was initially created by the Hegelian theory of culture, and subsequently by the positivist theory of progress, is in fact anti-historical, since it ignores memory's active role in giving birth to new texts.

4. In light of the aforementioned, one ought to pay attention to the fact that new texts are created not only in the present cross-section of culture, but in its past as well. This seemingly paradoxical proposition merely articulates a truth that is obvious and familiar to everyone. Throughout the entire history of culture, "unknown" monuments of the past have constantly been discovered,

---

ii This phrase comes from the Futurist manifesto "A Slap in the Face of Public Taste" [Poshchechina obshchemu vkusu], published by David Burliuk, Alexander Kruchenykh, Vladimir Mayakovsky, and Viktor Khlebnikov. See *Russian Futurism Through Its Manifestoes, 1912–1928*, ed. Anna Lawton, trans. Anna Lawton and Herbert Eagle (Ithaca: Cornell University Press, 1988), 51–52.

revealed, dug out of the earth or a library's dust. Where do they come from? Why is it that in critical editions we are constantly coming across headings like "An Unknown Monument of Medieval Poetry" or "Yet Another Forgotten Writer of the Eighteenth Century"?

Every culture establishes its own paradigm of what ought to be remembered (that is, preserved) and what is subject to oblivion. The latter is deleted from collective memory and "as if ceases to exist." But time and the system of cultural codes shift, and the paradigm of memory and oblivion changes. What had appeared to be truly extant can turn out to be "as if nonexistent" and subject to oblivion, and what was nonexistent can become extant and meaningful. They found ancient statues in the pre-Renaissance era, too, but they cast them aside and destroyed them and did not preserve them. Medieval Russian iconography was, of course, known in both the eighteenth and nineteenth centuries. But as high art and cultural treasure it entered the consciousness of post-Petrine culture only in the twentieth century.

It is not, however, merely that the set of texts changes, but the texts themselves change. Under the influence of new codes used in deciphering a text that had been set aside in the memory of culture in times long past, there is a permutation of meaningful and meaningless elements within the text's structure. In fact, texts that have attained the level of art through the complexity of their organization generally cannot be passive containers of stable information, insofar as they are not storehouses, but generators. Ideas in the cultural memory are not "preserved" so much as they grow. Texts that constitute the "shared memory" of a cultural collective serve not only as a means for deciphering the texts circulating in the contemporary, synchronous cross-section of culture, but they generate new ones as well.

5. The productivity of meaning-making in the process of collision between texts preserved in the memory of culture and contemporary codes depends on the extent of semiotic displacement. Insofar as cultural codes develop, being themselves dynamically involved in the historical process, texts first of all can precede and anticipate the dynamics of the codes' development. When classical sculpture or Provencal poetry flood the cultural memory of the Italian late Middle Ages, they provoke a disruptive revolution in the system of "the culture's grammar." In so doing, the new grammar influences the creation of the new texts appropriate to it, on the one hand, and, on the other, determines the perception, in no way adequate to the classical or Provencal, of the old ones.

A more complicated case arises when texts are brought into a culture's memory that, in their structure, stand far from its immanent organization, texts for the decipherment of which its internal tradition has no adequate codes. Among such cases are the mass penetration of translations of Christian texts into the culture of eleventh- and twelfth-century Rus or of Western European texts into post-Petrine Russian culture.

There emerges a rupture between cultural memory and its synchronic mechanisms of text-formation. This situation often has general typological features: initially there is a pause in text-formation (as though culture becomes a receptor, the capacity of memory increases with much greater speed than do the possibilities of deciphering texts); then there is an explosion, and the new text-formation assumes a remarkably turbulent, productive character. In this situation, the development of culture assumes the appearance of uniquely bright, almost spasmodic flashes. And yet the culture that is undergoing this flash period often rises from the periphery of the cultural arena toward its center and itself actively broadcasts texts into the dying craters of the former centers of text-formation.

In this sense, cultures whose memory is permeated on the whole by the texts they themselves have created are most often characterized by a slow and gradual development, whereas cultures whose memory is exposed periodically to massive saturation with texts devised in another tradition are prone to "accelerated development" (to use Georgy Gachev's terminology).[iii]

6. The texts that saturate a culture's memory are not generically uniform. What was said above about the impact of texts from another culture can be said, *mutatis mutandis,* of the incursion of painterly texts into the poetic process of text-formation, of theater into everyday behavior, or of poetry into music—that is, about any conflicts within the generic nature of texts in a dominant position in memory, and of the codes that determine the culture's present condition.

What I have said, even in so condensed a form, allows us to speak about the fact that memory is, for culture, not a passive container, but one of its mechanisms of text-formation.

---

iii Georgy Gachev (1929–2008) was a prolific Soviet author who worked at the crossroads between philosophy, literary history, and "culturology." *The Accelerated Development of Literature* (1964) was his first monograph. In it, on the basis of nineteenth-century Bulgarian literature, he worked out a theory according to which national literatures which had been hampered in their organic development by certain conditions (such as censorship) would then rapidly catch up on all stages of literary history once these conditions were removed. When it came out during the period of the Thaw, this theory was understood to apply likewise to Soviet literature. In his later years, Gachev devoted himself to working out the mentality of various nations conceived as distinct ethno-cultural types.

CHAPTER 5

The Language of Theater

Translated from Iu. M. Lotman, "Iazyk teatra," in Ob iskusstve *(St. Petersburg: Iskusstvo-SPB, 1998), 603–608, which was first published in 1989. The notion of performance as a "difficult dialogue" with the play text, on the one side, and the audience, on the other, captures the complexity of the performance act as a translation between mutually non-identical, partly heterogenous languages. This is a good example of what Lotman means by translation as the creative intersection between mutually incompatible languages.*

Theory isn't always necessary where practical knowhow stands in the foreground. For someone who knows how to walk, a theory of walking is unnecessary. All the more so if one sets oneself the goal of learning how to walk, when theory is quite unnecessary: those who know have no need of it, and it's not going to help those who don't know anyway. Simply put, "Watch, and do what I do"—this is more useful than any theory. Doesn't this mean that there is no need for a theory of walking at all? No, it is quite necessary, both for solving important theoretical questions, and for practical tasks—from designing robots to improving prostheses. It comes in handy to the doctor as well as to the physiologist and the physicist, but to the baby developing his skills or the invalid deprived of his mobility it is of little use.

Something analogous occurs in art. And when theoretical investigations are used for purposes they do not and cannot support—such as practical instructions on how to create a good artistic work—it inevitably leads to disappointment. And disappointments are a dangerous thing. In its time Ivan Krylov's monkey, disappointed with wearing glasses, "dashed them so hard against a rock that they gave off a spray of sparks."[i] Unfortunately, efforts to do precisely that with "quite impractical" theoretical investigations are more the norm than the exception. This does not mean that theoretical investigations do

i Reference is to Ivan Krylov's fable "The Monkey and the Spectacles" [Martyshka i ochki], a parable about people who buy things they do not know how to use.

not influence the practice of art. But they influence it not as instructions and recipes, but through their general impact on culture, shaping the thinking of artists and their audiences. For example, it would be strange to deny Mikhail Bakhtin's deep impact on contemporary art (and specifically on dramaturgy and cinema, to say nothing of the direct staging of Dostoevsky's novels). But this impact is realized through the reconstruction of our contemporary's philosophical consciousness.

It is worth approaching our present problem from these perspectives as well. If we are to await unambiguous answers to the questions of what theatricality is, how to create it (if it is "good") or how to avoid it (if it is "bad"), which styles of staging are considered theatrical and which not, and so forth; if we are to calculate that the outcome of a conversation can be transferred immediately to the stage, if only it has ended—then disappointment is inevitable. But if we are to treat the task as one of providing material for reflection—as beginning, and not ending, the conversation, the goal of which is to better understand what is much discussed in recent times, and often in vain—then one can hope that our exchange of opinions will bring a certain benefit.

As far as I am concerned, theatricality can be defined as follows. Any art speaks to us in a language peculiar to it alone. In order to transform a bouquet of flowers standing on a table into a painting, one must "retell" this bouquet through the language of painting, employing a specific perspectival mode, a specific genre tradition, all the means that allow the artist to create the "second reality" of the still-life. The peculiarity of the language of art consists in its never appearing to have been given in advance (except in clearly imitative texts), but always presents a certain mutable variant of itself that is indispensable specifically to the given approach. As such, the intention never offers itself as something molded into a finalized logic prior to the artistic act. The intention harbored by the artist is an *artistic* one. It is created in the given work and by the given work and cannot be separated from its text. Furthermore, the text is not a receptacle for the concretized intention, but is its generator, which, connected to its audience, on the one hand, and to its transmitter (the book, the theater, and so on), on the other, produces new messages, ideas, and feelings. In this way, the very concept of "the language of art" is complex and can only partially be understood by simple analogy with language in the linguistic sense (for example, in such expressions as the "Russian language," "English language").

Theatricality is the language of theater as an art. And it is in this that it can be neither bad, nor good: it is an integral part of theater as such, and one cannot make do without it, just as one cannot make do without language. It is possible to define the essence of theatricality (just as with the essence of art in general) from two points of view. From one, we can describe the internal architectonics of the work of art and define the structural properties that the text possesses so that we are able to perceive it as artistic within the bounds of the given culture. This is the structural aspect. From the other, we can say that everything that is perceived as art by a given audience is a work of art. Thus, medieval icons are perceived by us now as high art. In the nineteenth century, however, the academic school considered them unskilled works that fell outside of genuine art. Henryk Siemiradzki's canvases, which are of dubious taste, were then perceived as something infinitely more "progressive." Contrariwise, for the medieval viewer the icon was not art, either, but something infinitely higher. It evoked a religious feeling beside which, from the point of view of its original audience, an exclusively aesthetic perception was something blasphemous. We can call this second approach functional: from this point of view, an artistic work is that which is capable of serving an aesthetic function within the given culture. There are periods in the history of art—and not infrequently—when, in order to "be art" (to serve its function) the work is supposed to "not be art." When Belinsky was creating the "natural school's" poetics of the sketch,[ii] or Italian Neorealism was repudiating professional actors, film sets, everything that was connected with "cinematographicality," as in numerous other instances, the "repudiation of the language of art" was a "repudiation of the old language" and the path for creating a new one. The physiological sketch laid the path for the social novel, and the Neorealist disavowal of cinematographicality provided a powerful impulse for creating new forms of cinematic language.

For as long as the theater has existed, there has been a struggle between two concepts of theatricality: the viewer should forget that he is in a theater, the viewer should constantly feel that he is in a theater. This conflict is not about the nature of theater in itself, but concerns the subjective approaches of various theatrical performers. In fact, the viewers should simultaneously forget and always remember that they are in a theater. Depending on the aesthetic concepts, the cultural orientation, the individual task, stress may be placed on either part of this twofold formulation; the director may determine that he or she "ruins" or "creates" theatricality, but in fact so long as there is theater, both sides of its effect are present: belief that the illusive reality of the stage is real, and that it is not life, but "playing life." It is real—and we weep over Desdemona's

---

ii The so-called "Natural School" in Russia in the 1840s, interested in particular in sketches of urban life, was a precursor to High Realism. V. Belinsky was its main critical champion.

fate; it is illusion—and we do not rise to her aid. During the intermission, we draw ourselves out of the theatricality and calmly go out for a smoke, but the lights go down, and we return once again to the world of interrupted emotions, to the point where we had left off, to the world of illusory reality.

Theatricality's complexity when compared, for example, to poeticity, cinematographicality, or pictorality, consists in its connection to an art that is performative, that is, to a certain degree improvisational: every performance is unique. Additionally, performative art does not create, but rather "performs" a fixed authorial text. It is momentary: *The Inspector General* remains, but Mikhail Chekhov's Khlestakov, or else Igor Ilyinsky's, exists only so long as the performance does.

Theatricality has an especially complex nature.

First of all, it is created by the performance's relation to the play. Taken "on its own," the play is a finished artistic work, standing as an equal beside other genres of literary art: the novel, the epic, the lyric poem. Yet one need only begin to transform it into a performance, and it turns out that it contains a multitude of potential interpretations, that it is still as if unfinished, and we are to crown it with some instantiation. This instantiation removes the multiplicity of interpretations that exist for the reader who has not concretized Hamlet or Khlestakov in some personal image, and at the same time it creates a new multiplicity—the possibility of a distinct interpretation of the stage direction and acting.[1] The relation between play and performance is a complex and, as a rule, dramatic dialogue. In this relationship the theater is in a situation fundamentally different from that of the cinema. In the cinema, the screenplay is rarely presented as an artwork in its own right—it is a phase and element of the film's creation. A screenplay written specifically for some film hardly ever becomes the basis for repeat filming by other craftsmen. For a play, this is simply law. A film's success forever anchors the screenplay in *this* reel; the success of a performance prompts the same play to be put up on other stages. This is why the effort to replace the staging of plays with the theatricalization of works of artistic prose—bringing the working screenplay into the practice of the theater, combining the director and the author in a single person—is a consequence of the cinema's pressure on adjacent arts. Mixed marriages are useful to art, and adaptations are fruitful for the development of the repertoire. But we cannot help but note that in allowing the submissive scenarist to assume the place of the dramaturg, an equal partner in dialogue, the theater makes its own task easier. And easing is always to art's detriment.

A play's resistance is an enormous factor of art. The translation of a non-artistic text from one language to another is a technical matter and involves no kind of creative accrual; the translation of a poem from one language to another is difficult, almost always fraught with failures, but it creates a new (or almost new) artistic work. And transforming a novella by Mérimée into a Bizet opera or a story by Pushkin into an opera by Tchaikovsky is already a creative act, a product of the mutual tension between different kinds of art, which creates an explosion of artistic energy, a stream of new ideas. The further apart the languages from which the translation is realized—the more difficult and, what is more, impossible the translation—the more valuable the result, informationally, emotionally, culturally. A play and a show speak different languages, and a word written on a piece of paper is deeply inadequate to the one performed on the stage. Staging is one of the most difficult aspects of artistic translation. But it is precisely in its difficulty that its value lies. And any easing of this process (in particular, through a radical modernization of the defenseless classic) can provide a strong, if always short-lived and superficial effect. This, of course, does not apply to that indispensable modernization that does not ruin the play's internal structure and very often, as an instance of improvisation, crosses into the realm of its interpretation.

But theatricality has another "leverage point" as well. The performance is in dialogue with the play, on the one hand, and with the viewer, on the other. These are two different dialogues, and the performance tells different stories within them. No art is so immediately connected to the audience's reaction, or reacts to this reaction so promptly and actively, as the theater. The very possibility of dialogue is one of the most important and difficult achievements of culture, and the loss of dialogue with the viewer is the death of theater culture. Here we cannot avoid a harsh word for the awful role that theater criticism has sometimes played in ruining our culture of contact between the stage and the hall, the disdain for the viewer with which it has greeted performances to which droves of people were driven, while calling those performances that ran in empty halls artistic successes. We can all think of examples. I, for example, can still recall how the brilliant successes of Nikolay Akimov's theater in Leningrad were scratched out by a single newspaper article.

The disoriented viewer stops believing in the theater, and the disoriented theater no longer addresses the viewers sitting in the hall, but the potential future reviewer. The contact is cut off. Theatricality has left the theater.

The dialogue with the hall, however, does not boil down to this situation, which is so coarse as to be elementary. It has a more complex nature. In order for dialogue to occur, it is necessary first of all to have mutual trust among its participants. One researcher into the dialogue between a nursing baby and the mother feeding him has remarked that mutual love and the need for contact set the precedent for communicative language. Yet this is only the most common stipulation. There needs to be linguistic commonality, some shared cultural memory. That alone allows the text to be enveloped in an extratextual semantic atmosphere. On the stage, as in life, a significant portion of what is said is said with silence, and the most important actions are sometimes those that go unrealized. The viewer "from the sideline," excluded from the system of "stage-hall" communications characteristic of a given theater, a given performance, a given author, a given actor, perceives only a superficial layer of meaning, whereas the viewer actively participating in the performance perceives the whole depth of stage life. From this flows the fact that the theater ought to have its own viewer, a constant, active connoisseur and interlocutor.

Here I will permit myself a small digression. Criticism, often in the name of wide participation, orients the theater toward "no audience," toward the "average," mass consumer, whom the critic has not laid eyes on, and who does not exist. The people entering the hall do not yet constitute the masses; they are a random gathering of heterogenous individuals. And only the performance, the theater, the stage fuses them into a collective personality.

But the mutual understanding between the stage and the hall is but one side of the matter. Mutual understanding that is too complete, too easy, coming effortlessly as the heritage of past successes, testifies to the fact that the theater has come to a standstill, that it is exploiting yesterday's theatricality and not seeking a new one. A language's evolution, its alteration, its dynamism, is the law of any semiotic system. We will not touch upon the general reasons for this phenomenon, but when we talk about art, it is surely not the least of factors that one is always striving after the truth. Humanity is not moved by superficial fashion, not by the thoughtless desire for novelty for novelty's sake, not when for the entire stretch of its history it has been changing the artforms it has achieved for those as yet unknown. In so doing, the hard breaks within a tradition can themselves turn out to be more traditional than its conservation in museums. But evolutionary breaks are not to be confused with disrupting a continuity of development. No one senses novelty as much as someone who has a good memory of times past: for the one who has no memory, there is no novelty.

We were talking about the difficult dialogue with the author of a play; the dialogue with the viewer ought to be difficult as well. Not so difficult that the dialogue cannot take place, and not so easy that it were to become insipid. The first question of any dialogue is: In what language? The theater conducts a conversation in the language of theatricality.

But, in discussing this, one should remember the words of the Russian author who felt this theatricality more than anyone else and saw in it the pulse of theatrical life—Nikolay Vasilyevich Gogol. Gogol underscored that authentic stage life, authentic theatrical truth, is possible "only in such a case as when the matter is handled truly as required, and the full responsibility with regard to repertoire falls always to the first-class actor, that is, a tragedy will be led by the top tragic actor and a comedy by the top comic actor, when they will be the one and only chorus leaders of such an affair." And later: "[Otherwise] one gets instructions for an artist, written by someone who is not an artist at all, directions, where it is impossible even to comprehend what they are directed toward." And Gogol concludes: "In the matter of any kind of craft, the whole production of that craft must rest upon the principal craftsman, and by no means upon some functionary who has hitched himself to the side."

We began with the fact that the theater speaks in the language of theatricality. Only living and thinking beings possess the ability to speak. The theater should live and think.

Part Two

CULTURAL HISTORY

CHAPTER 6

The Role of Dual Models in the Dynamics of Russian Culture (until the End of the Eighteenth Century)

This article, which was first published in 1977, had a profound impact on understandings of Russian culture and society, although it has also been criticised for its very binarism. Scholars have in particular worried that this kind of reduction to binaries can serve to perpetuate dual ideological or mythological models of Russian culture. See, for example, Svetlana Boym, who asked whether these dualities "describe Russian culture or perpetuate its cultural mythology" (Svetlana Boym, Common Places: Mythologies of Everyday Life in Russia *[Cambridge, MA: Harvard Univeristy Press, 1994], 30). See also Catriona Kelly et al., "Introduction: Why Cultural Studies," in* Russian Cultural Studies: An Introduction, *ed. Catriona Kelly and David Shepherd (Oxford: Oxford University Press, 1998), 1–3. In truth, the difference between "culture" and "cultural mythology" is not always entirely clear. In its attempts to work out the "invariable mechanisms" of Russian culture, this article provides an excellent example of a structuralist approach to culture. Lotman never revised his views on the dual nature of Russian culture, nor his method of singling out the operations of binaries, albeit qualified and dynamized by their embedding into multiple layers of interlocking oppositions. However, the sections of* Culture and Explosion *included above demonstrate that he was aware of the pitfalls of binarism and hoped that Russian culture could transcend its intrinsic dualism. Rereading this article from a contemporary perspective draws attention to another interesting aspect, its argument about how cultures generate and, indeed, preserve a past that legitimizes their present, despite the rhetoric of a clean break. Our translation is based upon Iu. M. Lotman and B. A. Uspenskii, "Rol' dual'nykh modelei v dinamike russkoi kul'tury (do kontsa XVIII veka)," in Iu. M. Lotman,* Istoriia i tipologiia russkoi kul'tury *(St. Petersburg: Iskusstvo-SPB, 2002), 88–116.*

Culture can be understood in the broadest sense as the uninherited cultural memory expressed in a defined system of prohibitions and prescriptions.[1] Such an understanding in no way precludes, however, an axiological approach to culture; in fact, for the collective itself, culture appears in any event as a defined system of values. What separates the approaches we have suggested is reducible to the difference between the outside perspective of external observation and the inside perspective of the bearer of culture himself; the axiological approach inevitably assumes an account from precisely an inside perspective—that is, the self-consciousness of culture. Scholars of culture, too, naturally occupy the distanced position of the external observer in this instance: the position of internal observation itself becomes the object of study. The history of culture is, in this sense, not only the dynamics of one or another set of prohibitions and prescriptions, but also the dynamics of the culture's self-consciousness, which to a certain degree explains changes in its normative construct (that is, in its prescriptions and prohibitions).

As such, culture—a system of collective memory and collective consciousness—at the same time inevitably appears as a single value structure for the given collective. The need for self-description, bound to the need to order itself holistically at a certain stage according to structure and value, actively influences culture as a described phenomenon. Creating its own model by and for itself, the culture actively influences the process of self-organization; it organizes itself hierarchically, it canonizes some elements and excludes others. This model is thereafter made a fact of cultural history and, as a rule, influences how descendants imagine it and historians conceptualize it. The point, however, should be not that the models for culture's self-description are automatically transferred into a historical research text, but that they are transformed, as a kind of cultural mechanism, into a special object of research.

Observing the history of Russian culture in the time period under consideration convinces us of its sharp segmentation into dynamically interchanging stages,[2] such that each new period, whether the baptism of Rus or the reforms of Peter the Great, is oriented towards a decisive break from what precedes it. Yet at the same time the researcher runs up against series of repeating or highly similar events, historical-psychological situations, or texts. The regularity of such iterations does not allow us to brush them off as accidents without any deeper foundation. By the same token, one cannot chalk them up to the debris left over from earlier cultural periods: that would be contradicted by their durability and activity in the system of cultures contemporaneous with them. Analysis convinces us that new historical structures in Russian culture during the period under consideration invariably feature mechanisms that reproduce past culture all over again. The more dynamic the system, the more active the mechanisms of memory that ensure the homeostasis of the whole.

What interests us here is a specific feature of Russian culture in the era being discussed: its fundamental polarity, expressed in the dual nature of its structure. Basic cultural values (ideological, political, religious) in the system of the Russian Middle Ages are distributed across a field of values having two poles, divided by a sharp line, and devoid of a neutral axiological zone. Let's consider a specific argument that will make clear what we mean. The afterlife in Catholic, Western Christianity is divided into three spaces: Heaven, Purgatory, and Hell. Correspondingly, earthly life is thought of as allowing three types of behavior: the unequivocally sinful, the unequivocally holy, and the neutral, which allows for redemption beyond the grave, following some purifying trial. Thus, in the actual life of the Middle Ages in the West, there is a potential for a wide range of neutral behavior, neutral social institutions that are neither "holy," nor "sinful," neither "state," nor "anti-state," neither good, nor bad. This neutral sphere constitutes the structural reserve from which tomorrow's system develops. Insofar as the continuity here is obvious, it is unnecessary either to underscore it structurally or to reestablish it consciously and artificially.

The system of the Russian Middle Ages is constructed upon a pronounced duality. It had its own peculiar division of the afterlife, into Heaven and Hell, to continue with our example. It made no provision for intermediate neutral spheres. Correspondingly, in earthly life, too, one's conduct could be either sinful or holy. This extended to concepts beyond the church as well: thus one could regard secular power as divine or devilish, but never as neutral with regard to these concepts.[3]

The availability of a neutral sphere in the medieval West led to the emergence of a certain subjective contiguity between the rejected today and the awaited tomorrow. The ideals of anti-feudal thinkers drew on specific spheres of the reality around them—on the secular state apparatus, the bourgeois family—and were transferred into the ideal space of social theory, where they underwent a heroic and moralistic transformation. The neutral sphere of life became the norm, whereas the highly semiotized spheres at the top and bottom of medieval culture were pushed out into the zone of cultural anomalies.

A different orientation of values reigned in Russian culture of the corresponding period. Duality and the absence of a neutral axiological sphere led to the fact of the new being thought of not as a continuation, but as an eschatological substitution of everything. In this sense it is revealing that the opposition between the positive world of the family and the negative kingdom of medieval evil, which is common in Western culture, is entirely irrelevant to Russian culture. Therefore, while the medieval consciousness was disintegrating, the treatment of the image of the Mother of God through the prism of the poetry of private existence, of family life, which is important in Western Renaissance painting, found no echo in Russian art.

In this way, the dynamic process assumes a fundamentally different character under these conditions: change emerges as the radical rejection of the preceding stage. The natural result was the fact that the new arose not from a structurally "unused" reserve, but resulted from the transformation of the old—of its being turned the wrong way around, as it were. From here, in turn, repeated shifts could actually lead to the *regeneration* of archaic forms.

The potential for gradual development through this consistent and cyclically repeated "negation of negation" is conditioned by the fact that at each new stage, due to the changing historical situation and, in particular, to internal cultural influences, a new view of cultural development comes into being, one that actualizes one or another semantic parameter. As a result, the same concepts can be filled with new content at every stage, depending on the development's point of departure.

These deep structures of development, it happens, allow us to speak of the unity of Russian culture at various stages of its history. It is precisely in mutations that the immutable is revealed.

What we have been discussing largely explains the circumstance that, for Russia in various historical eras, what is typical is not its conservatism but, on the contrary, its reactionary and progressive tendencies.

1. One of the most stable oppositions constitutive of Russian culture across the whole span from the baptism of Rus to the reforms of Peter the Great is that of "ancient/modern." It proves so active and significant that, from the subjective position of a bearer of culture, at various stages it absorbs or subsumes other fundamental oppositions, such as "Russia/the West," "Christianity/paganism," "true faith/false faith," "knowledge/ignorance," "social top/social bottom," and so on.

The difference between the subjective experience of these concepts in the consciousness of participants in the historical process and the meaning they objectively take on in the holistic context of culture, the complex dialectic of their intersections and their relativity, will be in large part the subject of the present work.

1.1. The baptism of Ancient Rus was a decisive milestone in its self-consciousness. It is precisely in connection with this event that for the first time in the literature we encounter the characterization of the Russian lands as "new," and of Russians as "new people." In the *Primary Chronicle* [*Povest' vremennykh let*], Vladimir, in the prayer he uttered following the baptism, says, "O Christ, our God, who created Heaven and Earth, look upon these new people!"[4] In his "Sermon on Law and Grace" [Slovo o zakone i blagodati], Ilarion calls the Russian lands a "new wineskin" into which a new teaching has been poured.[5] In this instance, it is immaterial to us that the epithet "new" originated, through its reference to newly baptized people, in a specific outside tradition, insofar as it subsequently attained a significantly more idiosyncratic and broad significance in Russian history.

How this replacement of the "old" with the "new" is achieved is deeply significant. As Evgeny Anichkov has convincingly shown, the Christianization of Rus had been preceded by an attempt to create an *artificial* pagan pantheon:[6] it appears that in order to create the "new," Christian Rus, it was psychologically necessary to create a consolidated and, to a significant degree, conventional image of the "old" one.

Christianization itself unfolded as a demonstrative switching of places between the old (pagan) religion and the new (Christian). An outer manifestation of this, but nevertheless a significant one, was how sacred objects were spatially rearranged within the process of Christianization: the idol of Perun was toppled from the Kievan hills and into Podil, that is, into the place where the Christian Church of St. Ilya (Perun's Christian double) was then located, and a Christian church was constructed on high, on the site of the former pagan temple.[7] And so there is a radical inversion of "high" and "low." Vladimir (like Peter later on) would overturn the prevailing system of relations, changing pluses to minuses; he does not simply adopt a new system of values, exchanging old for new, but inscribes the old in the new—with a minus sign.

The baptism of Rus had the character of a broad cultural and political shift and was connected to the country's falling within Byzantium's sphere of influence. This makes the very early tendency to spurn Byzantine influence and the effort to place the Greeks and their empire hierarchically lower than the Russian lands all the more noteworthy. It is revealing that this aspiration engenders Byzantium's qualification as an "old" state and its contradistinction to the "new" Rus. Ilarion, jubilant at Rus being brought into the worldwide fold of Christianity, already speaks pejoratively of Byzantium, baptized of old, equating it with the *Old* Testament and with Hagar, who applied a fixed, despotic law, and juxtaposing Rus with Sarah and the grace of the New Testament.[8] [i] These tendencies subsequently gain an especially sharp expression when the notion of "Moscow as Third Rome" held sway, as Russia, following the fall of Constantinople, becomes aware of itself as the sole bulwark of Orthodoxy, and messianic attitudes are intensified.[ii] We must bear in mind that the collapse of the Byzantine Empire coincided roughly with the Russians casting off the Tatar yoke. And so, if what had happened in Byzantium was the triumph of Islam over Orthodoxy, then the opposite had been achieved in Rus—the triumph of Orthodoxy over Islam. It was as if Byzantium and Rus had traded places, resulting in Rus becoming the center of the Orthodox—and, by the same token, the Christian—world.[9]

Even earlier, Rus had witnessed the popularity of the words of Hrabar the Monk, who had affirmed the priority in holiness of the Slavonic tongue over the Greek, insofar as the Greek language had been created by pagans, whereas Church Slavonic had been made by holy apostles. In the original article on the creation of Russian writing that forms part of the *Explanatory Old Testament* [*Tolkovaia Paleia*][iii], but that appears in other records as well, Russian writing, alongside the Russian faith, is deemed a revelation, independent of Greek mediation. Here, it says:

> Let it be known in all tongues and to all people how the Russian tongue has accepted this holy faith from nowhere, and Russian writing was revealed by no one but God Almighty Himself, the Father, the Son, and

---

i The opposition between Hagar (the prophet Abraham's servant and concubine) and Sarah (his wife) goes back to Paul's Epistle to the Galatians 4:21–31, where the Apostle puts forward an allegory of Law and Grace, embodied by the two women. Hagar, born in bondage, with her son Ishmael "born of the flesh," represents submission to despotic law, while Sarah, born free, with her son Isaac "born of the promise," represents free, heavenly Jerusalem.

ii The idea that Moscow was the Third Rome, and that in keeping with the doctrine of *translatio imperii*, the succession of empires, it was destined to become the rightful successor to the Roman and Byzantine empires and to dominate the world as the preeminent Christian nation, emerged in Russia in the sixteenth century. How widespread and operative this idea was for sixteenth-century statecraft and beyond is disputed among specialists. This notion was revived in the second half of the nineteenth century, when it took on a life of its own as a confirmation of Russia's messianic aspirations. For a discussion of the origins and spread of this idea, see Marshall Poe, "'Moscow the Third Rome': The Origins and Transformations of a Pivotal Moment," *Jahrbücher für Geschichte Osteuropas*, Neue Folge 49, no. 3 (2001): 412–429.

iii The *Tolkovaia Paleia* is a compilation of excerpts from the Old Testament, enhanced with apocryphal stories and commentaries. The earliest copies date from the fourteenth century. Its author is unknown, and there has been scholarly controversy about its Byzantine or Russian origins.

> the Holy Spirit. The Holy Spirit inspired Vladimir to accept the faith, and baptism, and the rites of the church from the Greek. And Russian writing appeared, God-given, to a Rusian in Korsun, it was from it that the philosopher Constantine learned, and hence compiled and wrote books in the Russian tongue [according to another record, "voice"]. ... This man of Rus lived a godly life, through fasting and virtue in pure faith, alone in seclusion, and having the Russian tongue revealed to him became the first Christian, and no one knew from where he comes.[10]

1.2. The steady acknowledgment of the Russian lands as "new" coincides paradoxically with the activation of rather archaic cultural models. The very concept of the "new" turns out to be the realization of notions whose roots reach down into the deepest antiquity. In this one can observe two models for constructing the "new culture":

1. The underlying structure formed in the preceding period is maintained, yet it undergoes a decisive renaming while preserving all the old, fundamental structural contours. In this instance, *new texts* are created while preserving the archaic cultural framework.
2. The culture's underlying structure itself changes. Even as it changes, however, it demonstrates its dependence on the cultural model that had existed before, insofar as it is constructed as turning that model "inside-out," rearranging it by shifting the signs.

A vivid example of this is provided by the paths by which pre-Christian pagan notions penetrated the cultural system of Christianity. The pagan gods have a double fate: on the one hand, they can be identified with demons, thereby occupying a negative, yet wholly legitimized position within the system of the new religion. On the other, they can be associated with the Christian saints who functionally stand in for them. As demons, they can even retain their own names; as saints, only their function. Thus Volos/Veles ["Hair"] is turned into the "hair-worm" demon, a forest goblin, and so forth, and at the same time is transformed into St. Vlasy [Blaise], St. Nicholas, or St. George.[11] Mokosh lives on as an unclean force by the same name (there exists a dialect word *mokosh'*, meaning "unclean spirits";[12] it is interesting that in contemporary dialects the corresponding word carries the meaning of an "indecent woman"; compare the use of *venera* [Venus] in the same meaning in the urban slang of the eighteenth and nineteenth centuries) and, at the same time, is clearly associated with St. Paraskeva (Piatnitsa) of Iconium[13] and even with the Mother of God.[14]

Quite analogously, the places where pagan temples were located could have a twin fate, too: the function of the sacred could be retained, with the pagan deity being replaced with Christian saints (actually, with the deity being renamed), but the opposite might just as well occur: the deity's nature (sometimes including its appellation) might be maintained, but with a diametrically opposed function—the place could become "unclean," a demons' abode. What is interesting is how both of these perspectives, extant among diverse cultural audiences, could intersect, creating as it were a double "reading" of the very same cultural fact. On the one hand, there is the well-known custom, affirmed in Rus by the authority of St. Vladimir, of building Christian churches on the site of pagan temples. On the other, there is the revealing legend from the manuscript collection of the Kazan Theological Academy describing how the church was rattled by thunder during Mass, as it had been built upon an "idolaters' prayer-ground," and some birch and stone remained behind the altar.[15] In just this way, in Novgorod, on the site where the idol of Perun had been cast into the Volkhov River, a monastery was erected (the so-called Perun Monastery) in the same place where they were still holding annual pagan orgies in the sixteenth century.[16]

Of course, the site of a former pagan temple could be regarded by parishioners as enduringly sacred, but the clergy regarded putting a church there as consecrating an unclean place and banishing a demon from his own property.[17] What is essential, however, is that in both cases the site was regarded as hardly indifferent to the "sacred/unclean" opposition and was positioned against neutral territories. The possibility of flipping the poles of this opposition was confirmed by the transformation of the sacred into the unclean: derelict churches are the favorite abode of unclean powers (such as in Gogol's "Viy").

When it comes to the fates of pagan temples in the Christian world, interesting examples can be found in constructions like the bathhouse, the barn, and the smithy. There are grounds to assert that these places' perception as "unclean" is connected with their peculiar, sacral importance in the pre-Christian life of the Eastern Slavs, that is, with their special role as family (domestic) temples. In other words, pagan temples continued to maintain their cult function in the Christian period as well—albeit with a minus sign. It is particularly revealing that the persistent notion that the power in the bathhouse belongs to an unclean force, and not to a holy one (in the Christian consciousness this is conceived in such a way that the holy force turns its back, as it were, to the place, as it does to other "unclean" places: the efficacy of the unclean force is generally connected to divine acquiescence). Correspondingly, while the people are going to church on holidays, those sorcerers who never enter a church enter *the bathhouse*;[18] in the same way the bathhouse features as a traditional place for fortune-telling, sorcery, magical healing, and, of course, reciting incantations; the cult role of the bathhouse appears rather distinctly in the wedding ceremony as well, where bath rituals are in essence no less obligatory than the church service: one complements the other. In this light, it is utterly natural that in Russian folklore the moniker *bozhena* can be applied to the bathhouse, essentially signifying a "temple."[19] No less typical is the notion that people come to the bathhouse *to pray* to the unclean force (in essence, the incantations recited in the bathhouse can be regarded as their own kind of prayer), as is expressed, for example, in the following Belarusian song:

Amidst the village of Vouchkov,
Hey hey! [refrain with banging and stomping]
There stood an oaken bathhouse:
There, there, there! [refrain with banging]
The youth would come to give their prayers,
They'd kiss the stove and hug the post,
Before Sopukha[iv] they'd make the cross,
For, they thought, she is most clean,
Though Sopukha's really quite obscene![20]

Сярёд сяла Воучковскаго,
То то! [припев с стуком и топотом]
Туту стояла лазня дубовая:
Ту, ту, ту! [припев со стуком]
А ходили дѣтюшки богу помолиться,
Стоуб обнимали, печь цаловали,
Перяд Сопухой крыжом ляжали,
Яны думали: Прячистая,
Анож Сопуха—Нячистая!

In this way, pre-Christian forms of behavior could be preserved in the everyday life of Orthodox Rus, through sanctioned anti-behavior. In specific places and at specific times, the Christian *was compelled* to behave "inappropriately" as far as the norms of Christian behavior were concerned. Appropriate

iv "Sopukha" refers to soot and, by extension, to the smokestack.

behavior in an inappropriate place and at an inappropriate time would be regarded as blasphemous—that is, as sinful. Thus, for example, at Yuletide or at certain other moments of the calendar's ceremonial cycle, as well as during visits to "unclean" places, both within the Russian lands and when entering "heathen" lands, one was expected to manifest a particular behavior, the norms of which were opposed to what was "appropriate."[21] In practice, this led to the conservation of pagan behavioral norms.

The new (Christian) culture constituted itself to a significant degree in its opposition to the old, and in this way the old pagan culture, in the form of an anti-culture, appeared as an indispensable condition of culture as such. As a result, this "new culture," which thought of itself as the negation and utter destruction of the "old," was in practice a powerful means for preserving the latter, encompassing both inherited texts and preserved forms of behavior in their reversed mirror image.

In sum, everyday Orthodoxy is an undervalued source for the reconstruction of the pagan cult of the Eastern Slavs.

1.3. The dispute with ideologies inimical to one or another dimension of a culture inevitably becomes an essential moment in its self-determination, insofar as in the process of such a dispute a culture articulates its own position and subjects the position of another culture to a revealing transformation. The Christianization of Rus entailed not only the inevitability of the "new faith" defining itself against the pagan, but also implicated the Russian people in a polemic between Eastern and Western Christianity. It became necessary to assume a definite position in the defining ideological debate of the era. Paganism and "Latinism" were phenomena of a fundamentally different order. This difference was clearly felt by Old Russian scribes, who went so far as to assert that Latin heretics were worse than pagan ones, "for one cannot control them, as one can with the pagans. The Latins have the Gospels and the Apostles and other sacred things, and they go to church, but both their faith and their law are unclean; the whole land they have defiled."[22] In other words, "Latinism," in contrast to paganism, was regarded as a blasphemous parody of authentic Christianity, similar to it on the outside, yet filled with different content—Orthodoxy inside-out, so to speak. Paganism and Catholicism are thereby contrasted as the absence of information (entropy) versus false information.

But at the same time, a fundamentally different understanding of paganism becomes possible, one where it is treated as false faith. In this instance, paganism and Catholicism are, from the perspective of the Orthodox consciousness, united in their antithetical opposition to the true faith. For the

Orthodox Christian of Kievan Rus, both the pagans and the "Latins" appear as bearers of an "alien" faith; they are identified polemically, and they start to have certain general markers ascribed to them. This is how we get a certain syncretic image of "alien faith" in general. Old Russian scribes can speak of "Khors-the-Israelite" and "the Hellenic Old Man Perun."[23] Insofar as paganism was conceived as unorthodoxy, unorthodoxy, too, came to be conceived as paganism.

This led to interesting consequences. We have seen how Orthodoxy assumed specific norms of pre-Christian life in sanctioned forms of anti-behavior. Now the opposite was occurring: forms of anti-behavior were being ascribed to the "Latins," whose image was construed from how the Orthodox imagined the "unclean" world and forbidden actions. As a result, alongside other "unclean" things, actual features of Russian pagan behavior were ascribed to Western Christianity. This circumstance makes polemical compositions "against the Latins" a source that cannot be ignored in reconstructing East Slavic paganism.

Thus the Old Russian accuser of the Latins, starting from the familiar Russian expression "Moist Mother Earth" [*mat' syra-zemlia*], which in his ears rang distinctly of paganism, confidently ascribed similar notions to Catholics: "They call Earth their mother." And right away, from this initial premise, he flawlessly reconstructed the whole text of the myth: "If the Earth is their mother, then their father is the sky."[24] This example is exceptionally revealing both for the mechanism by which "Latin-ness" is reconstructed in the Old Russian consciousness, and as a testament to the fact that the anti-pagan inclination of Old Russian Christianity implied the latter's incorporating mechanisms for the autonomous generation of truly pagan texts, that is, the incorporation of paganism in the living cultural memory of Old Russian Christianity. Accordingly, if paganism is understood as an *alien* belief, then Catholicism, in its turn, actually assumes the markers of the *old* faith.

Also typical of the identification of Catholicism with paganism is the assertion that the "Latins" go to church in "Polovetsian vestments" and in "Hungarian hats."[25] Regardless of the historical authenticity of this telling, the very fact of equating pagan Polovetsian and Catholic Hungarian dress is significant.

We find a remarkable example of the same in the denunciation of Catholics in the Menology of Metropolitan Makary[v]:

v Metropolitan Makary (c. 1482–1563) was a key sixteenth-century churchman, state ideologist, and close associate of Ivan the Terrible. He is the author of several important compilations, including the Great Menology, which brought together saints' lives, sermons, letters, translations, and other such texts, arranged for daily reading throughout the year.

> On the very first night, the priest lies with his bride upon the altar behind the refectory, having lain her upon a rug, and crosses the woman's shame and kisses her shame. And he says: thou hath been my mother, and now thou art my wife. And thus he lies with her, and the filth having already come out of the bride onto the rug, and this rug having been washed and burned, the people then sprinkle that filth around the church.[26]

There is no need to say that Catholics had no actual analogues to the described rite. It is no less obvious that this testimony, with its fantastic details, contains information regarding deeply archaic customs whose roots reach back into the farthest antiquity. Though one cannot exclude the fact that recollections of some such ancient rites lingered in the consciousness of the given text's author, it is nevertheless more natural to think that comparable notions were generated on their own through the mechanism of prohibitions. In this case one might suppose that the Christianity of Kievan Rus comprised within itself mechanisms for the generation—to polemical ends—of pagan texts, which is to say, it included a structural memory of the cultural experience of times past.

"Novelty" not only incorporated antiquity in a complex way, but it was also its generator, subjectively apprehending itself as its antipode.

1.3.1. And much later, at various stages of historical development, a polemical or negative orientation can lead to the birth of pagan texts, and even to the regeneration of pagan rituals. In some cases this is due to anticlerical tendencies.[27] Thus, for example, Stepan Razin, pointedly repudiating church ritual, forced people during their wedding to perform a dance around a tree—that is, he essentially revived a corresponding pagan rite (the memory of which was preserved in folkloric texts, proverbs, and other genres).[28] By the same token, after the Revolution "there were instances when the young couple, wishing to dispense with the church ceremony, were afraid to tell their elders. They left their village, as if making for the church in a neighboring village several versts away, but they did not arrive there and, stopping in the woods, got down from the carriage and 'walked around a fir tree with lit candles.'"[29]

The resurrection of pagan rites can be observed among members of sects, including among certain extreme groups of Priestless Old Believers. A. F. Belousov has drawn our attention to the fact that among those of the priestless, celibate confession the rejection of a church wedding led to the institution of bride-abduction practiced up to modern times. And getting married by a tree or lake could become part of the custom of elopement [*svad'ba ukhodom*].[30] No less revealing is the fact that some Old Believer sects bury their dead in the *forest*, that is, where the "unclean" dead are buried;[31] at the same time, this custom coincides with the pagan Slavic custom of burying the dead in the forest or in a field, as reported already by Cosmas of Prague.[32]

Similar rites are observed among those Old Believer confessions that hold that the Antichrist's arrival has already occurred: insofar as radical inversion is ascribed to the world of the Antichrist, so too can spurning that world actually lead to a turning toward pagan forms. The rebirth (or continuation) of pagan burial, however, can be observed not only among sects. We find a curious example of this kind in the memoirs of Vladimir Pecherin, who describes how a clergyman refused to bury a suicide in the cemetery. "And so they dug him a place in one of the burial mounds," Pecherin writes.[33] The alternative to internment in the sacred ground of the cemetery is a grave in a *burial mound* [*kurgan*], which is conceived as a kind of pagan ("unclean") space. In precisely the same way, other instances of burying the "unclean" dead could entail essentially pagan behavior.[34]

2. The late Russian Middle Ages, unlike the early period, passed to a significant degree under the banner of "antiquity." It was precisely with the concept of the "old" and the "originary" that the highest axiological categories came to be associated. Yet the historian, undoubtedly convinced of this subjective focus on antiquity, would risk falling victim to the confusion of concepts already familiar to us.

2.1. Widely shared among various layers of the population in the seventeenth century, a dissatisfaction with the whole way of Russian life, which was practically expressed in several popular movements, assumed the form of demands for a return to antiquity. In the process, the understanding of "antiquity" was at times quite idiosyncratic. Quite common was the concept according to which the beautiful world of God contrasted sharply with the human world's awful disorder. A natural consequence of this was the demand to return to the primeval natural order. Thus it is characteristic that in *The Compendium of Kirsha Danilov* [*Sbornik Kirshi Danilova*] (the compilation is dated to the seventeenth century, the manuscript likely to the beginning of the eighteenth) the triumphal introductory refrain declaring the breadth, expanse, and splendor of the natural world is repeated thrice: "How high the height beneath the heavens ..." The function of this refrain, however, is transformed revealingly in all three texts. In the first, "About Salovei Budimirovich" [Pro Salov'ia Budimirovicha], it figures in harmony with the basic content of the heroic tale and offers a depiction of an epic expanse.[35] In the second, the tale "Arafonushka," it is inverted as a travesty:

How high the height of the ceiling above us,
So deep the depth of the floor beneath us,
And wide the breadth—the hearth before the stove,
So clean the field outstretched along the bench,
And so azure the sea in a tub of water ...[36]

Высока ли высота потолочная,
Глубока глубота подпольная,
А и широко раздолье—перед печью шесток,
Чистое поле—по подлавечью,
А и синее море—в лохани вода ...

The "expanse" from the epic tale is parodically set in opposition to the "restriction" of the actual world around us. And for the seventeenth century, restriction is a transparent metaphor for social evil. It is based to a certain degree on the opposition between the landlords' seizure of land in Russia's central regions and the expanse of "no man's lands" and waters in the unknown, distant country on the outskirts. This gives rise to the third use of the introductory refrain, a generalization of the opposition between the good in nature and the evil that reigns in human society, the harmony and beauty in the former and the dissolution of all connections in the latter:

How high the height beneath the heavens,
So deep the depths, the ocean-seas,
How wide the breadth across all land,
So deep the [D]nieper's pools,
How wondrous the Levanidov cross,
And long the river reaches of Chuvil,
So high the mountains of Sorochinsk,
How dark the forests of Brynsk
And black the soils of Smolensk,
The lower rivers running swift.
When reigned Tsar David Evtseevich,
And under Elder Makar Zakharyevich,
There was great lawlessness:
The nuns in cells were child-bearers,
The monks on roads were highway-robbers,
A son would take his father to court,

A brother against his brother would fight,
A brother would take his sister as bride.[37]

Высока ли высота поднебесная,
Глубока глубота акиян-море,
Широко раздолье по всей земли,
Глубоки омоты Непровския,
Чуден крест Леванидовской
Долги плеса Чевылецкия,
Высокия горы Сорочинския,
Тёмны леса Брынския,
Чёрны грязи Смоленския,
А и быстрыя реки понизовския.
При царе Давыде Евсеевиче,
При старце Макарье Захарьевиче,
Было беззаконство великое:
Старицы по кельям—родильницы,
Чернецы по дарогам—разбойницы,
Сын с отцом на суд идёт,
Брат на брата с боем идёт,
Брат сестру за себя емлёт.

Ideas like these were also close to those of Archpriest Avvakum:[vi]

Mountains high, cliffs rocky and exceedingly high—twenty thousand versts and more I dragged myself, and such mountains I saw not anywhere. Upon their peaks—tents and refuges, gates and pillars, and a fence, all made by God. Garlic grows upon them, and onion bigger than the Romanov kind, and well sweet. And hemp grows there, too, nourished by God, and in the yards grasses beautiful and bright, and exceedingly fragrant. Exceedingly many birds, geese and swans, float upon the sea like snow. There are fish, sturgeon and salmon trout, sterlet, cisco, and whitefish, and many other kinds, and exceedingly thick with fat: the sturgeon

vi Avvakum Petrov (1620–1680) was a priest and prominent foe of the liturgical reforms introduced by Patriarch Nikon. He was repeatedly exiled for this writings and eventually incarcerated and burned. Among other writings, he is the author of an important autobiography, *The Life of Archpriest Avvakum, Written by Himself* [*Zhitie Protopopa Avvakuma im samim napisannoe*]. He is seen by many Old Believers as one of their martyrs.

> is not to be fried in a pan, it will be all fat. The water is fresh, though with great seals and sea hares therein; I didn't see these in the ocean, when I lived in Mezen. And all this in Christ has been made for man ... And man, accustomed to vanity, passes his days like unto a dream: he leaps like a goat, puffs up like a bubble, grows fierce like a lynx, wants to lie like a snake, neighs like a foal when he sees another's beauty, is as cunning as a devil.[38]

The notion of the divinity and beauty of the natural order is also clearly expressed in Avvakum's story about how he prayed for the health of his chickens: "They are all necessary to God, both the livestock and the bird are for His glory."[39]

It is revealing that an idea that repudiates the entire real social order in the name of the natural, and that objectively harbors a negation that anticipates the ideas of Rousseau and Tolstoy, was experienced subjectively as an exhortation from antiquity. All of human history appears here as novelty, and the divine, primordial order as "antiquity."

The image of "antiquity" was deeply anti-historical and oriented toward a break with actual historical tradition.[40]

2.2. The notion that moving forward means returning to a lost truth (the movement into the future is a movement into the past) was so widespread that it swept up opposing social groupings. Thus, for example, the Nikonian effort to "correct" church texts rested upon the notion of a primordially correct—Greek—order. The subsequent history appeared as gradual corruption and the rebirth that followed it.

What is characteristic of the Old Believers is the inversion of historical time. Instead of the diachrony of "old/pagan" and "new/Christian," in their consciousness the opposition of another kind of diachrony emerges: the "old/Christian" and the "new/pagan," where "pagan" is equivalent to "satanic." The inversion of time among the Old Believers, expressed in the fact that in their consciousness paganism had taken root after Christianity, and not *before* it, undoubtedly flowed from the general eschatology of their thinking, which was focused on the end, and not the beginning of the historical process.[41] In turn, insofar as evil was conceived as having been imported into Rus from outside, a consequence of consorting with heretics, paganism and heresy were united into a single image of the heretical West. It is typical that Avvakum does not discern the internal division of the Western world: "the Roman people and all the West have fallen into sin"; "the whorish ramblings of the Roman Church and their whore-spawn, the Poles and Kievian Uniates, as well as our own Nikonians, for all their newfangled, heretical wizardry, we, the true faithful, thrice declare them anathema"; "all that is Frankish, that is, German."[42]

In this way, the problem of "old/new" is transformed into the antithesis "Russian lands/West." Insofar as the correct, the godly, is the primordial, and the sinful, the devilish, results from corruption—that is, novelty—the West is conceived as a "new" land. Positive concepts—piety, Orthodoxy—receive the epithet "ancient," whereas all that is sinful is interpreted as "newfangled." In connection with this, the polemic with pre-Christian notions—with ancient paganism—loses its currency: it vanishes completely from the literature, replaced by statements against the Nikonians, on the one hand, and against the Old Believers, on the other. Then again, the denunciation of the West acquires a peculiar urgency. The West is ultimately tagged with the notion not only of a primordially "new" land, but also of an "inverted," "left-hand" space—that is, a devilish space.[43]

To appreciate the sharply negative attitude toward the Nikonian Reforms in broad sectors of Russian society, one must bear in mind that in a whole host of instances new rituals could be interpreted as an inverse image of the old. Thus, moving in the direction of the sun is replaced with moving against the sun, in the execution of the liturgy the right and left sides switched places, and so on. Insofar as the "inverted," "left" world was interpreted within the Russian double-faith as belonging to the Antichrist, the Nikonian reforms could be joined with the rites of paganism and sorcery in the cultural consciousness (for example, various magical rituals employ moving against the direction of the sun and the action of the left hand). At the same time, to the extent that the Nikonian Reforms were associated with Latinism, Western culture itself could be interpreted as sorcery.

From the perspective of the New Belief, however, these notions, which were the consequence of "reading" the reforms in light of past cultural experience, had to be regarded as "ignorance." In this way, anything linked to the memory accumulated by past cultural development was called ignorance, and breaking from it was interpreted as "enlightenment." "To remember" meant to be ignorant, "to forget"—to be enlightened. It is interesting to note that a half-century later Peter the Great performed a great many acts that he could not have been unaware would be interpreted as signs of sacrilege or even as the mark of the Antichrist. But he deliberately ignored such a reading as ignorant.[44]

It is essential to note that originally, at the time of the church schism, the positions of both warring sides looked reasonably convergent: both camps reproached the other for one and the same thing—violating Orthodoxy. This led to the fact that the emotional innovator Avvakum could be counted in the same camp as the Old Believers, whereas the views of Nikon, as far as the followers of Joseph Volotsky were concerned, seemed rather traditional.[vii] To either party, the opposing group are pagans, in the broad sense, though their "ignorance" would be emphasized in one instance (for example, in Christian polemical literature pagans are traditionally dubbed as "ignoramuses") and their "demonism" in the other.

Subsequently, the Old Believers' position was preserved in stable traditional forms, while the ideology of the New Believers was open to new cultural influences. This circumstance allowed the increasingly wide penetration of the Renaissance-Baroque worldview into the New Believers' church culture.[45] These processes are quite noticeable in painting (as shown, especially, by Iosif Vladimirov's famous treatise) and in architecture.[46] Particularly significant in this sense is the controversy that arises in the mid-seventeenth century around "full-voweled" [*khomovoe*] and "speech-like" [*narechnoe*] (reformed) chanting, on the one hand, and monophony and polyphony, on the other.[47] [viii] It is quite characteristic in particular that the supporters of chanting "as spoken" direct their polemic against full-voweled chanting and polyphony at the same time—that is, these two phenomena, which are, in fact, utterly distinct from each other, are joined organically within the new cultural consciousness; at the same time, there is also a conflict with all manner of glossolalic interpolations preserved in church chanting ("anenaek"—*a-ne-ne-ne-na*—and "khabuv"—*o-kho-kho-bu-ve*). The reasons behind this become clear if we bear in mind that both full-voweled and polyphonic chant ("reading") are not essentially focused on the reception by a human audience. In such a performance, the literal content may be incomprehensible, which attests to its emphasis on the perspective of a Higher Addressee: the very instant of making an utterance in the sacred

vii Joseph (Iosif) Volotsky or Joseph of Volokolamsk (1439 or 1440–1515) was a monk and abbot known for his defense of monastic landownership and of the lavish decoration of churches. He also called for persecuting heretics and rejecting new teachings, and he supported the consolidation of the power of the tsars. Through his defense of monastic land holdings, he initiated a movement called the Possessors, opposed to the Non-Possessors who advocated foregoing land ownership and worldly possessions.

viii "Full-voweled" [*khomovoe*] singing consisted of filling in the soft and hard signs, which are normally unvoiced, with the vowels "e" and "o," respectively. This results in adding a syllable at the end of many words, thus producing a completely counterintuitive pronunciation. In contrast, "speech-like" [*narechnoe*] singing aims to stay closer to the pronunciation in normal usage.

language is what enjoys fundamental importance. The church service is understood, so to speak, as communication with God, and not with man, and accordingly the *objective* sense of the uttered text appears as uniquely important, abstracted as a matter of principle from its *subjective* interpretation. Meanwhile, the opposing manner of performance can be juxtaposed with the tendency for sacred texts to be translated into the language of the people and directed precisely toward their intelligibility to the human audience. From the position of the new Renaissance culture, neither full-voweled nor polyphonic chants could be regarded any other way but as unintelligible and ignorant. From the historical perspective, however, they are the fruit of an extensive and sophisticated cultural tradition.

One may note in this regard that from the perspective of one side of the conflict, "knowledge" consisted in mastering an extensive and finely developed tradition, and "ignorance" in its rejection. From the other position, "knowledge" was thought of as neglecting tradition in the name of what is concise and rational, of consciousness "clear as sunlight," whereas "ignorance" was perceived in following every twist in traditional thought. Both sides are united once again within the initial classification, diverging only in their assessments.[48]

3. The eighteenth century arrived under the banner of novelty. The "new" was identified with the good, the valuable, what was worthy of imitation, while the "old" was thought to be bad, liable to break down or be destroyed. The people of the Petrine era imagined Russia now as a creature "reborn in a new form," now as a newborn babe. In his "Encomium on the Battle of Poltava" [Slovo pokhval'noe o batalii Poltavskoi], Feofan Prokopovich invoked a "Russia reborn, strengthened, and completely grown up."[49] Feofan Prokopovich expressed the notion of Russia's complete and ultimate transformation with the famous words: "The Roman Emperor Augustus, as he lay dying, offered himself the greatest praise: *A Rome I found of brick*, he said, *but I leave one of marble.* But to utter these words would be vanity, and not praise, to Our Most Brilliant Monarch; for in truth it is fitting to profess that he found a Russia of wood, but he made one of gold" (from the "Encomium on the Day of Birth ... of Pyotr Petrovich").[50] In 1724, Peter I, contemplating the "point" of a ceremonial poem that poets ought simply "to disperse widely," found a different image—that of blindness and insight. In Peter's words, Russia's adversaries had vowed to keep her in blindness "so as not to admit us to the world of reason in all affairs, those of the military most especially." But God performed a miracle: they themselves went blind, and they did not notice Russia's miraculous transformation, "as though it had been closed to their eyes."[51]

All these images come down to Russia's instantaneous, miraculous, and complete transformation under Emperor Peter. Antiokh Kantemir found a synthetic formulation for it:

> The wise decrees of Peter will not our hands slip through,
> By them we've *suddenly become a nation new.* ...[52]
>
> Мудры не спускает с рук указы Петровы,
> Коими стали мы *вдруг народ уже новый.* ...

The image of the "New Russia" and the "new nation" turned into a distinctive myth that had arisen already at the beginning of the eighteenth century and was bequeathed to later cultural consciousness. The notion that eighteenth-century culture comprises a completely new stage, separate from the development that had preceded it, was so deep-rooted that, in actual fact, it was not subject to doubt; one could argue over whether the break with the old had occurred at the end of the seventeenth century or in its middle, whether its nature was instantaneous or gradual, and ultimately over how one ought to regard it within the framework of subsequent Russian history, whether as a positive event that ensured Russia's rapid cultural progress, or else as a negative phenomenon that brought about the loss of a unique national identity. Yet the fact itself is accepted by all, almost in the form in which the era we are examining had formulated it. It is assumed that the culture of the eighteenth century had a consistently secular, state-oriented, and anticlerical nature, and that it was thereby opposed to the pre-Petrine period. Meanwhile, the very same process appears to us as the consistent Europeanization of Russian culture.

A closer examination, however, convinces us that the new (post-Petrine) culture was significantly more traditional than is customarily believed. The new culture was constructed not so much according to models of "Western" culture (though it was subjectively experienced precisely as "Western") as along the "inverted" structural plan of the old culture. It is precisely here that we find the explicit separation of the more superficial cultural layer, which is subject to change, from all the deep forms that in the new hypostases of consciousness appeared only more brightly.

The new culture demonstrated its sacrilegious, anticlerical nature with pronounced zeal.[53] So it is all the more interesting that the construction of the new culture reveals invariable models of the medieval, ecclesiastical kind (these, of course, merely manifest the enduring models that organize the history of

Russian culture throughout, including, as one might suppose, that of both the pre-Christian and Christian periods).

3.1. We are already familiar with the crucial significance that the terms "enlightenment" and "enlightener," which are among the most fundamental notions of the "Age of Reason," held for eighteenth-century culture. Yet these words were not neologisms: they were known in pre-Petrine Rus. "To enlighten … means: to baptize, to grace with Holy Baptism."[54] It is in precisely this sense that the term "enlightener" is used in church singing directed toward St. Vladimir, "Tutor in Orthodoxy and Enlightener of All Russia, you who enlightened us all with baptism."[55] Joseph Volotsky called his own composition against heretics "The Enlightener" [Prosvetitel′]. The very same expression, however, was applied to Peter I as the creator of secular, Europeanized culture already in his own lifetime. In this sense, the creation of a new culture that demolished traditional Orthodoxy was conceived as a *second baptism of Rus*. Interesting in this regard is Feofan Prokopovich's tragicomedy *Vladimir*. Juxtaposing reform under Peter with the apostolic enlightenment of Rus was not Prokopovich's invention. In *The Journal, or: Daily Notes … of Peter the Great,* we read: "Then [1699—*Lotman and Uspensky*] I founded the Russian Order of St. Andrew the Apostle the First-Called, for the Russian nation had received from him the fundament of Christian beliefs."[56]

In Feofan Prokopovich's "tragicomedy," Vladimir, enlightener of Rus, appears in the obvious role of Peter I's alter ego. The reform of the Christianization (= "enlightenment") of Rus should evoke associations with the Petrine Reforms among the audience. At the same time, Peter's adversaries among the Orthodox hierarchs are depicted in the comedy in images of pagan sorcerers enlisting the help of demons to halt the enlightenment of Rus. A uniquely symptomatic role reversal occurs, while the broad conceptual scenario is maintained. The fact that the shamans Zherivol, Pyar, and Kuroyad are to be understood precisely as Peter's adversaries from the church is borne out by direct textual parallels. In the "tragicomedy," when Vladimir declares his desire "to change the law," Zherivol declares that there is no need:

> Change is not needed, as not the least
> Evil abides. In our own rule
> Where is the vice?[57]

> Непотребна измѣна, идѣже ни мало
> Зла не обрѣтается. В нашем же уставѣ
> кий порок ест?

Compare this passage from the "Words for the Opening of the Most Holy Administrative Synod in the Presence of His Imperial Majesty Peter I" [Slova pri nachatii Sviateishego Pravitel'stvuiushchego Sinoda v prisutstvii ego imperatorskogo velichestva Petra Pervogo, 1721]:

> Woe for these, our accursèd times! There are those, and many, who, with the ruinous remorselessness of learning, are unashamed to repudiate the sermons, the Christian precepts, that is, the only light for our paths—what need have we of teachers, of preachers? ... Thank God, all is well with us, and it is not the healthy, but the ailing, who need a doctor. ... For what kind of world do we have? What is our health? It has come to this, that anyone, be he the most lawless, thinks himself honorable and holier than others, like a maniac: this is our health. ... It has come to this, and in these times we were born, when the blind lead the blind, the most blatant ignoramuses theologize, and they write dogmas worthy of ridicule.[58]

An adherent to Orthodoxy is identified as superstitious, "like a maniac," who "is soon convinced of legend by an old wives' tale," whereas rationalism is thought of as "right faith," and the sovereign, champion of the Western Enlightenment, assumes the features of Prince Vladimir, equal to the Apostles.

3.2. It is no less revealing that the features of everyday freethinking, crossing into the practical godlessness that one encounters among the Russian nobility significantly more often than theoretical, philosophical atheism, often assume the character not of a rejection of faith, but of *crossing into another faith.* Attention is often focused not on arguments, but on the very fact of "receiving" the faithlessness and the personality of the one who has "delivered" it. People are not convinced of it, but are acculturated to it. Let us recall the words of G. Teplov about his dispute with an atheist, famously recorded by Denis Fonvizin: "The repudiator exclaimed, 'There's nothing to mull over—there is no God!' I interceded and asked him, "And who was it who told you that there is no God?' 'Pyotr Petrovich Chebyshev, yesterday, at Gostiny Dvor,' he replied. 'You got the right place!' I said."[59] In his conversation with Teplov, Fonvizin explained his method for deciding the question of God's existence as follows: "'I begin,' I replied, 'by examining what kinds of people reject God's existence and whether they can claim any authority.'"[60] That we are dealing not with the passage from religious to philosophical outlooks, but with the substitution of one belief for another, is demonstrated by the fact that the center of attention is shifted to the question of whom one can receive the true faith from, by whom a given conviction has been transmitted, and—what is quite revealing—whether it was received in an appropriate place.

What the historians of culture who study the consciousness of the typical eighteenth-century Russian nobleman take as the external veneer of Europeanization, beneath whose thin surface they discover the stratum of the pre-Petrine everyday, may have another nature as well.

Pre-Petrine culture did not exile the world of pagan notions from the consciousness of Orthodox Christianity. They were maintained as the lower—demonic—level of mythology, acknowledged as real though having their own limited and subordinate meaning. In this way, a person *was supposed to,* under specific circumstances, manifest non-Christian behavior. It is true that Christian behavior was open and demonstrative, while pagan behavior (for example, turning to a sorcerer or witch doctor, as was widely done not only among peasants, but also in the daily life of the landed gentry in the eighteenth century) was secret, hidden, and as if non-existent.

The "Age of Enlightenment" did not abolish this construction, but inverted it. The vigorous struggle that secular state authority and education waged against the church monopoly in the sphere of culture was unexpectedly refracted in the nobility's collective consciousness as a regeneration of paganism. The double-faith was maintained, but in reverse: public, official life, "fashionable" ethics, and secular everyday behavior were quickly suffused with reinvigorated pre-Christian or Eastern features ("pagan" ones, from the Orthodox point of view; this keeping of the perspective while altering the attitude's essence is revealing). Orthodoxy itself was maintained within the "closed," secretive aspect of life, from the penitential chains that state agents wore under their cambric shirts to Grigory Potyomkin's penitence and night prayers following masquerades and balls. Withdrawn into the strictly intimate and almost secretive sphere, it even got the upper hand (it is no accident that in respect to age its domains were childhood and old age).[61]

3.3. The subjective "Europeanization" of everyday life had nothing to do with an actual convergence with the Western lifestyle, and at the same time it markedly gravitated toward establishing anti-Christian forms that were decidedly impossible in the everyday life of the Christian West.[62] We see this, for example, in such phenomena as the serf-harem, an institution that was utterly impossible (in its openly displayed form) in pre-Petrine life but became commonplace in the eighteenth century. Serf-harems were not an inheritance from the past: they were born of the eighteenth century, and the harem's proprietor was, as a rule, an "enlightener" and Westernizer fighting against "entrenched ignorance."

Thus, in the diary of Ya. M. Neverov, we find a description of daily life in the home of the landowner P. A. Koshkarov, at the time of these memoirs (the early 1820s) already an old man, who maintained forms of life in his home that had apparently been established in the 1780s:

> ... Pyotr Alexeevich had a harem. Indeed, the daily life of female servants was arranged in his home purely as that of a harem. ... Twelve to fifteen young and beautiful girls occupied an entire half of the house and were appointed solely to Koshkarov's service [besides the landlord's constant, morganatic wife—they had no church marriage—Nataliya Ivanovna, a soldier's wife, from whom he had a daughter and seven sons, and his constant lover, Feoktista Semyonovna, "a girl of average age, quite beautiful, quick-tongued, and advanced, whose mother was the head of Koshkarov's harem," as Neverov notes—*Lotman and Uspensky*]; it was they who constituted what I have called a harem. The whole manor house was divided into two halves, male and female. ... The women's half of the manor house began as the drawing room, which was in fact a neutral room because Koshkarov would usually sit there on one sofa while Nataliya Ivanovna sat on another opposite him, while Feoktista had a special place. It was here that all other members of the family and the guests usually spent their time, and this is where the fortepiano stood. At the doors to the sitting room, leading into the hall, a footman usually stood duty, and at the opposite doors, those leading to Koshkarov's bedroom, stood a servant girl, and just as the footman was not allowed to cross the threshold to the bedroom, the girl could not step over the threshold into the hall. ... Not only the footman on duty or members of the male staff, but even male members of the family and guests were not allowed to pass the doors guarded by the servant girl. ... Usually in the evening, after dinner, the servant girl, at his bidding, announced loudly to the footman on duty, "His Lordship wishes to retire," which was a signal to the entire family to part for their rooms; Nataliya Ivanovna withdrew with a bow, the rest of us following her, and at once the footmen brought a simple wooden bedframe into the sitting room from the men's half of the house, and, setting it in the middle of the room, they withdrew at once, and the door from the sitting room to the hall was bolted, and the girls brought a feather duvet in from the bedroom, a blanket and other bedding necessities for Koshkarov, who during this

> time was performing his evening prayers from a prayer book, whilst the girl on duty held a candle, and during this time all the other girls brought in their own cots and placed them around Koshkarov's bed, as all of them besides Madame Ivanovna, the head of the harem, were to sleep in the same room with Koshkarov. ... Once a week Koshkarov would set off for the bathhouse, and all those who dwelled in his harem were to accompany him there, and not infrequently those of them who failed, owing to their recent arrival to that milieu, to master all the views held therein and in the bathhouse tried to conceal themselves out of modesty, returned from that place with a beating.[63]

One ought to emphasize that this harem's way of life was interpreted precisely as *Europeanized*, and on this basis it was differentiated from the peasant life from which the girls had torn themselves and which maintained certain features of the pre-Petrine structure:

> All the girls, without exception, were not only literate, but even quite sophisticated and well-read, and they had a reasonably large library at their disposal that, of course, consisted almost exclusively of belletristic works. Literacy was obligatory for a girl, otherwise she would not have been able to fulfil her duty to read aloud for Koshkarov, play whist with him, and so on, and thus every newcomer at once began to learn to read and write.

From the words of one of the girls, as a child Neverov "learned 'The Fountain of Bakhchisaray' [Bakhchisaraiskii fontan] by heart and subsequently kept an entire notebook of poems by Pushkin and Zhukovsky with him." "They were all clothed, of course, not in the national dress, but in pan-European clothing." It is revealing that when there was an offense the girls would return to their families, and their punishment would be "that they were forbidden to wear the so-called landlord's [European] clothes."[64] In this way, taking a girl into the harem meant bringing her into a "European" status, and excluding her from it meant returning her to her initial "uneducated" (peasant) existence and pre-Petrine dress.

Of course, the identification of the secular (= "European") with the pagan (whatever was non-Christian) was unconscious and on the whole prevailed in the undereducated milieu that had been deprived of direct contact with Europe. Yet this milieu was exceedingly large and actively exerted pressure on the culture of the nobility as such. The unconscious character of these notions underscored their connection not with one's individual level of education, but with deep culture-formative models. Alexey Arakcheev, who performed his pre-breakfast libation of a cup of coffee at the base of a bust of Paul I that stood in his garden, and who ordered that a place always be set for the late emperor at supper, likely had no idea of the pagan rites that his actions recalled. Deifying the emperors of Petersburg, he of course had not heard of the Hellenic notion of a deity's epiphany in the earthly kingdom. This was a different matter: in the double-faith system of Russian culture, deep-seated mechanisms had been established that gave birth to both pagan and Christian texts. A blow against any part of this duality inevitably led to the rapid development of the opposing tendency.

The bi-level structure of culture turned out to be significantly more stable than any of its concrete realizations. This is especially apparent in the nature of the Russian language situation.

3.4. One of the foundations of Russian culture in the pre-Petrine era was the specific bi-level correlation between the Church Slavonic language and spoken Russian. It is assumed that a characteristic marker of the new culture is the secularization of the language situation: the introduction of a civil alphabet, changes in the structure of literary language, and so forth: "A sharp blow was delivered against medieval fetishism in the sphere of Old Church Slavonic by reforming the alphabet (1708). It was a stark expression of the waning of the church's ideological hegemony."[65]

One may note, however, that in the given case the bi-level structure (the presence within the social sphere of a language marked by high prestige and a language deprived of this marker) is maintained, though its elements are altered. We will offer but one example: the famous censor and professor A. V. Nikitenko, surveying Arkhangelsk Province in 1834, saw "a cross made by Peter the Great himself and hoisted by him on the shore of the White Sea. Upon it is a Dutch inscription proclaiming that it was made by Captain Peter."[66]

It is obvious that the inscription on the cross, given the place where it was found, could only be in Church Slavonic and, beyond that, from the perspective of the medieval consciousness it would have been entirely out of the question to place an inscription in a "heretical" language on a cross. Yet Peter I made such an inscription, demonstrating that in his consciousness the Dutch language had functionally replaced the Church Slavonic. This position was later occupied by the German and French languages.[67]

3.5. The continuity of specific aspects of eighteenth-century consciousness relative to the traditional forms of pre-Petrine social thought was by no means manifest in the opposition between the "Europeanized" surface of life and its "Asiatic" depth, though just such a concept of a correlation between the old and the new was expressed more than once in post-Petrine culture:

> Reading these regulations, instructions, and decrees, you cannot rid yourself of the impression of the deep changes in the order of Russian life that are realized in the custodial authority's benevolent concerns. As if all of Russian life since its foundation is shifting before your eyes, a new, Europeanized Russia is growing up out of the debris of a ruined antiquity. Impressed by this imposing picture you then turn to study this Europeanized Russia, but not from those documents which record transformative dreams, but from those about the ordinary facts of life as it happens. And soon no trace of your mirage remains. And from these documents' half-faded pages, from beneath the outer cover of the new bureaucratic jargon, the old Muscovite Rus stares out at you, having stepped happily across the threshold of the eighteenth century and taken its place comfortably within the new frames of the Petersburg Empire.[68]

It is by no means for the sake of paradox that one may say that it was precisely the shift provoked by "Europeanization" (that is, by what was subjectively interpreted as Europeanization) that reinforced the archaic features within Russian culture. *Mutatis mutandis,* this shift did reveal certain archaic semiotic models that, albeit present in Russian medieval culture as it had taken shape since the fourteenth and fifteenth centuries, likely originated in a layer that was significantly more ancient still. In this regard, its prevailing surface manifestation notwithstanding, the eighteenth century was a deeply organic part of Russian culture as such.

An exceptionally convincing testament to the connection between the post-Petrine culture of the eighteenth century and pre-Petrine culture is the new culture's experience of geographic space. Despite the scientific-realistic portrayal of the Earth's surface as a kind of space marked out by various latitudes and longitudes delineating the ethnic nature of its inhabitants, their life conditions, their natural products and tradable commodities, yet not organized by a separation into "unclean," sinful lands and "holy," blessed ones, a sojourn in which promises perdition or leads to redemption,[69] in the consciousness of people in the eighteenth century—and in particular among the Russian nobility at large—a different idea lives on. In fact, geographic knowledge is, from this position, subordinate and technical. While Vasily Tatishchev did assert that "the gentry has need of geography"[70] (in Section 43 of the "Preamble" to his *Russian History*

[*Istoriia Rossiiskaia*], which bears the special subheading "On Geography, Both General and Russian"), apparently another opinion was nevertheless more widespread, as Prostakova famously formulated: "This science is not of the nobility."[71] [ix] And still, the medieval kind of notion that had ascribed religious-ethical or value markers in general to geographic space stubbornly persisted.

It was not only in the popular milieu, but also among the nobility at large that the notion of the West as a ruinous, sinful land persisted. Against this ideological background, notions of the West as the Kingdom of the Enlightenment, the source that ought to pour the light of Reason over Russia, stood out especially boldly. If, in the medieval consciousness, the holy lands (the East) were the source from which "the spark of godliness would reach even to the Russian kingdom,"[72] the eighteenth century began with the pointed assertion that the new enlightener of the Russian lands should make a pilgrimage to the West—with the "Grand Embassy" of Peter I. Later, a trip to Paris for a Russian nobleman of the eighteenth century assumes the character of a peculiar journey to holy places. It is no accident that those opposed to the Western orientation saw the main source of evils in precisely these journeys. What to some is joining in the Enlightenment—and to others joining in foppery—is achieved through a simple displacement in space, following the model of communing with a shrine during a pilgrimage.[73]

In the process, the West was conceived as "new" relative to the "old" Rus. Here it is essential to note, however, that the "New Russia" that Peter was creating was thought to be younger not only in relation to Muscovite Rus, but in juxtaposition with the Western world (here Ilarion's schema is repeated, with Byzantium replaced by the West). But if in this case "youth" and "novelty" meant embracing Western civilization, then for archaists[x] like Alexander Griboedov or, later, the Slavophiles, Russia's "youth" was conceived as a quality connected to freedom from spiritual communion with the West. In his sketch for a tragedy about 1812, Griboedov thought to have Napoleon, representing the West,

ix This is a reference to Fonvizin's comedy *The Minor* [*Nedorosl'*], in which Prostakova represents the unreformed, uneducated, despotic countryside gentry. She is perhaps not the best example of the "Russian nobility at large," which is in any case a problematic construct, given the huge differences in wealth, education, and lifestyle among the Russian nobility of the eighteenth and nineteenth centuries.

x The implied opposition between archaists and innovators goes back to a famous long article by Iurii Tynianov, "Arkhaisty i Pushkin," in his book *Arkhaisty i novatory* (Leningrad: Priboi, 1929). In this analysis of early nineteenth-century literary culture, the author proposed to replace the concepts of Neoclassicists and Romantics with those of innovators and archaists, two diffuse groups that are not necessarily aware of their shared values. Archaists aim to preserve certain traditions, but may, in fact, do so in very innovative ways.

voice "a meditation on this young, original nation, on the peculiarities of its dress, buildings, faith, morals. Left to itself alone—what could it produce?"[74]

3.6. The unfolding of the second half of the eighteenth century was dominated by ideas that exhibit a parallelism with the cultural models of the late Russian Middle Ages. Once again we are dealing with an effort to reject Culture in favor of Nature. Once more, a decisive rupture with the past has taken the guise of turning toward originary, "natural" forms of social being. A principled anti-historicism assumes the guise of turning toward an artificially constructed utopia of the past.

"The invention of memory"—the reconstruction of the utopia of the past—created the possibility of unexpected identifications. Thus, for Alexander Radishchev, the difference between different antiquities—ancient pagan, pagan Russian, or Orthodox Christian—becomes meaningless. They all fall into the ideal picture of fusing an originary national sovereignty with the world of heroes—of national leaders (*Songs Sung in Contests to Honor the Ancient Slavic Deities* [*Pesni, petye na sostiazaniiakh v chest' drevnim slavianskim bozhestvam*]), tyrant-killers, the ancient Stoics (the image of Cato the Younger that runs through all of Radishchev's works), or Christian martyrs (the hagiography of Saint Philaretos). Depicting a contemporaneous "strongman," F. V. Ushakov, Radishchev can pair the features of Cato with those of a Christian martyr (it is no accident that he called his tale "A Hagiography" [Zhitie]).

What will be typical of the completely different ideological positions of Paul I is the blending of Catholicism's ideal, chivalric past and Orthodoxy within a single utopian portrait. In the Chivalric Order of the Knights of Malta, which he had revived (revival itself being regarded as the restoration of an originary antiquity), Paul readily unites Catholic and Orthodox priories! It is hard to imagine a starker example of how historical nihilism can, from a subjective point of view, assume the guise of restoring antiquity.[75]

No less typical is the potential for some writers to identify Slavic mythology with Scandinavian,[76] and for others to place them in sharp opposition.[77] What is revealing is the potential *to choose* an appropriate antiquity for oneself (as in N. A. Lvov's dispute with Derzhavin, where the former refused to replace Greek with Scandinavian mythology in poetry, preferring Slavic myth as "originary").[78]

If one were to add the wide diffusion of eschatological feelings (from the social eschatology of Russian readers of Mably and Rousseau to the cosmic eschatology among readers of Semyon Bobrov), it will not appear baseless to think that a typological parallelism exists in the outcomes of Russian medieval culture and of eighteenth-century culture in their various historical-structural twists.

The topical problem that the end of the eighteenth century faced in seeking the originary foundations of national culture thus finds a resolution in various identifications that are at times incompatible from the position of the preceding historical tradition (compare, too, Yakov Galenkovsky and Nikolay Gnedich's somewhat later assertions about the originary identity between ancient Greek and Russian national characters, on the one hand, and, on the other, Shishkov's opinion regarding the identity between Church Slavonic and Russian literary cultures). All these identifications, however, are realized against the background of the sharp opposition between a reconstructed national culture and actual life among the nobility, a culture of secular "foppery" regarded as borrowed, foreign, and "Western." Although the latter was an explicit creation of the eighteenth century, it was felt to be "decrepit," and the reconstruction that opposed it was paradoxically thought of as simultaneously "originary" and "young," unspoiled by civilization. It is quite obvious that the concepts of "youth" and "age" had thereby been given an arbitrary meaning, and not one founded upon actual chronology (the historical).

There is no need to demonstrate that the eighteenth century in Russian culture was not merely a repetition of the medieval cycle; the distinctions within the very nature of these stages are too deep and obvious. In eighteenth-century culture, of course, actual Europeanization did occur. But it rarely coincided with what the bearers of culture themselves considered to be Europeanization. To the same degree, as we have seen, the historical tradition was often evident precisely where, subjectively, a break with tradition was implied, and innovation was at times manifest as a fanatical attachment to artificially constructed "traditions." If we take into account that all this mental labor depended on the historical experience accumulated by the culture, whether interpreted as direct or "inverted," then a complex and interesting picture emerges.

* * *

The essence of culture is such that the past within it, unlike the natural flow of time, does not "become past"—that is, it does not vanish. Fixed in the cultural memory, it enjoys a constant existence, albeit a potential one. Meanwhile, cultural memory is constructed not only as a storehouse of texts, but also as a specific generative mechanism. Culture, united with the past by memory, generates not only its own future, but also its past, in this sense serving as a mechanism for counteracting natural time.

Living culture cannot assume the shape of repetitions of the past: it is invariably giving birth to systems and texts that are structurally and functionally new. But it cannot help but to contain *memories* of the past within itself. The correlation between images of the past and future potentially present in every culture and the level of their action upon each other constitute an essential typological feature that must be taken into account when comparing distinct cultures.

The unique quality of Russian culture in the era we have considered manifested itself in the fact that a connection to the past was objectively felt most acutely when the complete break from it dominated subjectively and, in contrast, the focus on the past was tied to erasing actual tradition from memory and turning toward chimeric constructions of the past.

CHAPTER 7

The Symbolism of Petersburg and the Problems of Semiotics of the City

This chapter was included in Lotman's monograph Universe of the Mind, *although it was first published in 1984 in* Sign System Studies *[*Trudy po znakovym sistemam*]. In addition to the value of its analysis of Petersburg's cultural mythology, this piece also exemplifies the operations of a semiosphere. The similarities between Lotman's description of how a city operates as a generator of new information and his theoretical conceptualization of the semiosphere are obvious. Here Lotman works out the intrinsic "polyglotism" of St. Petersburg, the various "codes" that have inflected its cultural construction, from the rationalist city of urban planners to the military city preferred by Paul I, from the ghostly city of oral folklore to the "Roman" city of its architecture, and from the theatrical city to the official, bureaucratic one. Our translation is based on Iu. M. Lotman, "Simvolika Peterburga," in* Semiosfera *(St. Petersburg: Iskusstvo-SPB, 2000), 320–334.*

The city occupies a peculiar place in the system of symbols generated by the history of culture. Two basic aspects of urban semiotics should be noted: the city as space and the city as name. The second of these was addressed in the article "Echoes of the Concept of Moscow as Third Rome in the Ideology of Peter I," and we do not address it in the present work.[1]

The city as a closed space can find itself in a twofold relationship to the land surrounding it: it can be not only isomorphic with the state, but its personification, it can *be it* in a certain ideal sense (thus the city of Rome is at the same time the world of Rome), but it can also be its antithesis. *Urbis* and *orbis terrarium* can be perceived as two hostile entities. This last case is recounted in Genesis, where Cain is called the first builder of a city: "and he builded a city, and called the name of the city, after the name of his son ..." (Genesis 4:17). In this way, Cain is not only the builder of the first city, but also the one who gave it its first name.

Where a city's relation to the world around it resembles that of a centrally located temple to the surrounding city—that is, when it appears as an idealized model of the universe—the city is, as a rule, located at the center of the Earth. Or rather, wherever it is situated, it is ascribed a central location, it *is considered* the center. Jerusalem, Rome, Moscow—in various texts, they function precisely as the centers of certain worlds. The ideal embodiment of *one's own* land, it can simultaneously function as the prototype of the Heavenly City and be a holy site for the lands around it.

Yet, the City may also be eccentrically situated relative to the land it correlates to—it is located beyond its limits. Thus, Svyatoslav moved his capital to Pereyaslavets on the Danube, Charlemagne moved his from Ingelheim to Aachen.[2] Yet here, too, there is a discernible semiotic dimension. First of all, the existential code becomes sharper: what exists becomes non-existent, and what has not yet appeared becomes the only thing that is truly real. That's what Svyatoslav means when he declares that Pereyaslavets-on-Danube is located at the center of his lands—the state that he intends to create—while announcing that the actually existent Kievan lands were as though non-existent. What is more, there is a sharp increase in valuation: what is existent and bears the marks of the present and "native" is evaluated negatively, and what is to appear in the future, what is "foreign," receives a high axiological rating. At the same time, one may note that "concentric" structures tend toward exclusion, a separation from surroundings that are evaluated as hostile, while those that are eccentric tend toward inclusiveness, openness, and cultural contact.

The concentric positioning of the city in semiotic space is, as a rule, connected to the image of the city on a hill (or on hills). Such a city functions as a mediator between heaven and earth: clustered around it are myths of genesis (the gods, as a rule, participate in its founding); it has a beginning, but no end; it is the "eternal city," *Roma aeterna.*

The eccentric city is situated "at the edge" of cultural space: on the seashore, at the mouth of a river. What is realized here is not the antithesis of earth and heaven, but the opposition of the natural and the artificial. This is a city created in defiance of Nature, one that finds itself struggling against it, which provides two possibilities for interpreting the city: as the triumph of reason over the elements, on the one hand, or, on the other, as a perversion of the natural order. It is around precisely this kind of city that we find a concentration of eschatological myths, prophecies of destruction; the notion of doom and of the victory of the elements will be inextricable from this cycle of urban mythology. As a rule, it is a flood, sinking to the bottom of the sea. It is just such a fate that, in the prophecy of Methodius of Patara, awaits Constantinople (which steadfastly serves as the "un-eternal Rome"):

> ... and the Lord God's wrath upon it shall grow with a great fury, and He shall send his Archangel Michael, and he shall cut that city down with the scythe, smash it with the scepter, turn it over like a millstone, and thus sink it with its people in the depths of the sea, and that city shall perish; there shall remain a single pillar upon the square. ... Arriving on their ships, the sea-merchants shall lash their ships to this pillar and shall start to weep, speaking thusly: "O Constantinople, mighty and proud! How many years have we come to you, making trade, having grown rich, and now in but an hour the abyss has covered you and all your sumptuous edifices and rendered you without trace."[3]

This variant of eschatological legend became fixed in the mythology of Petersburg: not only the flood as a storyline maintained by periodic inundations, one that has given birth to a voluminous literature, but also the detail—the top of the Alexander Column or the angel of the Peter and Paul Fortress, rising out over the waves and serving as a mooring for ships—compel us to assume a direct reorientation from Constantinople to Petersburg. Vladimir Sollogub recalled:

> [Mikhail] Lermontov ... liked to sketch, with a quill or even a brush, a view of an enraged sea, from which emerged the extremity of the Alexander Column, crowned with an angel. Such an image resonated with his cheerless, grief-thirsty imagination.[4]

Compare Matvey Dmitriev-Mamonov's poem "The Underwater City" [Podvodnyi gorod], Vladimir Odoevsky's novella *The Mockery of a Corpse* [*Nasmeshka mertvetsa*], from *Russian Nights* [*Russkie nochi*], and many others.

The eternal struggle between the elements and culture, which is intrinsic to the idea of the doomed city, is manifest in the Petersburg myth as the antithesis of water and stone. The stone here is not "natural," not "wild" (unhewn); it is not rock standing in its place since time immemorial, but has been brought here, polished and "humanized," cultivated. Petersburg stone is an artifact, and not a natural phenomenon. This is why stone, rock, and the cliff are endowed in the Petersburg myth not with the customary markers of immobility, steadiness, and the ability to withstand wind and water, but rather with the unnatural marker of movability:

The mountain started moving, changing thus its place,
And witnessing the demise of what had been its grounding,
It passed across the Baltic's fathomless sounding,
Collapsing here, at the hooves of Peter's horse.[5]

Гора содвигнулась, а место пременя
И видя своего стояния кончину,
Прешла Бальтийскую пучину
И пала под ноги Петрова здесь коня.

The theme of the movement of the immobile, however, is but a part of the general picture of a perverse world where stone floats on water. Our attention is turned precisely to metamorphosis, to the moment when the "normal" world is transformed into the "inverted" one ("witnessing the demise of what had been its grounding").

The natural semantics of stone, of rock, is what we find, for example, in Fyodor Tyutchev's poem "Sea and Cliff" [More i utes]:

Insolent and unperturbed,
Not afeared by foolish waves,
Motionless and undisturbed,
A coeval of the universe
You, our giant, for all days![6]

Но спокойный и надменный,
Дурью волн не обуян,
Неподвижный, неизменный,
Мирозданью современный,
Ты стоишь, наш великан!

In this poem's symbolism, the cliff is Russia, which, for Tyutchev, is rather an antonym for Petersburg, and not its synonym.

Compare the typically "Petersburgian" oxymoron of the petrified swamp:

Against and despite the elements;
And with creative force, in a flash,
The swampy log has turned to stone,
A city has been erected ...[7]

Стихиям всем на перекор;
И силой творческой, в мгновенье,
Болотный кряж окаменел,
Воздвигся град …

Petersburg stone is stone on water, on swampland, stone resting on nothing, not "coeval to the world's creation," but placed there by a person. In the "portrait of Petersburg,"[i] water and stone change places: water is eternal, it was there before stone and will triumph over it, whereas stone is endowed with transience and the illusory. Water brings it to ruin. In Odoevsky's *Russian Nights* we find a portrait of Petersburg's demise: "Now the walls are swaying, a small window is smashed, and another, water has streamed through them, it has filled the hall. … Suddenly, the walls have come down with a crash, the ceiling gave way—and the coffin, and everything in the hall, the waves swept out to the boundless sea."[8]

The situation of the "inverted world," which inscribes such a model of the city into the exceptionally broad current of European culture from the sixteenth to the early eighteenth centuries, one ultimately correlated with the Baroque tradition, engendered conflicting appraisals from its audience.[9] This was demonstrated by Alexander Sumarokov when he provided parallel versions of his inscription, one heroic, one parodic. The "inverted world" in the Baroque tradition, which is bound up with the folkloric-carnival tradition (see the profound ideas of Mikhail Bakhtin, which have nevertheless enjoyed an unjustifiably broad interpretation in the works of his epigones), is perceived as a utopia, a "Land of Cockaigne"[10] or the "inverse world" [prevratnyi svet] in Sumarokov's famous chorus. But it could just as well have assumed the ominous contours of the world of Breughel and Bosch.

At the same time, there is the identification of Petersburg with Rome.[11] This notion enjoyed wide circulation toward the beginning of the nineteenth century, as in: "… one cannot help but be awed by the might and majesty of this new Rome! …"[12] Uniting two archetypes in the image of Petersburg, that of the "eternal Rome" and the "un-eternal, doomed Rome" (Constantinople), created the double perspective characteristic of Petersburg's cultural understanding: eternity and doom at the same time.

In its initial semiotic determination, Petersburg's inscription into this double situation allowed it to be treated simultaneously as both a "paradise,"

---

i Lotman means the conventional image of the city.

the utopia of the ideal city of the future, the embodiment of Reason—and as the ominous masquerade of the Antichrist. In both instances, what had occurred was complete idealization, only with opposite signs. One example offers a colorful illustration of the potential for a double reading of the "Petersburg myth": in the tradition of Baroque symbolism, the serpent beneath the hoof of Falconet's horseman[ii] is a trivial allegory of envy, enmity, of the hindrances placed in Peter's way by external enemies and internal opponents of reform. However, in the context of Russian audiences quite familiar with Methodius of Patara's prophecies,[iii] this image received a different, more sinister reading:

> This day our demise approaches ..., as says the patriarch Jacob, "I saw, said he, a serpent lying by the road and biting at the horse's heel, and I sat on the hind leg and awaited salvation from God." And so. The horse is the whole of the world, and the heel the last days, and the serpent the antichrist ..., he who will begin to bite, that is, to seduce by his evil deeds, he dares to make signs and wonders with his dreams before them all: he commands the mountains to come to the place.

Compare: "The mountain started moving, changing thus its place ..."[13] In this context, the horse, horseman, and serpent no longer oppose one another, and instead they make up the details of the end of the world, while the serpent moves from a second-order symbol to the main figure in the group. It is no accident that in the cultural tradition born of Falconet's monument the serpent would be assigned a role unlikely to have been foreseen by the sculptor.

The ideal artificial city, one created as the realization of a rationalistic utopia, was supposed to have been deprived of history, insofar as the reasonableness of the "regular state" signified the negation of historically established structures. This implied the construction of a city in a new place and,

ii Lotman refers to the Bronze Horseman, an equestrian statue of Peter I commissioned by Catherine the Great and designed by Étienne Maurice Falconet. Completed in 1782 and standing on Senate Square close to the Neva river, the monument has undergone extensive mythologization in the works of Pushkin, Dostoevsky, and Andrey Bely, among others, not to speak of artists such as Alexander Benois or Mstislav Dobuzhinsky. See Alexander Schenker, *The Bronze Horseman: Falconet's Monument to Peter the Great* (New Haven: Yale University Press, 2003). See also Grigorii Z. Kaganov, *Images of Space: St. Petersburg in the Visual and Verbal Arts* (Stanford: Stanford University Press, 1997).

iii Lotman refers to the *Apocalypse* of Pseudo-Methodius of Patara, a text of Syriac origin that was widely translated in the Middle Ages and influenced Christian eschatological thinking.

accordingly, the demolition of all that is "old" that might be found there. Thus, for example, under Catherine the Great, the idea of creating an ideal city where Tver had historically stood arose after a fire in 1763 had effectively destroyed the city. From the perspective of a planned utopia, such a fire could be regarded as a fortunate circumstance. The indispensable precondition of a working semiotic system, however, is the presence of history. In this regard, a city that has been created "suddenly," with a wave of the demiurge's hand, having no history and subject to a single plan, is, in principle, unrealizable.

The city as a complex semiotic mechanism, a generator of culture, can serve this function only because it constitutes a cauldron of texts and codes, variously arranged and heterogenous, belonging to different languages and different levels. It is precisely the theoretical semiotic polyglotism of any given city that makes it a field of diverse semiotic collisions that would be impossible under other conditions. Effecting a link between various national, social, and stylistic codes and texts, the city accomplishes diverse hybridizations, transcodings, and semiotic translations that transform it into a powerful generator of new information. The source of such semiotic collisions is not only the synchronic juxtaposition of manifold semiotic formations, but also the diachronic dimension: architectural edifices, urban rites and ceremonies, the city plan itself, the naming of streets, and thousands of other relics of bygone eras serve as coded programs that are constantly regenerating texts from the historical past. The city becomes a mechanism that is constantly recreating its own past, which is granted the possibility of coexistence, as though synchronously, with the present. In this regard, the city is, like culture, a mechanism working against time.[14]

The rationalist's city-utopia[15] was deprived of these semiotic reserves. The consequences of this would likely have baffled an Enlightenment rationalist of the eighteenth century. History's absence summoned a violent increase in mythology. Myth filled the semiotic void, and the situation of the artificial city turned out to be exceptionally mythogenic.

Petersburg is exceptionally typical in this regard: the history of Petersburg is inextricable from Petersburg's mythology, and in this instance the word "mythology" sounds far from metaphorical. Long before nineteenth-century Russian literature, from Pushkin and Gogol to Dostoevsky, made Petersburg's mythology a fact of national culture, the actual history of Petersburg had already been suffused with mythological elements. If one does not identify the city's history with the official-administrative history reflected in bureaucratic correspondence, but views it instead in its connection with the life of the population at large, one is immediately struck by how rumors, oral tales about unusual occurrences, and specific urban folklore play an exceptional role in the life of the "Northern Palmyra" from the very moment of its founding. The first collector of this folklore was the Privy Council. Pushkin evidently intended to turn his diary of 1833–1835 into an idiosyncratic archive of urban rumors; Anton Delvig was a collector of "horror stories," and Nikolay Dobrolyubov, in the handwritten newspaper *Rumors* [*Slukhi*] from his student years, laid the theoretical foundation for the role of orality in national life.

The peculiarity of "Petersburg mythology" in particular consists in the fact that the sense of a specifically Petersburg character enters into its self-consciousness, that is, it implies the presence of a certain external, non-Petersburgian observer. This might be the "view from Europe" or the "view from Russia" (= the "view from Moscow"). Yet what remains constant is the fact that culture constructs the position of the one observing it from outside. At the same time, the opposite perspective takes shape as well: the one "from Petersburg" on Europe or on Russia (= Moscow). Accordingly, Petersburg will be interpreted as "Asia in Europe" or "Europe in Russia." Both treatments merge in affirming the inorganicism, the artificiality of Petersburg culture.

It is important to note that the awareness of "artificiality" is a feature of the *self-assessment* of Petersburg culture, and only then does it pass beyond its limits, becoming an element of perspectives alien to it. Connected to this are such features, emphasized constantly in Petersburg's "image of the world," as spectrality and theatricality. It would seem that the medieval tradition of visions and prophecies ought to have been more fitting of the organic, traditionally Russian Moscow than of "rationalist" and "European" Petersburg. Yet it is precisely in the Petersburg atmosphere that it receives, *mutatis mutandis*, its most palpable continuation. The idea of spectrality is expressed quite clearly in the appropriately stylized legend of Petersburg's founding, which Vladimir Odoevsky put into the mouth of an old Finn:

> And they started to build a city, but they set a stone down, the swamp sucks it up; they've already heaped up many stones, rock on rock, beam on beam, but the swamp takes everything in, and all that remains upon the land is marsh. Meanwhile, the tsar had a ship built, saw for himself: he looks, and his city's not there yet. "You don't know how to do anything," he said to his people, and with these words he began to lift one rock on another and hammer away in the air. In this way he built the entire city and then set it down upon the earth.[16]

Of course, this story is characteristic not of Finnish folklore, but of the understanding of Petersburg within the circle of Petersburg literati close to Pushkin in the 1830s, of whom Odoevsky was one. The city forged in open air, having no foundation beneath it—such a position compelled one to regard Petersburg as a spectral, phantasmagoric space. An examination of the material demonstrates that in the oral literature of the Petersburg salon—a genre that blossomed in the first third of the nineteenth century and that undoubtedly played a large historical-literary role, but that has remained not only unexamined, but even unnoticed—a peculiar place was reserved for telling terrible and fantastic tales with an indispensable "Petersburg color." This genre's roots reach back to the eighteenth century. Thus the story told by Grand Prince Pavel Petrovich in Brussels on June 10, 1782, as recorded by the Baronness D'Oberkirch, undoubtedly belongs to this genre.[17] Here we find faith in the event's authenticity, an obligatory sign of the genre, as well as the appearance of Peter I's ghost, tragic forebodings, and, finally, the Bronze Horseman as a distinctive mark of Petersburg space. (Actually, the monument had not yet been erected, but Peter's shade leads the future Emperor Paul I to Senate Square and vanishes, promising a meeting in that place.)

We should count E. G. Levashyova's story about Anton Delvig's posthumous visit among the stories typical of this genre. Ekaterina Gavrilovna Levashyova is the cousin of the Decembrist Ivan Yakushkin, an acquaintance of Pushkin and Mikhail Orlov, and patroness of the exiled Alexander Herzen. Pyotr Chadaaev lived in her house on Novaya Basmannaya Street. She had an especially intimate friendship with Delvig, whose nephew would subsequently marry her daughter Emiliya. Ekaterina Gavrilovna Levasheva would say that her husband, N. V. Levashyov, had an arrangement with Delvig, about which Levashyov spoke as follows:

> … he [Delvig] loved to talk about life beyond the grave, about its connection to life here, about promises given in life and fulfilled after death, and once, with the aim of clarifying this theme to himself, of verifying the stories he had read or heard at some point, he extracted a promise from me, making the selfsame promise himself, to appear after death to whichever one among us remained alive after the other.
>
> I assure you that in making this promise, there were neither oaths, nor signatures in blood, no solemnity of any kind, nothing. … It was a simple, normal conversation, a *causerie de salon*. …[18]

The conversation was forgotten, Delvig passed away about seven years later, and, as Levashyov tells it, precisely one year after Delvig's death, at midnight, he appeared, saying nothing, in his study, sat down in a chair, and then, without uttering a single word, withdrew.

This story interests us as a fact of Petersburg's "salon folklore," one that it seems is not accidentally connected with the figure of Delvig. Delvig cultivated the oral "Petersburg" horror story. It is revealing that "The Solitary Little House on Vasilyevsky Island" [Uedinennyi domik na Vasil'evskom], by Pushkin and Vladimir Titov, is connected by specific threads to the atmosphere of Delvig's circle. Titov testified that it was at Delvig's insistence that it had been published in *Northern Flowers* [*Severnye tsvety*].[19]

The "Petersburg mythology" of Gogol and Dostoevsky rested on the tradition of oral Petersburg literature, canonized it, and, much like the equally oral tradition of the anecdote, brought it into the world of high literature.

The whole body of "oral literature" from the 1820s–1830s compels us to interpret Petersburg as a space in which the mysterious and the fantastic appear logical. The Petersburg tale is kin to the Yuletide tale, but in it the temporal fantastic has been replaced by the spatial.

Another peculiarity of Petersburg spatiality is its theatricality. The very nature of Petersburg's architecture, its unique consistency of massive complexes, without intermingling developments from different eras as cities with extensive histories do, gives off a sense of decorativeness. It is striking to the eye of both the foreigner and the Muscovite. But the latter regards this as a mark of "Europeanism," whereas a European, accustomed to the Romanesque style standing alongside the Baroque, the Gothic beside Classicism, to an architectural mix, looks with wonder upon the original, though for him also odd, beauty of large complexes. The Marquis de Custine[iv] writes of this as follows: "Je m'étonne à chaque pas de voir la confusion qu'on cesse de faire ici de deux arts aussi différents que l'architecture et la décoration. Pierre-le-Grand et ses successeurs ont pris leur capitale pour un théâtre."[20]

---

iv Astolphe-Louis-Léonor, Marquis de Custine (1790–1857), was a French aristocrat who wrote a scathing account of Russia under the reign of Nicholas I, *La Russie en 1839* (Paris, 1843). The text serves a strongly worded indictment of the despotic rule of the Tsar and the fear-induced abasement of his subjects. It was quickly forbidden in Russia, although smuggled copies in the original language circulated among the elite. Some excerpts started to appear in translation in 1891. For an extensive commentary, see Vera Mil'china and Aleksandr Ospovat, *Kommentarii k knige Astol'fa de Kiustina "Rossiia v 1839 godu,"* 3rd ed. (St. Petersburg: Kriga, 2008).

The theatricality of Petersburg space was evident in its sharp division into the "stage" and the "behind-the-scenes," in the constant awareness of the spectator and, what is especially important, in the replacement of what is there with what is "as-if there": the spectator is constantly present, but for the participants in the action on stage he is "as-if there" (noticing his presence means violating the rules of the game). Likewise, as far as the stage is concerned, the entire backstage space is not there. From the point of view of stage space, all that is real is life onstage; from the backstage point of view, that space is a game and a convention.

The feeling that there is a spectator—an observer whom one is not supposed to notice—accompanies all the ritual ceremonies that fill the routine of the "military capital." The soldier is like an actor, constantly in view, but nevertheless separated by a wall, transparent from one side, from those who are observing the review, the changing of the guard, or any other ceremony: they see him, and he exists for the spectators, but to him they are invisible and do not exist. The Emperor is no exception. The Marquis de Custine wrote:

> Nous devions être présentés à l'Empereur et à l'Impératrice.
>
> On voit que l'Empereur ne peut oublier un seul instant ce qu'il est, ni la constante attention qu'il excite; il *pose* incessamment, d'où il résulte qu'il n'est jamais naturel, même lorsqu'il est sincère; son visage a trois expressions dont pas une n'est la bonté toute simple.
>
> La plus habituelle me paraît toujours la sévérité. Une autre expression, quoique plus rare, convient peut-être mieux encore à cette belle figure, c'est la solennité; une troisième, c'est la politesse. ... On dirait d'un masque qu'on met et qu'on dépose à volonté. ... Je veux donc dire que l'Empereur est toujours dans son rôle, et qu'il le remplit en grand acteur ...; [ainsi le plus grand des maux que souffre la Russie] l'absence de liberté, se peint jusque sur la face de son souverain: il a plusieurs masques, il n'a pas un visage. Cherchez l'homme? vous trouvez toujours l'Empereur.[21]

The need for an auditorium presents a semiotic parallel to what the eccentric spatial location offers geographically. Petersburg has no perspective on itself: it is constantly required to construct a spectator. In this sense, both Westernizers and Slavophiles[v] are equally the creation of Petersburg culture. It

---

v Westernizers argued that Russia should adopt Western-style political and economic structures in order to catch up with civilizational development in the West. They argued for the

is characteristic that in Russia it is possible to have a Westernizer who has never been in the West, doesn't know its languages, and isn't even interested in the actual West. Ivan Turgenev, strolling around Paris with Vissarion Belinsky, was struck by the latter's indifference to the French life surrounding him:

> I remember, in Paris he saw the Place de la Concorde for the first time, and he immediately asked me, "It's one of the most beautiful squares in the world, don't you agree?" And at my affirmative reply he exclaimed, "Very well, then; now I know," and, as an aside, "basta!" And he started talking about Gogol. I pointed out to him that a guillotine had stood on this very square during the Revolution, and that this is where they cut off the head of Louis XVI; he looked around, said, "Ah!"—and recalled the scene in *Taras Bulba* when Ostap is executed.[22]

To a "Westernizer," the West is but an ideal point of view, and not a cultural-geographic reality. But this reconstructed "point of view" possessed a certain higher reality relative to the actual life observed from its position. Mikhail Saltykov-Shchedrin, recalling that in the 1840s he, "brought up on the articles of Belinsky, naturally sided with the Westernizers," wrote, "In Russia—though not so much in Russia as in Petersburg especially—we existed only in fact, or, as they said at that time, we had a 'lifestyle.' ... But spiritually we lived in France."[23] The formula that they "spiritually ... lived in France" did not exclude, but rather implied, that colliding with the real life of the West often turned out tragically and transformed the "Westernizer" into a critic of the West. Against this, the Slavophiles, having studied abroad, having heard the lectures of Schelling and Hegel, like Ivan and Pyotr Kireevsky, or like Yuri Samarin, who had no knowledge of the Russian language until he was seven years old—they, having hired university professors specially to learn how to speak Russian, constructed their Rus just as artificially, as an indispensable perspective on the real world of post-Petrine, Europeanized civilization.

The constant oscillation between the reality of the spectator and the reality of the stage, though each of these realities is presented, from the other

---

abolition of serfdom and reforms of the judicial system. Slavophiles started from the premise that the Russian people are intrinsically more collectivist than Westerners and hence that Russia should follow a unique path of development and should not emulate European institutions. Their ideas prepared the ground for the rise of Messianic ideas in Russia. For a brief exposition of the two philosophies, see Andrzej Walicki, *A History of Russian Thought from the Enlightenment to Marxism* (Stanford: Stanford University Press, 1979).

point of view, as illusory, engenders the Petersburg effect of theatricality. Its second aspect lies in the relationship between stage and backstage. The spatial antithesis between Nevsky Prospect (and the entire row of Petersburg palaces), on the one hand, and Kolomna, Vasilyevsky Island, and the outskirts, on the other, was interpreted literarily as a mutual relation of non-existence. Each of these two Petersburg "stages" had its own myth that was realized in stories and anecdotes and was attached to specific "sites." There was the Petersburg of Peter the Great, who filled the role of "his" Petersburg's patron deity or even as the *deus implicitus* invisibly present within his creation, and the Petersburg of the clerk, the pauper, the "non-citizen of the capital" (Gogol). Each of these characters had "his" streets, regions—his own spaces. A natural consequence of this is the emergence of plots in which two of these characters clashed in some way, due to extraordinary circumstances. Let's take up one story. Its gist is connected with the fact that the author E. P. Lachinova (under the pseudonym E. Khamar-Dabanov) published the satirical novel *Caucasian Escapades* (Prodelki na Kavkaze, 1844). The publication caused a stir. A. V. Nikitenko noted in his diary on June 22, 1844, "The Minister of War read the book and was horrified. He pointed it out to Dubelt and said, 'The book is all the more unwholesome for the fact that every line is true.'"[24]

N. I. Krylov, who had allowed this book through censorship, came under investigation. Krylov himself later told N. I. Pirogov the following about this episode. To understand Krylov's story, one must bear in mind the dogged rumors about how, in the Third Section, in the office of the chief of the gendarmerie, there is an armchair that drops the sitter halfway down a chute, after which concealed executioners, not seeing whose execution they are carrying out, flog him. Talk of such punishments meted out "in seclusion," which already circulated in the seventeenth century in connection with Sheshkovsky and resurfaced during the reign of Nicholas I, even penetrated Alexandre Dumas's "Russian" novels. Pirogov tells us:

> Krylov was a censor, and this year it had fallen to him to license some novel that had caused quite a stir. The novel had been forbidden by the censorship's central administration, and Krylov was summoned to see Orlov, the chief of the gendarmerie. ... Krylov travels to Petersburg, understandably in the darkest frame of mind, and presents himself initially to Dubelt, and then, together with Dubelt, sets out to see Orlov. The weather was damp, chilly, gloomy.

Driving through Isaac Square, past the monument to Peter the Great, Dubelt, wrapped in an overcoat and having nestled himself into a corner of the carriage, says, as if to himself—this is how Krylov tells it: "He's the one they ought to hew down—Peter the Great—for his prank, building Petersburg in a swamp."

Krylov listens and thinks to himself, *Right, my good man, right, you can't fool me, I'm not saying a word.*

And along the way Dubelt attempted several times to resume the conversation, but Krylov remained mute as a fish. At last they arrive at Orlov's. They receive a very warm welcome.

Dubelt leaves Krylov with Orlov.

"Forgive me, Mr. Krylov," says the chief of the gendarmerie, "for our disturbing you over such a trifle. Be so kind as to have a seat, and we'll talk."

"And I am standing there," Krylov tells us, "neither alive nor dead, and I'm thinking over what to do next: not to sit—no way, if he invites you, and you sit for the chief of the gendarmerie, then you might be hewn down anyway. In the end, there's nothing to be done. Orlov again invites me to, and he points to the armchair standing beside him. So I," according to Krylov, "gingerly and carefully seat myself upon the very edge of the chair. My heart was in my throat. Fine, so then I'm waiting for the cushion I'm sitting on to drop down and—you know the rest … And Orlov most likely noticed—he smiles mildly and assures me that I can be quite at ease. …"[25]

Krylov's story is interesting in many respects. First of all, despite being the report of a participant in a true event, it is already quite clearly compositionally organized and is already halfway toward its transformation into an urban anecdote. The *point* of the story consists in the fact that within it Peter I and an official meet as equals, though it falls to the Third Division to decide which of them ought to be hewn down (Dubelt's formulation—"He's the one they ought to hew down"—testifies to the fact that he is caught in the moment of choosing), though the choice evidently lands against the "sovereign founder." It is crucial that the question is discussed in what is the traditional Petersburg locus for such reflections—on Senate Square. At the same time, the ritual thrashing of the statue is not simply a form of passing judgment on Peter, but also a typically pagan, magical action upon a deity conducting itself "improperly." In this respect, Petersburg anecdotes about blasphemous pranks against the monument to Peter I (such as the famous anecdote about Countess Tolstaya, who after the 1824 flood made a special trip to Senate Square to stick her tongue out at the Emperor)[26] are, like any blasphemy, a form of divine veneration.

The "Petersburg mythology" developed in the background of other, deeper layers of urban semiotics. Petersburg had been conceived as Russia's seaport, the Russian Amsterdam (the parallel with Venice was firm as well). But it was simultaneously supposed to be the "military capital" and the royal residence—the country's administrative center—and furthermore, as the analysis convinces us, also the New Rome, with all the imperial pretensions that come with it.[27] Yet all of these layers of practical and symbolic function contradicted one another and were often incompatible. It was inevitable that a city would be founded that was functionally to have replaced Novgorod, destroyed by Ivan IV,[vi] and to have restored both the cultural balance between two historic centers (something that was traditional for Rus)[vii] and the equally traditional links with Western Europe. Such a city was supposed to become both an economic center and the meeting place of diverse cultural discourses. Semiotic polyglotism is law for a city of this kind. Meanwhile, the ideal of the "military capital" demanded a singularity of vision, the strict adherence to a single semiotic system. Any deviation from this could, from this perspective, appear only as a dangerous breach of order. One ought to note that the first type always gravitates toward "irregularity" and the contradictions characteristic of an artistic text, the second toward the normative "regularity" of metalanguage. It is no accident that the philosophical ideal of the City, which was one of the codes of Petersburg in the eighteenth century, was beautifully congruent with the "military" or "bureaucratic" (official) Petersburg and did not coincide with the cultural, literary, or commercial Petersburg.

The struggle between Petersburg the artistic text and Petersburg the metalanguage suffuses the city's entire semiotic history. The ideal model struggled for real embodiment. It is no accident that Custine perceived Petersburg as a military encampment where the tents had been replaced by palaces. Yet this tendency met persistent and effective resistance: life suffused the city with both the private residences of the nobility, with their independent, "private" cultural life, and with the non-noble intelligentsia, with its distinctive cultural tradition,

---

vi Ivan IV ordered a massacre in Novgorod in 1570, prompted by his fears of treason from church authorities and boyars in the city. Ivan's personal army, the *oprichnina*, looted the churches and executed the population randomly. The massacre set off the decline of Novgorod as a major center.

vii Until the rise of Moscow in the fourteenth century, Kiev and Novgorod were the two major centers of medieval Rus.

which traced its roots to the religious milieu. Transferring the royal residence to Petersburg, completely unnecessary to its role as the Russian Amsterdam, complicated the contradiction all the more. As the capital, the symbolic center of Russia, the New Rome, Petersburg should have been the country's emblem, its expression, but as the royal residence, endowed with the features of an anti-Moscow, it could only be the antithesis of Russia. The complex interweaving of the "native" and the "foreign" in Petersburg's semiotics left an imprint on how the entire culture of this period assessed itself. "By what dark magic have we made ourselves foreigners among our own!" wrote Alexander Griboedov, articulating one of the fundamental questions of the era.[28]

Over the course of its historical development, Petersburg distanced itself ever more from the contrived ideal of the "regular government's" rationalist capital, of a city organized by statutes and having no history. It became overgrown with history; it acquired a complex topo-cultural structure supported by its population's differences in class and nationality. With exceptional speed, the life of the city grew more complex. The motleyness of Petersburg already frightened Paul. The city was ceasing to be an island within the empire, so Paul decided to make an island within Petersburg. In an analogous sense, Mariya Fyodorovna strove to transfer a scrap of cozy Montbéliard to Pavlovsk.[viii] By 1830, Petersburg had turned into a city of cultural-semiotic contrasts, and this served as ground for an exceptionally intense intellectual life. By the quantity of texts, codes, connections, associations, by the volume of cultural memory accumulated over the historically trivial span of its existence, Petersburg can rightly be considered a unique object in which semiotic models have been embodied in architectural and geographic reality.

viii Mariya Fyodorovna, née Sophie Dorothea of Württemberg (1759–1828), was the empress, Paul's wife. Montbéliard was a family estate of the dukes of Württemberg, where she spent part of her childhood. Her ideas contributed substantially to the design of Pavlovsk, a beautiful landscape estate in the Brownian style in the vicinity of St. Petersburg that served as one of Paul's residences. After his death, Mariya Fyodorovna continued to reside in Pavlovsk.

CHAPTER 8

The Duel

This chapter is drawn from Iu. M. Lotman, Besedy o russkoi kul'ture: Byt i traditsii russkogo dvorianstva (XVIII–nachalo XIX veka) *(St. Petersburg: Iskusstvo, 1994), 164–179, although Lotman had written about duels before, notably in his biography of Pushkin (1981).* Besedy o russkoi kul'ture [Conversation on Russian Culture] *started as a TV program on the culture of the nobility before becoming a monograph, which explains its more conversational style. Lotman's text contains both footnotes and endnotes, which we have merged into endnotes to accommodate the explanatory glosses. Lotman's analysis of the duel provides an interesting test case of the articulation between individual agency and social pressure. As Lotman describes it, many participants in duels acted against their explicit intentions and were caught in a logic over which they had lost control.*

A duel is a battle conducted by two persons according to defined rules, with the goal of restoring honor, of removing from the offended party the shameful stain that an insult has left. In this way, the role of the duel is socio-symbolic.

The duel is a defined procedure for restoring honor and cannot be understood outside of the specifics of how "honor" is understood in Europeanized, post-Petrine Russian noble society's general system of ethics. Naturally, from a perspective that has ostensibly rejected this understanding, the duel has lost its meaning and transformed into ritualized murder.

The Russian nobleman of the eighteenth and early nineteenth centuries lived and acted under the influence of two counterpoised regulators of conduct. As a loyal subject, a servant of the state, he submitted to orders. The psychological spur for this submission was the fear of the punishment that would befall the disobedient. But at the same time, as a nobleman, a member of an estate that was simultaneously a ruling body socially and a cultural elite, he submitted to the laws of honor. Here the psychological spur toward submission is shame. The ideal which the culture of the nobility establishes for itself implies the complete banishment of fear and the affirmation of honor as the fundamental legislator of conduct. In light of this, activities that demonstrate fearlessness gain in significance.

Thus, for example, whereas the "regular state" of Peter I continues to regard the nobleman's conduct in war as service for the good of the state, and his bravery merely as a means for achieving that aim, with respect to honor bravery becomes an end in itself. The chivalric ethics of the Middle Ages have, from these vantages, undergone a certain restoration. From a similar point of view (reflected distinctly both in the *Lay of Igor's Campaign* and in the *Devgenian Deed*) the knight's conduct is not measured against his defeat or victory, but has value in and of itself. This is particularly apparent with respect to the duel: danger, coming face-to-face with death, becomes the cleansing agent that rids a person of an offense. The offended party is himself supposed to decide (making the right choice testifies to how well he has mastered the laws of honor) whether it is a dishonor so insignificant that demonstrations of fearlessness are sufficient to redeem it—by showing readiness for battle (reconciliation is possible after the challenge and its acceptance; in accepting the challenge, the offender shows by the same act that he thinks his opponent equal to himself and, consequently, rehabilitates his honor)—or with a symbolic display of battle (reconciliation follows an exchange of shots or blows with swords, with no bloody intention on either side). If the offence has been more serious, the kind that must be cleansed with blood, the duel can conclude with the first injury (to whom makes no difference, insofar as honor is restored not by the harm or vengeance inflicted on the offender, but by the fact of spilling blood, including one's own). Ultimately, the offended party can qualify the offense as mortal, the redemption requiring the death of one or another party to the dispute. It is essential that the determination of the degree of the offense—insignificant, to the blood, or to the death—should correlate with the determination of the social milieu (for example, with the opinion of the military regiment). A person who arrives too easily at reconciliation might be taken for a coward, and one who is unreasonably bloodthirsty for a pugilist.

As an institution of corporate honor, the duel encountered opposition from two sides. From one side, the government's attitude to dueling was unwaveringly hostile. In the "Warrant on Duels and the Instigation of Fights," the forty-ninth section of the Petrine *Military Statute* (1716), the following was prescribed: "If it happens that two come out to a designated place, and one bares his sword against the other, We command that they both, though neither having been brought to injury or death, shall, without mercy, along with the seconds or witnesses they shall implicate, be punished with death, and forfeit all chattels and possessions. ... If they commence to battle, and in that battle be killed and wounded, then both living and dead shall be hanged."[1] K. A. Sofronenko considers that the "Warrant" was directed "against the old feudal aristocracy."[2] N. L. Brodsky agrees, maintaining that "the duel is a custom of bloody revenge and reprisal, born of feudal-chivalric society, that has been preserved in the milieu of the nobility."[3] Yet, the duel in Russia was not a holdover, insofar as nothing analogous existed in the everyday life of the Russian "old feudal elite." Catherine II indicated unambiguously that the duel represents an innovation: "A prejudice received not from our forebears, but adopted or borrowed—foreign" ("Manifesto on Duels" from April 21, 1787; see also "Legislative Instruction," Article 482).

Nicholas I's pronouncement is characteristic: "I despise duels; it is barbarity; in my view, there is nothing chivalric about them."[4]

Montesquieu likewise indicated the reasons for an autocratic power's negative attitude toward the custom of dueling: "Honor cannot be a principle of despotic states: all people are equal there, and therefore they cannot elevate themselves above one another; there, all people are slaves, and therefore they cannot elevate themselves above anything. ... Can a despot put up with honor in his own state? Honor claims its glory in its contempt for life, yet the despot's entire strength lies merely in his ability to deprive one of life. How would honor itself be able to put up with a despot?"[5]

Naturally, in the official literature duels have been prosecuted as displays of the love of freedom, "the revived evil of conceit and the freethinking of this era."[6]

On the other hand, the duel was subject to criticism from the intellectual-democratic camp, which saw in it a display of the nobility's estate prejudice and which opposed the nobleman's honor to a human one based on Reason and Nature. From this position, the duel became an object of enlightened satire and critique. In his *Journey from Petersburg to Moscow,* Alexander Radishchev wrote: "... you have a strong spirit, and you will not consider it an offense when the ass kicks you or the swine touches you with its fetid snout."

"It has happened that someone gets the least bit brushed inadvertently by sword or hat, or has but a single little hair on his head disturbed, or the cloth upon his shoulder ruffled, and it's pistols at dawn ... Someone with a toothache gives an answer under his breath, or one with a cold will say something through his nose ... They pay you no mind ... Well, see the sword up to the hilt! ... And either he's deaf or nearsighted, but when, God forbid, he does not answer or does not see the bow ... How can this be?! Right away it's swords in hand, hats on heads, and it's clang and chop!"[7] This position is also recorded in Alexander Izmailov's fable "The Duel" [Poedinok]. Alexander Suvorov's negative attitude toward the duel is well known.[8] [i] The Masons, too, had a negative attitude toward the duel.

In this way, what could come to the fore in the duel is, on the one hand, a narrowly estate-based idea of defending the honor of the group, and, on the other, a notion of defending a human dignity that, despite its archaic forms, is universal. Facing a duel, V. D. Novosiltsev—creature of the court, darling of the emperor, aristocrat, and aide-de-camp—turned out to be the equal of K. P. Chernov, a second lieutenant in the Semionovsky Regiment, from provincial nobility, with neither a fortune, nor connections.[ii]

Owing to this, the Decembrists were of two minds when it came to single combat. Theoretically allowing for negative pronouncements in the spirit of the Enlightenment-era critique of the duel, the Decembrists in practice made wide use of the law of dueling. Indeed, E. P. Obolensky killed a certain Svinyin in a duel;[9] K. F. Ryleev repeatedly challenged various persons to duel and fought with several; A. I. Yakubovich had a reputation for being a pugilist. The duel between Novosiltsev and Chernov, which took on the character of a political conflict between a member of a secret society defending his sister's honor and an aristocrat scorning the human dignity of simple people, caused a loud ruckus among their contemporaries. Both parties to the duel succumbed to their wounds within a few days. The Northern Society turned Chernov's burial into Russia's first street protest.

Pushkin, too, was not unfamiliar with the view that the duel was a means of defending one's own human dignity. While he was living in Chisinau, Pushkin found himself in a situation that offended his pride, that of a young civilian surrounded by people in officers' uniforms who had already proven their unquestionable courage in war. This is how we explain his overblown punctiliousness in matters of honor and his almost pugilistic behavior during this period. His time in Chisinau is noted in his contemporaries' memoirs for the many times

i Alexander Suvorov was a military commander during the reigns of Catherine II and Paul I. As a general under Catherine he won several important victories during the two Russo-Turkish wars. Under Paul he became a field marshal and played a critical role in containing the advance of the French revolutionary army in 1799. He is seen as one of the most talented military leaders in Russian history.

ii It was not always the case that socially disparate nobles fought duels against each other. Sometimes high-placed nobles frowned upon challenges issued by low-level counterparts. Discussing such a case, the Chevalier de Corberon attributed this to the great inequalities in Russian society and saw in it a significant difference with France. See *Un diplomate français à la cour de Catherine II 1775–1780, Journal intime du chevalier de Corberon*, 2 vols (Paris: Librairie Plon, 1901), vol. 1, 111.

Pushkin challenged people.[10] A characteristic example is his duel with Lieutenant-Colonel S. N. Starov, of which V. P. Gorchakov has left a record. Pushkin's poor behavior while dancing at a gathering of officers, his having insisted on a dance of his own choosing, against the officers' wishes, became the pretext for a duel. It is revealing that the challenge directed to the poet was not from one of the younger officers taking part in the spat directly, but—on their behalf—from S. Starov, the commander of the 33rd Egersky Regiment, which was then stationed there. Starov was nineteen years Pushkin's senior and outranked him significantly. Such a challenge contradicted the requirement that the adversaries be equals, and it clearly represented an attempt to knock the insolent civilian kid down a peg. It was assumed, of course, that Pushkin would be frightened of dueling and would make a public apology. Events unfolded in the following manner:

> [Starov] approached Pushkin, who had just finished dancing his figure. "You were impolite to my officer," S[taro]v said, having cast Pushkin a determined glance, "so see clear to apologize to him, or else you will have to deal with me instead." "What I am to apologize for, Colonel, I do not know," Pushkin responded quickly. "As far as concerns you, I am at your service." "Till tomorrow, then, Alexander Sergeevich." "Very well, Colonel." Having shaken each other's hand, they parted. ...
>
> When they met at the dueling place, a blizzard with a strong wind hindered their aim, the adversaries took their shots, and both missed; they fired again, and again they missed; then the seconds firmly insisted that, if they did not want to allow that to be the end of it, the duel be postponed without fail, and they confirmed that there were no firing charges left. "Well then, until next time," they both said in a single voice. "Goodbye, Alexander Sergeevich." "Goodbye, Colonel."

The duel had been conducted according to all the rules of a ritual of honor: there had been no personal hostility among the shooters, and the irreproachability of how the ritual was observed in the course of the duel evoked mutual respect in them both. This, however, did not impede a second exchange of shots and, insofar as possible, a repeat of the duel:

> A day later ... reconciliation came quickly.
>
> "I have always respected you, Colonel, and that is why I accepted your proposal," Pushkin said.

> "And well done, Alexander Sergeevich," S[taro]v replied, "for by doing so you elevated my respect for you all the more, and I should say that, in truth, you are as good under fire as you are with a pen." These words of honest regard moved Pushkin, and he rushed to embrace S[taro]v.

Care in observing the ritual of honor had equalized the status of the civilian youth and the veteran lieutenant-colonel, having given them an equal right to public respect. The ritual cycle was closed by Pushkin demonstrating his readiness to fight the duel, thereby preserving Starov's honor:

> About two days after they were reconciled there was talk of his duel with S[taro]v. They were praising Pushkin and casting aspersions on S[taro]v. Pushkin flared up, threw his billiard cue, and walked quickly and directly up to the young men. "Gentlemen," he said, "how things ended up with S[taro]v is our affair, but I do declare that if you permit yourselves to pass judgment on S[taro]v, whom I cannot help but respect, then I shall take it as a personal insult to me, and each of you will answer for it to me as required."[11]

It was specifically for its ritual "classicism" that this episode attracted the attention of his contemporaries and was widely discussed in society.[12] Pushkin had lent it an artistic finish, having concluded the exchange of fire with a rhyming epigram:

> I live.
> Starov
> Does thrive.
> Duel unfinished.
>
> Я жив.
> Старов
> Здоров.
> Дуэль не кончен.

It is characteristic that precisely this episode enjoyed a ready formula in the folkloric memory of his contemporaries:

> The Colonel Starov,
> Thank God, does thrive.

Полковник Старов,
Слава богу, здоров.

The image of the poet composing a verse during a duel is a variant of the dueling legend that poeticizes one's carefree immersion in extraneous activities as the apex of brilliant conduct in defending one's honor. In "The Shot," Count B. eats cherries while standing at the line;[iii] in Edmond Rostand's play *Cyrano de Bergerac,* the hero composes a poem during the duel. Pushkin demonstrated the very same thing in his duel with Starov.

Pugilistic behavior as a means of defending oneself socially and affirming one's personal equality in society may have drawn Pushkin's attention during these years to Vincent Voiture, a seventeenth-century French poet who had affirmed his own equality in aristocratic circles through a pronounced zeal for dueling. In reference to this poet's passion for dueling, Tallemant des Réaux wrote, "No man of bold spirit can count so many instances of dueling as our hero, for he has fought duels at least four times, day and night, in bright sun, under the moon, and by torchlight."[13]

Pushkin's attitude toward dueling was contradictory: as an heir to the eighteenth-century Enlightenment, he saw it as a manifestation of "polite enmity," which "is wildly … fearful of misplaced shame." In *Eugene Onegin,* the cult of the duel is upheld by Zaretsky, a man of questionable honesty. Yet at the same time the duel is also a means of defending an aggrieved party's dignity. It places the mysterious pauper Silvio and Count B., the darling of fate, on the same footing. The duel is a prejudice, but the honor that is forced to turn to it for help is not.

It is owing precisely to its duality that the duel presupposed the availability of a strict and painstaking ritual for its execution. Only an exacting compliance with procedure distinguished the duel from murder. But the need to observe the rules exactly stood in contradiction to Russia's lack of a strict codification of the system for dueling. By official decree, no printed Russian codices for dueling could appear, nor was there a juridical body that could assume the power to regulate the rules for it. Of course, one could use French codices, but the rules they set forth were not entirely consistent with the Russian dueling practices. One achieved a strict observation of the rules by turning to the authority of

iii "The Shot" is one of the stories in Pushkin's *Belkin Stories* [*Povesti pokoinogo Ivana Petrovicha Belkina*]. This is the story of a deferred duel, caused by the count's provocative indifference to the proceedings, which enraged his opponent Silvio. Silvio had aborted the duel and waited several years until the count would be married and more attached to life before resuming his fight with him.

connoisseurs, the living bearers of tradition and the arbiters in questions of honor. In *Eugene Onegin,* such a role is filled by Zaretsky.[14]

The duel would begin with a challenge. As a rule, this was preceded by some altercation that resulted in one side or the other considering himself offended and, as such, demanding redress (satisfaction). From that moment the adversaries were to have no communication: that was to fall to their representatives (known as seconds). Having chosen a second, the offended party discussed the gravity of the offence that had been inflicted upon him, the nature of which would determine the duel to come, from a purely formal exchange of fire to the death of one or both participants. Afterwards, the second issued a written challenge (cartel) to the adversary.

The role of the seconds came down to the following: as intermediaries between adversaries, they were first of all obliged to apply maximum effort toward reconciliation. It was the seconds' duty to seek out every possibility of resolving the conflict peacefully without betraying the interests of honor and especially while making sure that their parties' rights were preserved. Even on the field of battle the seconds were obliged to undertake a final effort toward reconciliation. Beyond that, the seconds work out the conditions of the duel. In this, unwritten rules prescribe that they endeavor that the agitated adversaries not choose forms of duel bloodier than would be minimally demanded by the stringent rules of honor. If reconciliation has proven impossible, as it was, for example, in Pushkin's duel with D'Anthès,[iv] then they draw up written conditions and see carefully that all procedures are strictly followed.

As an example, the conditions signed by the seconds for Pushkin and D'Anthès (originally in French) were as follows:

1. The adversaries will stand at a distance of twenty paces from each other and five paces (each) from their lines, which will be separated by a distance of ten paces.
2. Armed with pistols, at the given signal the adversaries may fire while approaching each other, though in no case may they cross their lines.
3. Furthermore, it is understood that, upon firing, the adversaries are not permitted to change position, so that he who has shot first is exposed to his adversary's fire at the same distance.[15]

iv This is the duel that prematurely terminated Pushkin's life. George-Charles de Heeckeren d'Anthès (1812–1895) was a French officer serving at the Russian court. Pushkin challenged d'Anthès to a duel over the latter's open courtship of his wife. D'Anthès was subsequently expelled from Russia and proceeded to make a political career in France.

4. When both sides have taken their shots, and if there has been no result, the duel is reenacted as before: the adversaries stand at the same distance of twenty paces; the same lines and rules are preserved.
5. The seconds are obligatory intermediaries in all discussions between the adversaries on the field of battle.
6. The seconds, here undersigned, and invested with complete authority, guarantee with their honor, each for his own side, a strict observance of the conditions hereby set forth.[16]

The conditions for Pushkin's duel with D'Anthès were maximally severe (the duel was designed to have a fatal outcome), but, surprisingly, the conditions for Onegin's duel with Lensky were quite severe as well, though here there was clearly no cause for mortal enmity. So long as Zaretsky separated the friends by thirty-two paces, and assuming the lines were drawn at an "honorable distance," that is, ten paces apart, each could take eleven steps. But one cannot be sure that Zaretsky did not settle on a distance of fewer than ten paces between the lines. There was apparently no requirement that the adversaries not move after the first shot, which spurred them toward the most dangerous tactic: not firing while walking, but running quickly up to the line and aiming at the motionless adversary from the closest possible distance. It was precisely in cases like this that both duelists would become casualties. So it was in the duel between Novosiltsev and Chernov. The requirement that the adversaries remain on the spot where they had been standing when the first shot was fired was the least possible softening of the conditions. It is characteristic that when Griboedov exchanged shots with Iakubovich, despite there not having been any such requirement in the conditions, he nevertheless remained on the spot where he had been fired upon, and he fired without approaching his line.

In *Eugene Onegin*, Zaretsky is the duel's sole administrator, and it is all the more remarkable that he, "in dueling a classic and pedant," conducted the affair with great negligence, or rather, that he consciously ignored everything that might have precluded a bloody outcome. Already at Onegin's first visit, when the cartel is delivered, he would have been obliged to discuss the possibilities for reconciliation. Before the duel had begun, he was likewise directly obligated to attempt to conclude the matter peacefully, all the more so because no one had endured an offense worthy of blood, and it was clear to everyone, except the eighteen-year-old Lensky, that the matter amounted to a misunderstanding. Instead, he "rose without explanation … /Having much to do at home."[17] Zaretsky could also have put an end to the duel at another moment: Onegin's appearance with a servant instead of a second was a direct offense to him (seconds, like adversaries, should be social equals; Guillot, a Frenchman and a freely hired footman, could not be formally rejected, though his appearance in this role, as well as the justification that he was at least "a decent fellow," were an unambiguous insult to Zaretsky) and at the same time a flagrant violation of the rules, since the seconds were supposed to have met the day before, without the adversaries, to draw up the rules for the duel.

Ultimately, Zaretsky had every grounds not to allow a bloody outcome, by declaring Onegin a no-show: "Forcing others to wait for you at the dueling place is extremely impolite. Having appeared on time, one is obliged to await his adversary for a quarter hour. After such a term has passed, he who has appeared first has the right to quit the dueling place, and his seconds should draw up a report testifying to his adversary's absence."[18] Onegin was late by over an hour.[19]

In this way, Zaretsky behaved not only as someone who disregarded the strict laws of the art of dueling, but as a person maximally interested in an outcome that was scandalous and sensational—which, when it comes to the duel, meant fatal.

Here is an example from the "classics of dueling": in 1766, Casanova fought a duel in Warsaw with a favorite of the Polish king, a certain Branicki, who appeared on the field of honor accompanied by a splendid retinue, whereas Casanova, a foreigner and a traveler, could bring only one of his servants in the role of witness. He rejected such a decision, however, as outright impossible, offensive to his adversary and his seconds and hardly flattering to himself: his second's doubtful merit would cast a shadow over his own irreproachability as a man of honor. He preferred to ask his adversary to appoint him a second from among his own aristocratic retinue. Casanova risked having an enemy for a second, but he did not agree to admit a hired servant to be a witness in an affair of honor.[20]

It is rather curious that an analogous situation was partially repeated in Pushkin's tragic duel with D'Anthès. After having difficulty finding a second,[21] on the morning of January 27, 1837, Pushkin wrote to d'Archiac that he would bring his second "only to the meeting place," and then contradicting himself, albeit quite in the spirit of Onegin, he went on to entrust Heeckeren [D'Anthès] to choose his second for him: "... I accept him in advance, be he a liveried lackey" (XVI, 225 and 410).[v] Unlike Zaretsky, however, d'Archiac decisively

v Lotman uses the following edition: Pushkin, *Polnoe sobranie sochinenii.*

precluded such a possibility, declaring that "the meeting among the seconds, *mandatory before the duel*" [d'Archiac's emphasis—*Lotman*], is a precondition, the refusal of which is tantamount to a refusal to duel. D'Archiac's meeting with Danzas took place, and the duel became formally possible. Zaretsky's meeting with Guillot occurred only on the field of battle, but Zaretsky did not call off the combat, though he could have.

Onegin and Zaretsky both violate the rules of the duel. The former, in order to demonstrate his irritated contempt for the affair into which he had fallen against his own wishes, and the seriousness of which he did not yet believe, and Zaretsky because he saw in the duel an amusing affair, if at times also a bloody one, a subject of gossip and practical jokes ...

Onegin's conduct in the duel testifies undeniably to the author's wanting to make him an unwitting murderer. Both for Pushkin and for those of the novel's readers familiar with the duel from more than just hearsay, it was obvious that one who categorically wishes the death of his antagonist does not fire right from the get-go, from a greater distance, while the other person is pointing a gun at him, distracting him, but that he accepts the risk, allows himself to be fired upon, requires his adversary to approach the line, and shoots him as a stationary target at close range.

Thus, for example, in Alexander Zavadovsky's duel with Vasily Sheremetyev, renowned for its role in Alexander Griboedov's biography (1817), we see a classic case of pugilistic behavior:[vi]

> When, at their furthest distance from one another, they started to come closer together, Zavadovsky, who was a superb shot, walked slowly and calmly. Either Zavadovsky's sangfroid enraged Sheremyetev, or the latter's sense of spite overwhelmed his reason, but it was he who, as they say, could stand it no longer, and he shot at Zavadovsky without having yet reached his line. The bullet passed close to Zavadovsky, because it tore away part of the collar of his frock coat, just at the neck. At that, quite understandably, Zavadovsky became angry. "*Ah*," he said. "*Il en voulait à ma vie! A la barrière!*" (Aha! He is making an attempt on my life! To the line!)
>
> There was nothing to be done. Sheremetyev approached. Zavadovsky fired. The shot was fatal: he had hit Sheremetyev in the stomach![22]

vi The duel between Zavadovsky and Sheremetyev over the dancer and actress Avdotya Istomina (1817), to which Sheremetyev succumbed, was then continued by a duel between their respective seconds, the poet Griboedov and the future Decembrist Alexander Yakubovich.

To understand the pleasure a person like Zaretsky could find in this whole affair, we must add that Pushkin's friend Pyotr Kaverin (a member of the Union of Welfare, whom Onegin meets at the Talon Restaurant in the first chapter of *Eugene Onegin*, and a famous debauchee and pugilist), who was present at the duel as a witness, upon seeing how the wounded Sheremetyev "jumped in place several times, then fell and started to roll around in the snow," went up to the wounded man and said, "What is it, Vasya? Bit of turnip?" Turnip was a delicacy among the lower classes, and he used this expression ironically, in the sense of "How's that? Taste good? How do you like that?"[23] One should note that, contrary to the rules of the duel, it was not uncommon for the public to gather at a duel, as though for a spectacle. We have reason to believe that a crowd of curious onlookers was present at Mikhail Lermontov's tragic duel, turning it into an extravagant spectacle. The requirement that there not be extraneous witnesses had serious grounds, insofar as they could prod the participants in the spectacle, now having assumed a theatrical character, into bloodier actions than what the rules of honor demanded.

If in fact an experienced shot fired first, then, as a rule, it testified to the agitation that had led him to pull the trigger accidentally. This is how the duel is described in Edward Bulwer-Lytton's famous novel, conducted according to all the laws of dandyism; the English dandy Pelham and a French fop, both experienced duelists, are shooting at each other:[vii]

> The Frenchman and his second were on the ground first. ... [This is a deliberate insult; the norm for refined courtesy was to arrive at the dueling place at precisely the same time. Onegin exceeded all allowances by being over an hour late.—*Lotman*] I saw that the former was pale and agitated, not, I think, from fear, but passion. ... I looked steadily at D'Azimart, and took my aim. His pistol, owing, I suppose, to the trembling of his hand, went off a moment sooner than he had anticipated—the ball grazed my hat. My aim was more successful—I struck him in the shoulder—the exact place I had intended.

But this raises the question: why did Onegin shoot at Lensky anyway, and not past him? First of all, a demonstrative shot to the side was a fresh insult and could not facilitate reconciliation. Secondly, in the case of an inconclusive exchange of fire the duel began all over again, and the adversary's life could be

vii *Pelham; or, Adventures of a Gentleman* (1828) is Edward Bulwer-Lytton's second novel.

spared only at the cost of one's own death or injury, whereas the legends of combat that had shaped public opinion poeticized the killer, not the killed.[24]

There is one more essential circumstance that must be taken into account. With its strict ritual, the duel, presenting a whole theatricalized act, a sacrifice for the sake of honor, follows a rigid script. Like any strict ritual, it deprives its participants of individual will. The individual participant has no power to suspend or change anything in the duel. Bulwer-Lytton's description contains the following:

> When we took our ground, Vincent [his second—*Lotman*] came to me, and said, in a low tone, "For God's sake, suffer me to accommodate this, if possible?"
>
> "It is not in our power," said I. ...

Compare that to *War and Peace:*

> "Well, then, begin!" Dolokhov said.
>
> "Why not?" Pierre answered, still smiling.
>
> It got awful. It was obvious that the affair, having begun so lightly, could no longer be forestalled by anything, that it was moving forward of its own accord, now independently of human will, and had to see itself through.

Revealingly, Pierre, having spent all night thinking, "What is the point of dueling, of this killing?"—once he landed upon the field of battle, he *fired first* and *wounded* Dolokhov on his left side (a wound that could easily have proven fatal).[viii]

Extremely interesting in this regard are the memoirs of H. Muravyov-Karsky, a competent and precise witness who conveys Griboedov's words about his own feelings during his duel with Iakubovich. Griboedov felt no personal enmity toward his adversary, with whom he dueled merely to complete the "quadruple duel"[25] initiated by Sheremetyev and Zavadovsky. He proposed a peaceful resolution, which Iakubovich refused, also underscoring that he felt no personal animosity toward Griboedov and was merely fulfilling the promise he had made to the dead Sheremetyev. And it is all the more noteworthy that, having arisen with peaceful intentions, in the course of the duel

viii In Leo Tolstoy's *War and Peace* Pierre Bezukhov, a wealthy orphan educated abroad, struggles repeatedly to understand the purpose of social conventions and to abide by them.

Griboedov felt the desire to kill Yakubovich—the bullet passed so close to his head that "Yakubovich supposed himself wounded: he clutched at the back of his head, looked at his hand. … Griboedov told us afterwards that he had aimed at Iakubovich's head and wanted to kill him, but that this had not been his initial intention when he took his position."[26]

In Alexander Bestuzhev's *Novel in Seven Letters* [*Roman v semi pis'makh*, 1823], we find a striking example of a duelist who, influenced by dueling logic's power over a person's will, changes his plan for how to conduct himself. On the night before a duel, the hero resolves to sacrifice himself and anticipates his own demise: "I will die, I say, because I have decided to wait for the shot … I offended him." The following chapter of this epistolary novel, however, narrates an entirely unexpected turn of events: the hero has performed a deed diametrically opposed to his intentions. "I killed him, killed this noble, magnanimous person! … We approached one another from twenty paces, I with a firm step, but with no thought, without any intention: hidden in the depths of my soul, the feelings completely clouded my reason. At six paces, I don't know why, I don't know how, I released the fateful charge—and the shot resounded in my very heart! … I saw Erast shudder … When the smoke had cleared—he already lay upon the snow, and his blood, which had spurted, hissing, from his wound, was hardening within him."[27]

For the reader who had not yet lost the living link with dueling tradition and was still capable of understanding the shades of meaning in the picture Pushkin had drawn in *Eugene Onegin*, it was obvious that Onegin "loved him [Lensky] and, aiming at him, did not want to injure him."[28]

This capacity of the duel to deprive people of their own will and to transform them into toys and automatons, dragging them in, is very important.[29]

It is especially important for our understanding of Onegin's image.

The novel's hero—who pushes aside any external pressure on his personality, and who is in this way the opposite of Tatyana, organically connected to national customs, beliefs, and habits—betrays himself in the sixth chapter of *Eugene Onegin*: against his own wishes, he admits the dictate of the behavioral norms thrust upon him by Zaretsky and "public opinion," and immediately, losing his will, he becomes a puppet in the hands of the impersonal ritual of the duel. Pushkin has an entire gallery of statues coming to life, but there is also a procession of live people transformed into automatons.[30] In the sixth chapter, Onegin comes off as the forebear of these characters.

The fundamental mechanism by which the society that Onegin despises nevertheless exercises complete control over his actions is the fear of being ridiculous or of becoming the subject of gossip. One ought to take into account that the unwritten rules of the Russian duel of the late eighteenth and early nineteenth centuries were significantly more severe than, for example, those in France, and were in no way comparable to the nature of the late Russian duel as indicated by the act of May 13, 1894 (see A. I. Kuprin's *The Duel* [*Poedinok*]). The common distance between lines at the beginning of the nineteenth century had been ten to twelve paces, and it was not uncommon to have cases in which adversaries were separated by just six paces[31]; in the period between May 20, 1894, and May 20, 1910, out of the 322 instances of dueling that took place, not one had been conducted at a distance of fewer than twelve paces—and only one at twelve paces. The overwhelming majority of instances of dueling occurred at a distance of twenty to thirty paces, that is, at a distance from which no one in the early nineteenth century would have thought to shoot. Naturally, only fifteen of the 322 encounters had a fatal outcome.[32] Meanwhile, at the beginning of the nineteenth century inconclusive duels provoked an ironic attitude. In the absence of firmly fixed rules, there was a sharp rise in the significance of the atmosphere that pugilists, the keepers of dueling tradition, had created around the duel. It was they who cultivated the bloody, brutal duel. Having walked up to the line, a person had to display exceptional spiritual independence to maintain his own personal mode of behaving, and not to assume the norms that had been approved and imposed upon him. Thus, for example, Onegin's behavior was shaped by his oscillation between the kinds of natural human feelings that he felt toward Lensky and his fear of appearing ridiculous or cowardly by having broken the conventional norms of behavior in a duel.

In Russia, any duel, and not only an "irregular" one, was a criminal act. Every duel subsequently became the object of a legal proceeding. Both the adversaries and the seconds bore criminal responsibility. Following the letter of the law, the court would sentence duelists to death, but for officers this was then most often commuted to demotion to the rank of soldier with the right of promotion (a transfer to the Caucasus offered the possibility of quickly recovering the rank of officer). Onegin, as a non-serving nobleman, would most likely have gotten away with a month or two in a fortress and a subsequent period of church penance. Judging from the text of the novel, however, Onegin's duel with Lensky was not the subject of a legal proceeding at all. This could happen if a parish priest were to register Lensky's death as the result of an unfortunate accident or suicide. Chapter 6, stanzas XL and XLI, despite their link to the common elegiac clichés of the tomb of the "young poet," allow us to suggest that Lensky had been buried outside the cemetery fence, that is, as a suicide.

We find a real encyclopedia of the duel in Alexander Bestuzhev's story "The Test" [Ispytanie, 1830]. In the tradition of the Enlightenment, the author denounces the duel and simultaneously, in almost documentary detail, describes the entire ritual of preparing for one:

> Valerian's old servant melted the lead in an iron ladle, standing on his knees before the fire, and poured out the bullets—a task he would interrupt with frequent prayers and signs of the cross. At the table, some artillery officer was trimming, molding, and fitting the bullets for the pistols. Just then the doors opened cautiously, and a third figure, a member of the cavalry-guard, came in and interrupted their business for a minute.
>
> "*Bonjour, capitaine,*" the artillerist said to the one who entered. "Do you have everything ready?"
>
> "I brought two sets with me, one by Küchenreuter, the other from Le Page: we'll inspect them together."
>
> "It is our duty, Captain. Have you fitted the bullets?"
>
> "The bullets were made in Paris and, surely, with especial care."
>
> "Oh, do not count on that, captain. I've been fooled by similar credulity in the past. The second bullets—I now blush at the memory—wouldn't go into the barrel, and however much we tried to pound them into place, it was no use. The adversaries were forced to shoot with saddle guns, each nearly the size of a mountain licorne, and it was a good thing that one got the other right in the forehead, where any bullet, whether smaller than a pea or bigger than a cherry, brings about the same result. But judge for yourself, what censure would we have exposed ourselves to if this grapeshot had blasted an arm or a leg to smithereens?"
>
> "A classic truth!" the cavalry officer replied, smiling.
>
> "Do you have refined gunpowder?"
>
> "Of the finest grain."
>
> "All the worse: leave it at home. In the first place, for consistency we will take common rifle powder; in the second, the refined stuff doesn't always ignite quickly, and it can happen that the spark skips off it altogether."
>
> "What shall we do about the set triggers?"[33]
>
> "Yes, yes, these accursed set triggers are eternally knocking my mind off from my aim, and they've put more than a few good men into deep storage. L-oi, the poor devil, got killed by his set trigger before my very eyes: his pistol fired into the ground, and his rival took him right to the line, like a grouse. And then I once saw another fellow fire reluctantly into

the air when he could have put the muzzle right to his adversary's chest. Not letting them cock the set triggers is almost impossible and always useless, because an imperceptible, even an unconscious movement of the finger can do so, and then a cool-blooded shooter has all the advantages. And letting them, it won't be long before you lose your shot! Bastards, these gunsmiths: seems they imagine that the only reason pistols were invented is for the shooting club!"

"But then wouldn't it be better to forbid them from cocking their set triggers? We could warn the gentlemen as to how to deal with the spring; and beyond that it's on their honor. What say you, sir?"

"I am in favor of anything that will soften the duel. Will we have a physician, Captain?"

"Yesterday I called on two, and I was appalled at their mercantile self-interest ... They started with a preface on responsibility—and finished by demanding an advance; I decided against entrusting the fate of the duel to such hucksters."

"In that case I will endeavor to bring a doctor with me—a most eccentric fellow, but the most noble person in the world. I've had occasion to drag him out of bed straight to the field, and he decided without hesitation. 'I am well aware, sir,' he said, winding bandages around an instrument, 'that I can neither forbid it, nor put a stop to your recklessness, and I willingly accept your invitation. It is my pleasure to purchase, albeit at my own risk, relief for humanity's suffering.' But the most amazing thing of all is that he refused a rich gift for his journey and treatment."

"That is an honor to humanity and to medicine. Is Valerian Mikhailovich still asleep?"

"He was writing letters for a long time, and it hasn't been more than three hours since he fell asleep. Be so kind and advise your comrade not to eat anything before the encounter. In case of misfortune the bullet can slip and shoot clean through, causing no harm to the innards, if they maintain their elasticity; besides, the hand is truer on an empty stomach. Have you seen to the four-seat carriage? In a two-seater there's nowhere to help the wounded, nor to put the killed."

"I ordered that a carriage be hired from the far end of town, and that they choose a driver too dim to figure it out and let on to anyone else."

"You've done as well as could be, Captain; the police are no worse than a crow when it comes to smelling blood. Now, about the conditions: the line as before, at six paces?"

> "Six, yes. The prince doesn't even want to hear of a greater distance. Only a wound on even-numbered shots ends the duel—flare-outs and misfires do not count."
>
> "How pigheaded they are! If only they were fighting over something serious—then you wouldn't begrudge the gunpowder. But all for a woman's whim and their own caprice."
>
> "Have we seen many duels for a just cause? They are all over an actress, over cards, over horses, or over a scoop of ice cream."
>
> "One has to admit that all these duels, whose causes are difficult or shameful to recount, don't do us much honor."[34]

The conventional ethics of the duel existed in parallel with universal moral norms without confusing or abolishing them. This led to the fact that the victor in a duel was, on the one hand, ringed in a halo of public interest, which was expressed characteristically in the words recalled by Karenin in *Anna Karenina:* "He had performed excellently; his was the challenge, his the kill."[ix] On the other hand, all the customs of dueling could not make him forget that he is a *killer.*

For example, in Kiev, where he lived out the rest of his life, a Romantic legend proliferated around Nikolay Martynov, Lermontov's killer—Martynov, whose character was like that of Grushnitsky,[x] apparently promoted this himself—one that reached Mikhail Bulgakov, who told it in his *Theatrical Novel:* "What mournful eyes he has … He had once killed a friend in a duel in Piatigorsk … and now that friend comes to him at night, nodding his head by the moonlight at the window."

V. A. Olenina recalled the Decembrist Evgeny Obolensky: "This unfortunate had a duel, and he killed—from then on, like Orestes pursued by the Furies, he, too, never found his peace anywhere." Olenina knew Obolensky before the Fourteenth of December, but the ward of Mikhail Muravyov-Apostol, A. P. Sozonovich, having grown up in Siberia, recalled, "This lamentable affair haunted him his entire life." Neither education, nor the trial, nor the prison colony softened the experience. One can say the same about a raft of other cases.

---

ix From part 4 of Tolstoy'a *Anna Karenina.* This refers to a scene in which Anna's husband Alexey Kurakin struggles to decide how he should behave, having discovered that his wife was engaged in an affair with Vronsky. Karenin contemplates both the Christian requirement of forgiveness and the social convention of the duel.

x A character from Lermontov's *A Hero of our Times* [*Geroi nashego vremeni*]. In the novel Grushnitsky gets killed by Pechorin in a duel.

CHAPTER 9

A Woman's World

This chapter was similarly first presented as a part of a TV program on the life of the nobility and then published within Conversations on Russian Culture. *Lotman's tone here is markedly more conversational, which we tried to retain in the translation. This format also explains the very light referencing. This translation is based on Iu. M. Lotman, "Zhenskii mir," in* Besedy o russkoi kul'ture: Byt i traditsii russkogo dvorianstva (XVIII–nachalo XIX veka) *(St. Petersburg: Iskusstvo, 1994), 46–74. Lotman's text contains both footnotes and endnotes, which we have merged into endnotes to accommodate the explanatory glosses. The editor comments at length on this piece and its gendered language in the introduction to this volume. Its main interest lies in the ways in which it traces how reading literature has forged a new consciousness among women.*

We have already discussed how the moral composition of a person changed, developed, and took shape from the eighteenth to the early nineteenth centuries. But in doing so, despite our saying "person" throughout, we have actually been talking about men. Meanwhile, not only were the women of this period swept up in the flow of a rapidly changing life, just as the men were, but they were starting to play an increasingly large role in that life. And women were changing a great deal.

A woman's character is correlated in a rather distinctive way to the culture of the era. On the one hand, women, with their intense emotionality, keenly and immediately absorb the peculiarities of their time, getting ahead of it to a significant degree. In this sense, a woman's character can be called one of the most sensitive barometers of social life. On the other hand, a woman's character, paradoxically, also makes manifest qualities that go in the other direction. Women—wives and mothers—are connected to the utmost degree to the superhistorical qualities of a person, to what is deeper and broader than the imprint left by an era. This is why a woman's influence on the era's composition is in principle contradictory, flexible, and dynamic. The flexibility appears in the variety of connections a woman's character shares with the era.

Female influence is rarely addressed as a historical problem in its own right. If, in speaking of the eighteenth and early nineteenth centuries, a historian paints a portrait of Saltychikha,[i] then it is most likely with the goal of characterizing the mores of serf-ownership. The fact that we are speaking of a woman will appear as an accident of the historical process. If this question should nevertheless arise, then, as a rule, the researcher exhausts it with general remarks about the underdevelopment (the developmental delay) of women in one or another period at some remove from ourselves, and he sometimes notes the rare exceptions to this rule.

What will interest us is both those peculiarities that the era imposed upon a woman's character, as well as those that the woman's character imparted to the era.

Undoubtedly, a woman's world was quite distinct from a man's, and first of all by the fact that it was excluded from the sphere of state service. Women did not serve, and they had no ranks, though the state endeavored to extend the ranking principle to them, too. In the Table of Ranks, there is a special, detailed stipulation that women have the rights bound to the rank of their fathers (until marriage) and husbands (in matrimony): "Contrariwise, all maidens whose fathers are of the first rank are to outrank, until they have been given in marriage, all wives who are of the fifth rank, specifically those lower than Major-General but above that of Brigadier, and maidens whose fathers are of the second rank outrank wives at the sixth rank, that is, below that of Brigadier and above that of Colonel; and maidens whose fathers are of the third rank will outrank wives of the seventh, that is, below that of Colonel and above that of Lieutenant Colonel, and so forth."[1] These bureaucratic ranks subsequently expanded all the more. Under Anna Petrovna and Elizabeth Petrovna, it was established what class a lady had to be in order to have the right to wear gold stitching on her dresses, what class for silver, how broad her lace should be, and so on. The expression "a lady of a certain class" appeared. Later, Pyotr Vyazemsky recorded in his journal the words of a foreigner who spoke with wonder of

i Darya Saltykova (1730–1801) was a landowner from an elite family who developed a habit of subjecting her serfs to cruel and sadistic punishment, leading to the death of at least thirty-eight of them. After many serf complaints were rejected by officials, Catherine II eventually ordered an inquiry, which led to a trial in the Senate, where Saltykova was convicted of the torture and death of thirty-eight serfs. Catherine condemned her to life imprisonment, as well as loss of nobility and name. Although Catherine in fact strengthened the power of landowners over their serfs, which worsened the ill-treatment of serfs, she sought to turn this case into a show trial against the abuse of serfs.

having loved—in Petersburg, on Vasilyevsky Island, on the Seventh Line—a twelfth-class lady.

Thus a woman's rank, if she was not attached to the court, was determined by the rank of her husband or father.[2] In documents from the era we come across the words "Madame/Miss Colonel," "Madame/Miss State Councilor," "Madame/Miss Privy Councilor." Yet these words designate not the independent status of the woman herself, but the status of her husband (for a maiden, that of her father). In Denis Fonvizin's comedy *The Brigadier* [*Brigadir*], Madame Brigadier and Madame Councillor are the wives of the Brigadier and the Councillor, respectively.

In one of Nikolay Leskov's stories,[ii] there is talk of a certain hierarch's habit of playing with his subordinates, making them answer him in verse, "in rhyme." At one point, out for a walk, he pronounces:

> The monarch's chambers I do spy.
>
> Чертоги зрю монарши.

His companion answers in rhyme:

> Madame Secretary made Foma die.
>
> Погиб Фома от секретарши.

It would be natural for the contemporary reader to understand the words "Madame Secretary" as indicating the woman's role or place of work. Yet such an interpretation would have been utterly impossible in the late eighteenth and early nineteenth centuries. They are talking about the secretary's wife.

This kind of exclusion of women from the world of service did not deprive them of significance. On the contrary, a woman's role in the life and culture of the nobility becomes all the more evident during the years that concern us. A woman could not fill the purely male roles connected with service and state affairs.[iii] But then what culture had handed over completely to women gained all the more significance in the general course of life.

---

ii This episode, in fact, comes from S. M. Solovyov's *Notes for my children* [*Zapiski dlia detei moikh, a esli mozhno, i dlia drugikh*], though there it is Stepan, not Foma who perishes.

iii Lotman does not mention that women discharged important functions as owners and managers of country estates, especially as their husbands might be serving in the capitals or in dislocation in an army regiment. See Michelle Lamarche Marrese, *A Woman's Kingdom: Noblewomen and the Control of Property in Russia, 1700–1861* (Ithaca: Cornell University Press, 2002).

Still, one ought not think that Russia had no cases in which a woman fought for her right to purely male roles. The celebrated Nadezhda Durova, "The Cavalry Maiden," first earned her right to the biography of a combat officer and, thereafter, in a second instance, to the "male" right to the biography of a writer. Her third victory, as early as the 1830s, was the right to go out in men's clothing.[iv] Durova's example is rare, but not unique. We know of cases in which girls, running away from home, dressed up as men in order to set off for holy places with a crowd of bearded monks, or even, dressing in men's clothes, of them sharing all the burdens of military campaigns with their fiancés or sweethearts. This, however, did not shake things up, but rather underscored the division of the culture into "male" and "female" zones.

Women's entrée into a world previously considered "male" began not with these instances, which were quite rare anyway. It began with literature. The Petrine era had drawn women into the world of letters: of women it had demanded literacy.

Of course, one ought not think that women were illiterate in the pre-Petrine era, or that literacy could not occupy a significant place in their lives. For example, we still have a Bible that had been transcribed by Tsarevna Sophya Alexeevna; her letters to Prince Vasily Golitsyn are well-known. Of course, Sophya was a unique woman, both in her education and in her political aspirations. But then, at Pushkinsky Dom (the Institute of Russian Literature), there are the letters of Peter I's first wife, Evdokiya, to the officer Stepan Glebov, her lover. These moving letters of a woman in love seem to break away from their own era. They tell us what a woman of any time brings into the world around her, and it would be strange to suggest that the women of pre-Petrine Rus lacked these feelings or means to express them. Intimate correspondence is a phenomenon that comes a great deal earlier than eighteenth-century epistolary culture, and, needless to say, it continued to exist in both the Petrine and the post-Petrine eras.[3] Thus Alexey Razumovsky, the Empress Elizabeth's beloved (and possibly her secret spouse), destroyed Elizabeth's intimate letters to him before he died.

There is more to discuss, however, in regard to a woman's world in the era that concerns us. Toward the end of the eighteenth century, it was no longer just a matter of literacy, nor of the ability to express one's intimate feelings in

---

iv Nadezhda Durova (1783–1866) dressed as an officer to join the Russian cavalry during the Napoleonic wars. She wrote extraordinary memoirs about her experience: Nadezhda Durova, *The Cavalry Maiden: Journals of a Russian Officer in the Napoleonic Wars,* trans. Mary Fleming Zirin (Bloomington: Indiana University Press, 1989).

correspondence. By this time private correspondence (familial, romantic), expanding gradually, had become an integral feature of the life of the nobility. These letters were not preserved, and an enormous number of them have been lost, but what has been retained testifies to the fact that, for a woman, an unlettered life had become impossible. Already in Fonvizin the illiterate woman is a satirical image.

The letter became a definite genre with a great many variations. With the rise of correspondence as a feature of polite behavior, a division emerges between the printed word, directed from the state toward the literate part of society, and the epistolary word, from one private individual to another. But the picture gradually becomes more complicated. On the one hand, unofficial literature appears—books targeted toward society and nonetheless lacking the imprimatur of state authority. Literature separates itself from statehood. The first sign of this was Vasily Trediakovsky's *Journey to the Island of Love* [*Ezda v ostrov Liubvi*, 1730]. On the other hand, there arises a literature in manuscript that is intended for the circle, the salon, society.

The complex processes that directly concern the world of woman's culture also occur within literature. At that time, the two basic types of literature were divided by a line, on one side of which fell print that was endorsed by the state—official, scientific, military, and so forth—and, on the other, artistic literature, which was allowed (if it were not prescribed a didactic, educative function that was useful to the very same state) as innocuous entertainment. Its role was to serve a leisure purpose. But once allowed in, the guest begins quite quickly to make designs on the role of host. Artistic literature, maintaining and in fact increasing its independence from the state's direct mandates, wins the place of spiritual leader for the society. This is why it was as though Russian society of the second half of the eighteenth century had a "double leadership": from the pages of official letters, one continues to hear the voice of the state, but artistic literature becomes the voice of ideas, at first of independent ones, and later of those that were directly in opposition.

In the house of every educated person of the eighteenth century one finds both printed books and those in manuscript.[4] The book is expensive, and frequently they do not buy it, but transcribe it. Many translations from foreign authors also remain in manuscript. The map of culture becomes increasingly diverse: it encompasses acts of state, as well as historical narratives, as well as romance novels, letters, and official papers. The circle of printed and manuscript materials expands so much that certain parts of the library are now maintained in the landowner's study, and others with his wife, even if "she loved Richardson. / Not that she had read him. ..."[v]

Thus an entirely new concept appears toward the end of the eighteenth century, that of the women's library. Remaining as it had been the world of feelings, the world of the nursery and the household (as noted previously, with rare exceptions), "a woman's world" was becoming ever more spiritual.

Women became readers. But there were different kinds of books, and of readers as well. We are familiar with outstanding Russian women of the late eighteenth and early nineteenth centuries, who were accustomed to the greatest manifestations of European and Russian literature, those like Tatyana Larina[vi] or Polina from Pushkin's story *Roslavlev*. But we also have documentary sources about numerous girls and women already in Pushkin's era who did not distinguish themselves through personal talents. They were not writers like Yekaterina Rostopchina[vii] or participants in historic events like Nadezhda Durova. They were mothers. And while their names have remained unknown, their role in the history of Russian culture, in the spiritual life of subsequent generations, is enormous. The domestic libraries of women of the late eighteenth and early nineteenth centuries shaped the temperament of the people of 1812 and the Decembrist era; the domestic reading of mothers and children in the 1820s cultivated the agents of Russian culture in the middle and second half of the nineteenth century.

But it was not only the habit of reading that was changing a woman's temperament. Women's daily life was changing massively, and the fashions, attire, and behaviors of their grandmothers seemed like caricatures to their granddaughters and provoked laughter. One would think that a woman's world, bound to a person's eternal functions—love, family life, childrearing—ought to be more stable than the vain world of men. But things went differently in the eighteenth century: Peter I's reforms overturned not only the life of the state, but the domestic way of life, too.

The first consequence of the reforms for women was endeavoring to change their *outward* temperament, to approximate the conduct of society

---

v A quotation from book 2 of Pushkin's *Eugene Onegin*, which describes the outlook of Tatyana Larina's mother. Samuel Richardson's novels were seen as the epitome of Sentimentalism and provided a repertoire of gendered behavioral roles.

vi At the beginning of *Eugene Onegin*, Tatyana Larina is presented as a socially awkward young woman who spends her time reading and daydreaming. As she falls in love with Eugene, she construes his image through the male protagonists of the novels she has been reading.

vii Ekaterina Rostopchina (1776–1859) is the author of several works of spiritual literature. She was the wife of Fyodor Rostopchin, the governor of Moscow in 1812 who gave orders to set fire to the city, and the mother of Sophie, la Contesse de Ségur, the famous author of children's literature in French. She converted to Catholicism.

women in Western Europe. Clothing and hairstyles change; for example, a wig becomes obligatory. Incidentally, in order for wigs to sit properly, they were fitted to a cropped head. Therefore, when you see beautiful headdresses in eighteenth-century portraits of women, they are wigs made from someone else's hair. Wigs were powdered. You will recall that in "The Queen of Spades" [Pikovaia dama] the old countess, despite the fact that the story's action is set in the 1830s, dresses according to the fashions of the 1770s. Pushkin puts it this way: "... they removed the powdered wig from her gray and close-cropped head." That is actually how it was.

Dresses, needless to say, also changed. As did the whole way of behaving. During the Petrine reforms and in the years following, a woman endeavored to resemble her grandmothers (and peasant women) as little as possible.

In fashion, artificiality reigned. Women spent a great deal of effort on changing their appearance. Fashions varied. Merchants' wives, for example, dyed their teeth black, and in the world of merchants this was considered the ideal of beauty.[5]

In more Europeanized society, of course, they did not blacken their teeth. But here, too, there were ways of altering one's appearance. For example, they stuck beauty marks made of taffeta or velvet on their faces. The spot where beauty marks were affixed was not accidental. For example, a beauty mark at the corner of the eye meant, "I am interested in you"; a beauty mark on the upper lip, "I want to kiss you." And insofar as a woman held a fan, the movement of which also carried a special meaning (for example, abruptly snapping her fan shut meant, "You do not interest me!"), the combinations of beauty marks and fan-play created a distinctive "language of coquetry."

Ladies were coquettish, ladies whose main business was how people spent the evening. And in the evening, by candlelight, one required bright makeup, because faces go pale in candlelight (all the more so in Petersburg, with its noxious climate!). This is why ladies used so much rouge, face powder, and various other cosmetics (upwards of twenty pounds per annum!). They laid it on very thick.

During the Petrine period, a woman was not yet accustomed to reading much; she did not yet aspire to a variegated spiritual life (this applies, of course, to people as a whole: there were then already female writers in Russia). The spiritual needs of the majority of women were still satisfied as they had been in pre-Petrine Rus: the church, the church calendar, fasts, prayers. Naturally, until the end of the eighteenth century, the "age of Voltairism," everyone in Russia was a believer. This was the norm, and it established the moral tradition within the family.

At the beginning of the eighteenth century, however, the family was also quite rapidly undergoing the very same surface-level Europeanization as clothing was. Women started to regard it as necessary, as fashionable, to have a lover, without whom they would be "behind the times." Coquettishness, balls, dances, singing—these are women's occupations. Family, household, childrearing—these moved into the background. Very quickly, the custom of not breastfeeding became standard in the upper echelons of society. That is for the wet-nurses. Consequently, a child grew up almost motherless. (Of course, not in the provinces, and of course, not in the house of some poor female landowner, with twelve children and thirty serfs, but mostly among the Petersburg upper nobility.)

And, suddenly, rapid and quite important transformations took place. Around the 1770s, the air of a new time sweeps over Europe. Romanticism is born and, especially after the works of Jean-Jacques Rousseau, it becomes customary to aspire to nature, to a "naturalness" of mores and conduct.

These tendencies penetrated into Russia, too. The consciousness of people in the last quarter of the eighteenth century begins to be penetrated by the notion that the good is in nature, that human beings, created in the image and likeness of God, are born for happiness, for freedom, for beauty. "Unnatural" fashions start to provoke a negative attitude, and "naturalness" becomes the ideal, specimens of which were sought in the female figures of antiquity and in "theatricalized" peasant life. Clothes are now simple: there are no longer sumptuous petticoats with a farthingale, nor corsets, nor brocade. Women's clothing is made from light material. To the defenders of the cult of Nature, a shirt with a very high waist seems "natural." The era of the French Revolution propagandizes a simplicity of dress. Paul I tried in vain to quash the fashion: at the last supper before he was assassinated, Empress Mariya Fyodorovna came to him in a forbidden European dress—a simple shirt, high waist, exposed décolletage, exposed shoulders—a child of nature. The empress's evening attire became the first public testimony to the end of the Pauline era. The first gesture of rebellion, as was often the case in eighteenth-century Russia, was made by a woman.

In the portraits from this period we see how the new way of attiring oneself was bound to naturalness, simplicity of movement, the living expression of the face. Thus, in Vladimir Borovikovsky's[viii] portrait of Mariya Lopukhina, it is hardly an accident that, instead of the then-customary bust of the empress

viii Vladimir Borovikovsky (1757–1825) was a talented portrait painter who left a series of depictions of the ruling family and aristocratic elite that often caught them in a moment of subtle dreaminess.

or a rather stately architectural construction in the background, we have ears of rye and cornflowers. The girl and nature are associated through their naturalness.

Dresses appeared that were later called "Onegins," though they had already come into style at the turn of the century, long before the publication of *Eugene Onegin*. Along with the change in style, hairdos change as well: women (as well as men) repudiate wigs; here, too, "naturalness" triumphs. This fashion crosses borders and, though there is a war on between revolutionary Paris and the rest of Europe, attempts to halt the fashion at political borders prove to be in vain. Here women had won a brilliant victory over politics.

The change in tastes also affected cosmetics (and, generally, everything that altered a woman's appearance). The Enlightenment ideal of simplicity abruptly cuts off the use of makeup. Paleness (if not natural, then that which is created with great artistry!) became an obligatory element of the feminine allure.

An eighteenth-century beauty shines with health and is prized for her stoutness. To people of this period, it seems that a full-bodied woman is a beautiful woman. It is precisely a solid, full-bodied woman that is considered the ideal of beauty—and portraitists, not infrequently committing a sin against truth, bring those they portray closer to the ideal. We know of cases in which the artist of a solemn portrait (which we can establish by comparing it with sketched profiles or other portraits) endows his female client with a full figure quite unlike her own. Exhibiting their preference for lavish forms, they treat their appetite much the same. The woman of this period eats a lot and is not ashamed to.

With the approach of the Romantic era, the fashion for health comes to an end. Now paleness, a sign of the depth of one's sincere feelings, seems beautiful and starts to please. Health, however, appears as something vulgar. Vasily Zhukovsky would say in *Alina and Al'sim*:

It pleases one's gaze, lively color,
Days of youth fulfilled;
But color pale, a mark of dolor,
Is more pleasant still.

Мила для взора живость цвета,
Знак юных дней;
Но бледный цвет, тоски примета,
Еще милей.

The woman of the Romantic era was supposed to be pale, pensive, melancholic. Men liked it when tears shone in women's mournful, pensive blue eyes, and when a woman, reading poems, was carried somewhere far off in her soul, into a more ideal world than that which surrounded her.

Yet the Romantic ideal of the woman-angel had its double, too:

> The angel is by demon groomed
> And by demoness attired.[6]
>
> Ангел дьяволом причесан
> И чертовкою одет.

The Romantic conjunction of the "angelic" and the "demonic" also joins the norms of feminine conduct.

Literature and art of the late eighteenth and early nineteenth centuries create an idealized image of the woman that clearly diverged from what lived reality provided.[ix] But, on the one hand, this dramatically elevated a woman's role in the culture. The image of the poetic maiden becomes the ideal of the era. On the other hand, this image has an ennobling effect on actual young women. Isn't this why their names, however few, are unforgettable in Russia's history? The heroic deeds of women in the Decembrist era are largely the fruit of how the poetry of Zhukovsky, Ryleev, and Pushkin penetrated women's libraries at the turn of the eighteenth and nineteenth centuries and in the first decades of the nineteenth.

The change in the general style of culture was reflected in the most diverse aspects of daily life.

The striving for "naturalness" demonstrated its influences first of all on the family. Throughout Europe, breastfeeding had become a sign of naturalness, a mark of good mothering. From this point one started to value the child, to value childhood.

Formerly, in the child they had seen only a small adult. This is quite noticeable, for example, in children's clothes. At the beginning of the eighteenth century, children's fashion does not yet exist. Children are clothed in small uniforms: their clothes are small in size but adult in cut. It is believed that children should have a world of adult concerns, and the very condition of childhood

---

ix On this point, and its consequences, see Barbara Heldt, *Terrible Perfection: Women and Russian Literature* (Bloomington: Indiana University Press, 1987).

is that which one must pass through as quickly as possible. Whoever tarries in this condition is a Peter Pan [Mitrofan],[x] a layabout, immature and stupid.

But Rousseau once said that the world would perish were it not that every person has been a child at some point in life ... And the culture gradually picks up the notion that a child—that is just a normal person. There appear children's clothes, the nursery, and there arises a notion that playing is a good thing. It is not just the child who needs instruction through play, but the adult as well. Instructing with the rod is a contradiction of nature.

Thus the attitudes of humaneness, of respect for the child, are brought into domestic life. And this is primarily a woman's doing. The man serves. In youth, he is an officer and is rarely at home. Later he is discharged, a landlord, home only in passing, ever occupied with managing the estate or with hunting. It is the woman, however, who creates the child's world. And in order to create it, the woman is required to have lived through and contemplated a great deal. She must become a reader.

So, from the 1770s through the 1790s, women do become readers. To a significant degree, this occurs under the influence of two people: Nikolay Ivanovich Novikov[xi] and Nikolay Mikhailovich Karamzin.

Novikov, having devoted his life to propagating the Enlightenment in Russia, gave rise to a new era in the history of Russian women's culture as well. To be sure, women had read books before Novikov, too, but he was the first to set himself the goal of turning women—the mothers and ladies of the house—into readers, of preparing them a well-considered system of useful books in a form they would find accessible. Let us recall that Alexander Sumarokov was still dreaming of the ideal kingdom, where "even the maidens study in school" (those "of noble birth," the writer stipulated). Novikov realized Sumarokov's pedagogical dreams with unheard-of energy and extraordinary skill. It was he who created a genuine library of women's reading.

---

x Mitrofan is the minor in Fonvizin's comedy *The Minor*, a young noble who could not care less about education and demonstrates little aptitude for anything at all.

xi Nikolay Novikov (1744–1818) was a writer, journal editor, and publisher, who energetically advanced the cause of education and enlightenment in Russia. A prominent Freemason, he was instrumental in introducing Rosicrucianism to Russia, publishing Masonic literature, along with the works of the French *encyclopédistes* and other kinds of literature, including for children. In the late 1780s Catherine II started to watch his activities with disquiet. He was subject to several investigations and eventually, in 1792, his printing press was confiscated, while he was arrested and sentenced to fifteen years of imprisonment. Paul I released him upon his accession to power, but Novikov never resumed his public activities, in part because his fortune had been expropriated.

Karamzin began his Enlightenment activity in Novikov's school and under his supervision.[xii] Along with his friend A. P. Petrov, he edited Novikov's journal *Children's Reading for Heart and Mind* [*Detskoe chtenie dlia serdtsa i razuma*, 1785–1789]. The journal's readers were—for the first time in Russia—children and their mothers.

Yet Karamzin soon parted ways with Novikov. Novikov, seeing literature primarily as applied pedagogy, believed that Russia needed morally instructive, useful books—didactics merely pretending to be art. Karamzin, however, a poet and one of the most brilliant figures in Russian literature of the eighteenth century, could not, and did not want to, assign art a purely subservient role. Beauty, in his opinion, has a moral significance in and of itself. Art is moral even without tiresome instruction in virtue. It is pedagogical precisely when it is not fussing over pedagogy.

Karamzin lays the theoretical foundations for and creates a literature whose moral and pedagogical effect was not grounded in straightforward edification. Furthermore: certain of Karamzin's works that had boldly addressed questions of love and ethics even struck the diminishing ranks of Novikov's followers as immoral. Now it is almost impossible for us to imagine the indignation provoked by Karamzin's stories, in which the author touched upon such "forbidden" topics as a brother's love for his sister ("The Island of Bornholm" [Ostrov Borngol'm, 1794]; the ballad "Raisa," 1791) or romantic suicide ("Sierra-Morena," 1795). Yet it is precisely these works, whose influence on readers had struck the literary Old Believers as immoral, that were, as history has shown, not only deeply moral, but even moralistic. It is no accident that for the generation of the Romantics Karamzin had already begun to seem naïve and his morality heavy-handed.

The relationship between literature and morality is one of the most acute questions to arise at the dawn of Romanticism. It struck an especially painful note as the problems of "art and family," "art and women," and "art and children" were being discussed. I will offer one example.

---

xii Nikolay Karamzin (1766–1826) was a writer, editor, and historian. The travelogue and short stories he wrote in the 1790s had a huge impact on Russian literature and on the evolution of the Russian language. In the 1800s, he abandoned fiction and first devoted himself to editing a journal, before receiving a commission by Alexander I to write a history of the Russian state, to which he devoted the last twenty years of his life. *The History of the Russian State* was similarly very influential, if controversial. Liberal minds detected in it a defense of autocracy. The work is also useful in light of its rich source base, especially as some of the sources he used subsequently perished in various calamities.

The young Anna Evdokimovna Karamysheva (whose fate will be considered in detail later, in the chapter "Two Women") was being raised in the family of the writer Mikhail Kheraskov. Novels seemed so perilous to virtue that when they mentioned them in Kheraskov's house (but novels back then were so innocent, so boring, so virtuous!),[7] they would simply shoo Karamysheva, already a married woman, out of the room! This was the 1770s. So it was in a family oriented toward the patriarchal way of life. But by this time Karamzin's mother was already reading and having her son read those fashionable novels that ten years later inundated the majority of ladies' libraries.[8] These novels were also naïve, but Karamzin would subsequently say that a person who cries over the hero's fate will not be indifferent to another person's misfortunes. In naïve books that were already laughable in Pushkin's era, a humanitarian thought shone through, and they may have performed better than moral lessons laid out in the form of direct admonitions.

A bit more time would pass, and Tatyana Larina, a girl of the 1820s, would appear before readers "with a French book in her hands, with a mournful thought in her eyes." Pushkin's heroine lives in a world of literature:

Imagining each heroine
Of her own most belovèd authors,
Clarissa, Julie, and Delphine,
Tatyana silent forests wanders,
In hand a risky volume caught. ...
(3, X)[xiii]

Воображаясь героиней
Своих возлюбленных творцов,
Кларисой, Юлией, Дельфиной,
Татьяна в тишине лесов
Одна с опасной книгой бродит. ...

For a young lady of the 1820s, a provincial young lady living somewhere near Pskov, her thoughts and feelings are through and through those of the heroes of the best literary works. No wonder Pushkin would say of Tatyana:

xiii Clarissa is a reference to Samuel Richardson's novel *Clarissa; or, the History of a Young Lady* (1748); Julie refers to Rousseau's *Julie, ou la Nouvelle Héloïse* (1761); and *Delphine* (1802) is an epistolary novel by Madame de Staël.

She sighs to make of stranger's sorrow,
Of stranger's rapture, her own plight. …
(3, X)

Вздыхает и, себе присвоя
Чужой восторг, чужую грусть …

A different kind of person, a different kind of woman, is created. Fyodor Rokotov[xiv] demonstrated this very well in one of the first Romantic portraits, that of Alexandra Struyskaya[xv]. Let us recall Nikolay Zabolotsky's poem written in reference to this portrait:

Remember how, from bygone hazes,
Out of Rokotov's portrait frame,
Just barely enshrouded in atlas,
Struyskaya looked on us again?

Her eyes, alike to two mists swirling,
Half-smiling, half as if she'd wept,
Her eyes, alike to two deceptions
Befoggèd now by each misstep.

A marriage made of two enigmas,
Both half-enraptured, half-dismayed,
Delirium of insane kindness
Anticipating mortal pains.

When day at last is growing dimmer,
And the storm clouds begin to roll,
Her fascinating eyes still shimmer
Up from the bottom of my soul.
"A Portrait" [Portret]

---

xiv Fyodor Rokotov (1736–1808) is another important eighteenth-century portraitist. His background is disputed, though it is likely that he hailed from a serf family. Educated at the Academy of Arts in St. Petersburg, he taught there in the 1760s, but subsequently moved to Moscow, where he had more creative freedom. During the 1770s and 1780s he painted a prodigious series of members of the main muscovite aristocratic families, many represented through some mysterious, dreamy haze. His late work of the 1790s is more in line with classicist values of clarity of line and texture and more assertive poses.

xv This portrait is dated 1772.

Ты помнишь, как из тьмы былого,
Едва закутана в атлас,
С портрета Рокотова снова
Смотрела Струйская на нас?

Её глаза—как два тумана,
Полуулыбка, полуплач,
Её глаза—как два обмана,
Покрытых мглою неудач.

Соединенье двух загадок,
Полувосторг, полуиспуг,
Безумной нежности припадок,
Предвосхищенье смертных мук.

Когда потёмки наступают
И приближается гроза,
Со дна души моей мерцают
Её прекрасные глаза.

And after a few more years we see how a young woman, a girl, will sometimes turn out to be able to do what men cannot, men bound to the life of the state and to service, brave men who perish in their redoubts.

Perhaps the most terrifying thing of all occurred once the ranks of the Decembrists were scattered by buckshot on Senate Square. It was not arrest and exile that turned out to be terrifying. The moral disintegration of humanity was occurring in the palaces of Petersburg, where those who yesterday had been friends to the Decembrists hastened to affirm their loyalty to the power of the new emperor, while their recent pals and close kin were bearing their cross in the snows of Siberia. (A rarity among those who took part in Petersburg parades or balls at the Winter Palace was he who had neither brother, nor kin, nor bunkmate in a Siberian cell!) The deportees lived under awful conditions in Siberia, but they had nothing to be afraid of: the most terrifying thing *had already come about.* But those in Petersburg who just yesterday had been having freedom-loving conversations with today's exiles, and who now knew that it was mere happenstance protecting them, that everything could change in a minute, and one who was sitting in his Petersburg study could find himself shackled in a prison colony—they were the ones who took fright. Ten years of fright—and society degrades: the men will start to be afraid; a different person will appear, the "constrained" person of the era of Nicholas I. Mikhail Saltykov-Shchedrin would later tell how his hero dreams he is sleeping, and that a pyramid of people in uniform has been erected on his head. This pyramid crushed his head, flattening it ...[xvi]

But the women were not afraid. One, Princess Volkonskaya, writes a letter to Alexander Benckendorff. She writes in French: she is a society lady, and he is a man of society (Benckendorff himself loathed wearing the gendarme's uniform); he, of course, would never permit himself to put a lady of society "in her place."[9]

Women prove to be more resilient than men. They are mentally stronger, have no fear, they travel to Siberia under awful conditions. In Petersburg they are warned that all the children of exiles who are born in Siberia will be registered as belonging not to the nobility—but to the peasantry. They menace them by saying that they'll be defenseless against the criminal inmates, and the Decembrists' wives would later recall that the officials were far worse than the criminals in the prison colonies, among whom there were human beings, whereas there were almost none among the officials.

The behavior of women in the post-Decembrist era is a fact not only of "woman's culture." To a significant degree, girls and women of the 1820s created the general moral atmosphere of Russian society. When we talk about where the people of the Decembrist circle come from, people whom Alexander Herzen called "a generation of the heroic forged from pure steel," one can point to many causes. There are historical events, as well as wars, and also books, but there is also the humanistic atmosphere that had barged so unexpectedly into family life. Of course, one ought not to think that such women were quite so numerous. There were also "wild landowner-women," and there were even more of them. There were also kind, quiet women, not at all bad, the whole meaning of whose lives was in salting pickles and stocking up for the winter—old-fashioned proprietresses, agreeable, good. But the fact that society already had people, and to a significant degree women, who were living life in the spirit—this was creating a completely different way of life.

What is more, just as a woman's letter written in French to the sovereign or the official was shifting the text into a space beyond class considerations, so too was it as though all feminine behavior in this era, in its higher manifestations, broke away from the social sphere of its time and became an expression of universal principles.

---

xvi Refers to Saltykov-Shchedrin's novella "A Complicated Affair" [Zaputannoe delo] (1848).

Pushkin made bold use of this in his unfinished novel *Roslavlev* (1831), in which we find an exceptionally interesting dialogue of ideas, a polemic with Mikhail Zagoskin's novel *Roslavlev, or Russians in 1812* [*Roslavlev, ili Russkie v 1812 godu*, 1831].[xvii]

Mikhail Zagoskin, whose talent as a prose author Pushkin valued rather highly, was near in his attitudes to Nikolay Nadezhdin (a famous critic and Belinsky's "mentor"). What set their position apart was the combination of an immature democratism seeking its own path and a negative attitude toward revolutionary and liberal ideas. Accordingly, Zagoskin's patriotism was, on the one hand, acceptable to the democratic camp taking shape in Russia and, on the other, slightly tinged with an officious and pro-government hue. This defined, for example, Zagoskin's position in the story of the persecutions of Pyotr Chaadaev[xviii]: Zagoskin had sided with those who accused the author of *Philosophical Letters* [*Filosofskie pis'ma*] of lacking patriotism. His accusations did in fact extend to the entire circle of the heirs to liberalism and Decembrism, who had survived an era of exile and executions, people including Mikhail Orlov, the Turgenev brothers, and Pushkin himself.

In response to Zagoskin, Pushkin blamed him for the fact that the novelist seemed to have monopolized the right to be patriotism's mouthpiece. It is quite characteristic that Pushkin would select a female heroine as the embodiment of his understanding of patriotism. It is precisely Polina, the heroine of *Roslavlev*, a highly spiritual woman who has risen above the political factionalism of the day, who could become an exponent of Pushkin's point of view, which fused high patriotism with a universal morality.

Pushkin himself, in a somewhat joking form, conflated his own perspectives with a woman's point of view—a naïve one, though in fact a profound one. In his unfinished *Novel in Letters* [*Roman v pis'makh*, 1829], Liza (and, in her

---

xvii Zagoskin's novel *Roslavlev, or Russians in 1812* is a historical novel about the patriotic response of the Russian people to the invasion of Napoleon's army. The novel reflects a traditional absolutist theory of the state, enhanced with an unassailable sense of the distinctive national character of Russians, so that even Roslavlev, a Romantic hero influenced by French Enlightenment, comes around to join the visceral, exceptionalist patriotism of the people. Pushkin's fragment undermines this notion through the character of Polina, a self-confident young woman who takes after Madame de Staël and demonstrates the hypocrisy of the nobility's patriotism, advancing the notion that extensive exposure to Enlightenment thought had in fact prepared her to become a genuine patriot, transcending the tribalism of her kin.

xviii Pyotr Chaadaev (1794–1856) was declared insane and condemned to house arrest for his "First Philosophical Letter," a savage indictment of Russia's lack of civilizational progress.

words, Pushkin himself, being more than a little arch) says: "Now I remember why V[yazemsky] and P[ushkin] are so fond of the daughters of provincial landowners. They are their natural audience."

One may note that in the following era, when women were winning the right to participate more broadly in political life, they competed with men in their ability "to dispute taxes / Or to prevent emperors from fighting among themselves,"[xix] but they constrained what was eternal within themselves, what remains in a person for all times. In the era of Romanticism and Decembrism, however, Russian women, having risen to the intellectual level of an educated man of their time, took another step forward—toward a universal point of view.

But the heroic generation of the Decembrists' wives was yet to come. Now, at the turn of the century, we are dealing with their mothers, "gentle daydreamers," but without these mothers we would not have their daughters.

The world of women played a conspicuous role in the destinies of Russian Romanticism. The Romantic era allotted women a supremely important place in the culture. The era of the Enlightenment had posed the question of defending women's rights. The woman, the child, the common man—such were the typical heroes for whose equality and rights the creature of the Enlightenment fought. The "wards" had to be cultivated, defended, and taught, and the educator and defender was a man—of course, the kind who had already adopted the ideas of the "Age of Enlightenment." Pushkin loved to repeat the words of the French historian and philosopher Ferdinando Galiani on woman: "An animal weak and sickly by nature."[xx]

The era that Karamzin initiated in Russia allotted women a completely new role. Zhukovsky's poetry affirmed the notion of the woman as a poetic ideal, an object of worship. Together with the Romantic taste for the age of chivalry, there arises the poeticization of the woman.

---

xix This is a quotation from Pushkin's "From Pindemonti" [Iz Pindemonti], a poem about the lyrical I's desire to withdraw from public affairs and abide purely by his commitment to poetry (A. S. Pushkin, *Polnoe sobranie sochinenii*, vol. 3, 420). There is no explicit reference to the public role of women in the poem.

xx Ferdinando Galiani (1728–1787) was in fact born in Naples, though he wrote and published both in Italian and French. He was an economist who took on the then-fashionable ideas of the Physiocrats and insisted on the need to regulate trade, but was known also for his wit. Pushkin quoted this saying in a letter to his wife Natalya. The saying itself comes from Galiani's essay "Fragment of a Dialogue on Women" (1784). For more context on Pushkin's attitude towards his wife, see Catriona Kelly, "Educating Tat'yana: Manners, Motherhood and Moral Education (Vospitanie), 1760–1840," in *Gender in Russian History and Culture*, ed. Linda Edmonson (Basingstoke: Palgrave Macmillan, 2001), 1–28.

The creature of the Enlightenment affirmed the equality of woman and man. In woman he saw a *person,* and he strove to make her equal in her rights to her father and her husband. Romanticism revived the idea of the inequality of the sexes, which was constructed according to models of the chivalric literature of the Middle Ages. Elevated to an ideal, woman was allotted the realm of elevated and refined feelings. It was man who should be her servant and defender. Of course, the Romantic ideal had difficulty adapting to Russian reality. As a rule, it enveloped the world of the girl from the nobility, a reader of novels, her soul submerged in vicarious literary experiences and partaking "of a stranger's sorrow, of stranger's rapture." Thus, for example, in her youth Sophie Saltykova, Delvig's future wife, lived through a stormy passion for the Decembrist Pyotr Kakhovsky. Kakhovsky, a poor officer with no connections, of course could not be considered as a suitor for a high-society noblewoman. But the two young people have no thought for marriage. They are bound by an ideal love. Their declaration of love unfolds as an exchange of poetic quotations.

Here we cannot help but recall the tragic and, at the same time, characteristic fate of the two Protasov sisters, Masha and Sasha. One would subsequently marry Ivan Moyer, professor at the Dorpat Imperial University, famous surgeon, teacher of Nikolay Pirogov. Moyer was an excellent person: Pirogov left very warm reminiscences of him. The other sister would marry Alexander Voeykov, a professor and man of letters and, alas, a cruel and immoral person.

Masha, still almost a child, would fall in love with her relation, the poet Zhukovsky. Zhukovsky belonged on his father's side to an ancient noble family. His father was the landowner Bunin (apparently an ancestor of the writer Ivan Bunin, of which the latter was especially proud), but his mother was Salkha, a captive Turk living in the house in something like a serf's capacity. The future poet was illegitimate—on the whole, precisely what was regarded as "of doubtful provenance." The child could not receive his father's surname, and the poet's father proposed to the poor nobleman Zhukovsky, who was a dependent living in the Bunin home, that he become the child's godfather and give him his surname.

Zhukovsky had a very good upbringing as an equal member of the family. His elementary education and arrangements for his future were seen to by his older married sisters, Ekaterina Protasova and Avdotya Elagina.[xxi] What is more, in this house of Bunin, Protasov, Elagin—a large nest of culture where the tone was set by the young, the aunties and cousins—Zhukovsky was the

xxi Zhukovsky's sister was in fact Avdotya Alymova (1754–1813). Avdotya Elagina (1789–1877) was his niece, the daughter of his sister Varvara.

only boy, everybody's favorite. They cared for him tenderly, fought hard for his nobility, provided him an education in what was then the best institution of learning, the Moscow Boarding School for Nobility.

In 1805, already a famous poet, Zhukovsky becomes the domestic tutor to his nieces, the daughters of his stepsister, Ekaterina Protasova. And here is where the drama unfolds. Reading of the love of Zhukovsky and Masha Protasova, it is impossible not to sense how tightly literature and life, the poetry of the real and the poetry of poetry, are intertwined therein. Actual sufferings become literary storylines, and literary heroes explain the meaning of lived feelings and sufferings to those taking part in the drama.

It is as though life were acting out a storyline before the lovers, one that by that point had already passed into literature and, after Jean-Jacques Rousseau's *The New Heloise,* had been lived by all of Europe's "tenderhearted" female readers. The commoner teacher falls in love with his noblewoman pupil, and she with him. But their marriage is impossible because society has its own laws, its own prejudices.[10]

And so a wall arises between Masha and Zhukovsky that is even more solid than class prejudice. Masha's mother, a deeply religious woman, considers a marriage between such close relations impossible. The hospitable Protasov home suddenly becomes foreign. Zhukovsky's sister extracts a secret promise from him that he will renounce his claims on Masha. They give him to understand that he will be tolerated in the house only so long as he hides his love. The tragic feeling will torment the poet for the rest of his life. It will form the content of Zhukovsky's poems, of Masha's poems, of their passionate correspondence.

It is as if Zhukovsky's life in literature and in actuality unfolded in parallel. Tristan, the hero of the medieval romance of Tristan and Iseult, gives up his beloved queen. The life of Tristan and Iseult, rife with separation and suffering, is crowned by their posthumous union. For Zhukovsky, this image becomes the literary embodiment of his actual real-life sufferings. But at the same time, the poet's actual real-life sufferings are reflected in his work as generic "chivalric" storylines. Thus art spilled over into life, and life, into art.

But the Romantic woman does not remain a passive participant in this "game" of literature and life. Life's prose cannot break Masha of the habit of looking at everything that is happening through the eyes of poetry. A half-century will pass, and to the common reader, the admirer of Dmitry Pisarev,[xxii]

xxii Dmitry Pisarev (1840–1868) is a member of the radical, revolutionary intelligentsia of the 1860s. He wrote a number of acerbic articles on the literature of his day, including a famous

such a view will start to seem "impractical." But it was precisely this "impracticality," the inseparability of the lived and the poetic, which both created the high spirituality of Romantic girls in the early nineteenth century and allowed them to play an ennobling role in Russian culture.

It fell to Sasha Protasova to continue the "novel-life." The youngest of the sisters, a charming scamp called at home by the name of the heroine of Zhukovsky's ballad "Svetlana," she marries Zhukovsky's friend, the Dorpat University professor Alexander Voeykov. The family moves to Dorpat (today's Tartu). There, Masha, yielding to her mother's pressure, marries Professor Ivan Moyer. Zhukovsky, suppressing his own feelings, gives her his blessing on the marriage and (as Tristan had done!) himself delivers his beloved into the arms of his friend.

Moyer is an honorable person. He spares Masha's feelings, he holds her in great esteem. He is himself not only a fine surgeon, but also a musician. This is not the self-interested and cold Voeykov. But an extremely tormenting situation comes about. All three of them are decent people. All three suffer. Zhukovsky arrives in Dorpat. His relationship with Masha is always platonic, but the feeling remains strong and tragic.

And then Masha dies after giving birth to her second child. She is buried in Dorpat, where her grave remains to this day. One of Zhukovsky's best poems, "March 19, 1823," is dedicated to Masha Moyer's death:

> You stood before me,
> You stood in silence.
> Your gaze was doleful
> And full of feeling.
> It brought my mind back
> To pleasant pastimes. ...
> It was the last time
> In the world we live in.
>
> You drew away then,
> A silent angel;
> Your grave is peaceful,
> As Paradise is!
> Therein all earthly

---

article on Turgenev's *Fathers and Sons*, "Bazarov," where he states that a pair of shoes are infinitely more useful than the works of Pushkin.

Reminiscence,
And there all holy
Thoughts of heaven.

The heavenly stars,
A silent night! ...

Ты предо мною
Стояла тихо.
Твой взор унылый
Был полон чувства.
Он мне напомнил
О милом прошлом ...
Он был последний
На здешнем свете.

Ты удалилась,
Как тихий ангел;
Твоя могила,
Как рай, спокойна!
Там все земные
Воспоминанья,
Там все святые
О небе мысли.

Звезды небес,
Тихая ночь!

In speaking of women at the beginning of the last century, it is necessary also to say a few words about children. A peculiar childhood took shape in this cultural universe. Not only did they start sewing children's clothes, not only did they cultivate children's games, but children started to read very early. A woman's world was inextricable from a child's, and the woman-reader gave birth to the child-reader. Reading a book aloud, and later the separate children's library—such was the path that the future people of letters, warriors, and politicians would follow.

Generally, it is difficult to name a time when the book would play the kind of role it would in the late eighteenth and early nineteenth centuries. Having burst into the child's life in the 1780s, by the beginning of the following century the book had become childhood's obligatory companion. Children had very interesting books—of course, first and foremost, novels: after all, children read what women read. The woman's library, the woman's bookshelf, shaped the extent of the child's reading and the child's tastes. Novels turned one's head: they had heroic knights who rescue beauties, serve the good, and never bow to evil. Impressions from books became quite easily bound to the fairytale children had heard from a nanny. The novel and the fairytale did not contradict one another.

By the close of the eighteenth century, the Russian children's book, inaugurated by Novikov's work in publishing, had already become quite diverse. Here there are both classic works, such as *Don Quixote* and *Robinson Crusoe,* and literature that is largely primitive: translations of works for children culled from didactic books in German and French. But children most often fall under the influence of the best of what they have read—and so the young Muravyovs, future Decembrists, are already dreaming of going to Sakhalin, which to them seems to be an uninhabited island (the world of Robinson!), and of establishing there the ideal Republic of Choka.[xxiii] On the island the brothers would start all of human history anew: they would have neither lords, nor slaves, nor money; they would come to live for the sake of equality, fraternity, and liberty.

A different book would also enter children's reading during this era: *The Children's Plutarch* [*Plutarkh detei*].[11] Plutarch is a famous classical prose writer, the author of the *Parallel Lives* of the great people of ancient Greece and Rome. Having just lived through a "first wave" of literary impressions, having felt that one was a medieval knight fighting villains, warlocks, and giants—a crusader warring against the Moors—the child becomes absorbed into the world of historical heroics. In the eyes of children and adolescents, the most fascinating image becomes that of the Roman republican.

A revealing episode in this regard comes from the biography of the famous Decembrist Nikita Muravyov. He transports us to a children's ball. The time of the action is the beginning of the nineteenth century. The story's hero is six years old.

"Children's balls" are special balls put on during the first half of the day, whether in private homes or at the dance master Iogel's. Even quite small

xxiii Choka was the name of a society of dreamers Nikolay Muravyov-Karsky (1794–1866) founded in 1810. The members lovingly concocted plans to set up a republic organised along the principles of Rousseau's social contract on the island of Sakhalin. Choka was a code word for Sakhalin.

children were taken, but the dancers also included girls of twelve, thirteen, or fourteen years who were considered ready for betrothal, since fifteen years old is already a legitimate age for marriage. Let us recall how, in *War and Peace,* the young officers Nikolay Rostov and Vasily Denisov, on leave, arrive at Iogel's for a children's ball. Children's balls are celebrated for their gaiety. Here the unencumbered atmosphere of child's play passes imperceptibly into an absorbing coquetry.

Little Nicky, the future Decembrist, stands at the children's party and does not dance, and when his mother asks him why, the boy inquires (in French), "But really, Mommy, did Aristides and Cato dance?" To which his mother responds, also in French, "One must suppose they did when they were your age."[12] And it is only then that Little Nicky goes to dance. He has not yet learned much, but he already knows that he will be a hero like an ancient Roman. As yet he is poorly prepared for it, though he knows geography, as well as mathematics and several languages.

In 1812, the sixteen-year-old Nikita Muravyov decides to run off to the active army in order to realize a heroic deed:

> Aflame with the desire to defend the Fatherland by taking part in the war personally, he decided to report to Commander-in-Chief Kutuzov and ask him for an assignment. ... He obtained a map of Russia and, given his inexperience, kept with him a separate note that contained the names of the French marshals and their divisions; having furnished himself with this intelligence, at night he stole away from the house on foot and walked in the direction of Mozhaysk. On the way he was intercepted by peasants who were afraid of spies and, after tying him up, led him to their district court. However much Nikita explained himself or his status, they paid no heed to anything he said: they took him, bound, to Moscow, to the hard-hearted Count Rostopchin, the capital's supreme commander, who ordered that he be tossed in jail until it was sorted out. As he was being taken there, he was spotted by his Swiss tutor, Monsieur Petra, who spoke with him in French, so that the enraged folk not only refused to hand the young man over, but, showering abuse upon them both, led them to jail, calling them spies. Petra, having somehow broken free of the crowd, ran off to Ekaterina Fyodorovna [Nikita Muravyov's mother—*Lotman*], who immediately rushed to Count Rostopchin, begging him to return her completely innocent son.[13]

Nikita Muravyov and his coevals had a peculiar childhood, a childhood that creates people who are prepared in advance not for career, not for service, but for heroic deeds—people who know that the worst thing in life is the loss of one's honor. To commit an unworthy act is worse than death. Death does not scare the adolescents and youth of this generation: all the great Romans had perished heroically, and such a death is enviable. When General Ypsilanti, a Greek in the Russian service, a combat officer whose arm had been torn off near Dresden, raised the Greek rebellion against the Turks, Pushkin wrote to Vasily Davydov: "Al[exander] Ypsilanti's first move is magnificent and brilliant. He's made a happy start—henceforth, whether dead or triumphant, he belongs to history—twenty-eight years old, arm torn off, a lofty goal!—an enviable lot."[14]

People live so that their names will be recorded in history, and not to wangle an additional hundred serfs out of the tsar. Thus a new psychological type is created in the nursery.

It is striking, but even Ypsilanti's torn-off arm, a testament to his heroism, is an object of the young Pushkin's envy. Pushkin belongs to a generation thirsty for heroic deeds and afraid not of death, but of obscurity. The thirst for fame is a widespread feeling, but for people of the Decembrist era it is transformed into a thirst for freedom. Of the hero of his epic *Prisoner of the Caucasus* [*Kavkazskii plennik*], Pushkin wrote:

O Freedom! He alone pursued
You yet in this deserted world.

Свобода! Он одной тебя
Ещё искал в пустынном мире.

With this, he immediately made his hero a mouthpiece for the feelings of his generation. But it is a characteristic feature of the time that the Romantic thirst for freedom enveloped women, too. There will be no women on Senate Square on the Fourteenth of December. But this day will become a fateful end to Romantic youth not only for their husbands, brothers, and sons, but for them as well.

The second half of the eighteenth and first half of the nineteenth centuries, as we have seen, opened a peculiar space for women in Russian culture, and this was connected with the fact that a woman's character in these years was shaped by literature as never before. It was precisely then that the notion that a woman was the most sensitive barometer of an era took hold, a view later adopted by Ivan Turgenev and a characteristic feature of nineteenth-century Russian literature.

It is especially important, however, that women also constantly and actively adopted the roles that epic poems and novels have assigned them. In characterizing the contemporaries of Zhukovsky or Ryleev, we can therefore evaluate the everyday and psychological reality of their lives through the prism of literature. The heroes of literature become the heroes of life. One can demonstrate, for example, the sort of role that Kondraty Ryleev's epic poem *Voinarovskii* played in shaping the Decembrists' behavior.[xxiv]

The female image gave literature a positive hero. It was here in particular that the artistic (and real-life) stereotype whereby a man embodies socially typical flaws, whereas a woman embodies the society's ideal, took shape. This stereotype became not only active, but long-lasting: many generations of Russian women lived "after the heroes" not only of Ryleev, Pushkin, and Lermontov, but—later—of Turgenev and Nekrasov.

The end of the era that concerns us created three stereotypical images of women that moved from poetry into girlish ideals and real women's biographies, and that later—in Nekrasov's era—moved back from life into poetry. The first image, imported from Zhukovsky's biography into his poetry, is connected to the Protasov sisters (who were discussed earlier). This is the image of the affectionately loving woman whose life and feelings have been crushed. The heroine is imbued with ideal feeling, a poetical nature, tenderness, emotional sensitivity. Society's cruelty has destroyed her soul, her health, and her life. Resigned to her fate, the poetic child perishes. In the consciousness of her contemporaries, this ideal evoked the image of an angel who has happened to visit earth and is ready to return to her heavenly home.

The second ideal is the demonic character. In literature (and in life) it was associated, for example, with the heroic image of the "lawless comet"[xxv] that boldly destroys all the conventions of a world created by men.

xxiv Ryleev's poem is about the inner doubts of Andrey Voynarovsky, a freedom-loving, rebellious, and despot-hating exile, who finds himself alienated from his people and wonders about the meaning of his political actions.

xxv The image of a "lawless comet in the clear circle of planets" comes from Pushkin's poem "Portrait" (1828). It refers to Agrafena Zakrevskaya, whose beauty and turbulent behavior made her stand out from other women. Lotman quotes the entire poem and discusses Zakrevskaya below.

The everyday life of Russian high society at the beginning of the nineteenth century cannot be regarded as entirely uniform. Although the ideal norms of behavior that society demanded of a lady and that combined the behavioral rules of pre-Revolutionary French high society with Petersburg primness were rather strict, here, too, real life turns out to be significantly more diverse. For example, the conceited coldness of Petersburg society contrasted the freedom and spontaneity of "Moscow behavior," and the freedom permitted at festivities in the countryside turned out to be decidedly unacceptable at a ball or even at a house party in the capital. After their confidential chat in the garden, Tatyana and Onegin

> Set off for home along the garden,
> Arrived together, and no one broached
> The thought that they deserved reproach:
> A village freedom freely pardons,
> With happy rules devoid of pride,
> What haughty Moscow can't abide.
>
> (4, XVII)

> Пошли домой вкруг огорода;
> Явились вместе, и никто
> Не вздумал им пенять на то.
> Имеет сельская свобода
> Свои счастливые права,
> Как и надменная Москва.

In point of fact, by the eighteenth century higher society, and especially Moscow's, permitted the originality and individuality of a woman's character. Only in Moscow were there such women as Nastasya Ofrosimova, whose unusual behavior attracted Lev Tolstoy (as Mariya Akhrosimova in *War and Peace*) and Griboedov (as Khlyostova in *Woe from Wit*). There were other women as well who allowed themselves scandalous behavior and openly broke the rules of propriety. Until the Romantic era, however, they were perceived as harmlessly (if a first offense) or scandalously crossing the bounds of the cultural norm. In the world of ideology, it was as though they didn't exist.

In the Romantic era, "unusual" female characters wrote themselves into the philosophy of culture and simultaneously became fashionable. In literature and life, the image of the "demonic" woman appears, the rule-breaker who scorns the conventions and falsehood of high society. Having appeared in literature, the ideal of the demonic woman actively invaded everyday life and created an entire gallery of women wrecking the norms of "proper" high-society behavior. This image falls into the same rank as that of the male protester. In his poetry, Pushkin draws together "the citizen of noble spirit" and "the woman not of beauty cold, / But ardent, enchanting, bold."[xxvi] This character becomes one of the main ideals of the Romantics. At the same time, an interesting and rather ambivalent relationship emerges between the real and the literary "demonic woman."

Agrafena Fyodorovna Zakrevskaya (1800–1879) is the wife of Arseny Zakrevsky, Governor-General of Finland, from 1828 Minister of the Interior, and after 1848 the military Governor-General of Moscow. An extravagant beauty, Zakrevskaya was famous for her scandalous liaisons. Her image attracted the attention of the best poets of the 1820s and 1830s. Pushkin wrote of her (in his poem "A Portrait" [Portret]):

With soul ablaze and set aglow,
With passions stirred into a tempest,
O northern women, unembarrassed
Will she appear among you now
And then, and flaunting social profit
Keep striving till her strength expires,
Akin to some unlawful comet
Amidst enumerated stars.

С своей пылающей душой,
С своими бурными страстями,
О жены Севера, меж вами
Она является порой
И мимо всех условий света
Стремится до утраты сил,
Как беззаконная комета
В кругу расчисленном светил.

It is to her that Pushkin's poem "The Confidant" [Napersnik] is dedicated. Viazemsky called Zakrevskaya "a bronze Venus." Evgeny Baratynsky created the following image of the tragic and demonic beauty:

xxvi From Pushkin's poem "Of alien lands an inexperienced lover" [Kraev chuzhikh neopytnyi liubitel'] (1817).

How much you lived in not much time,
So much you caught in deepest feeling.
In restless flame of passions flung,
How passionate your fire's fading!
Enslaved to your tormenting goal,
In the longing of an empty soul,
What more could your soul still be after?
Alike to Magdalene, your dole,
And like a siren's, your raucous laughter![15 xxvii]

Как много ты в немного дней
Прожить, прочувствовать успела!
В мятежном пламени страстей
Как страшно ты перегорела!
Раба томительной мечты!
В тоске душевной пустоты,
Чего ещё душою хочешь?
Как Магдалина плачешь ты,
И как русалка ты хохочешь!

It was Agrafena Zakrevskaya who served as the prototype for Princess Nina in Baratynsky's epic poem "The Ball" [Bal]. And, finally, according to Vikenty Veresaev's hypothesis, it was she whom Pushkin sketched in the guise of Nina Voronskaya in the eighth chapter of *Eugene Onegin*. Nina Voronskaya is a vivacious, extravagant beauty, the "Cleopatra of the Neva," the ideal of the Romantic woman who has positioned herself both outside the conventions of behavior and outside of morality.

It is utterly obvious that Zakrevskaya, in her real-life behavior, patterned herself according to the image of her that Pushkin, Baratynsky, and other artists had created.

The experience of another "demonic" love became a completely different, passionate, and tormenting one for Pushkin. This story has two realities, for it was traced by two utterly separate gazes, one set of eyes belonging to political spy craft, the other to Pushkin. Both versions are Romantic, though their Romanticisms are diametrically opposed.

From a third, biographical perspective, the matter appeared as follows. Count Adam Rzewuski, a Polish aristocrat, had married, in Romantic

---

xxvii From Baratynsky's poem "To ..." [K ...] (1827).

fashion, a captive Greek woman. The story of this marriage had everything familiar to us from the epic poems of Byron and his epigones: a purchased bondwoman for a wife, adventurism, crime, and the main thing—two daughters of unheard-of beauty, even in this era rife with enchanting women. From their parents the daughters had received nothing but their beauty, guile, and some innate passion for perfidy and risk. In these sisters Pushkin and Mickiewicz saw the heroines of Byron; in actuality, they were more the demonic heroines of Balzac. One of the sisters (Eveline) did become Balzac's wife at a later time and bound herself closely to his creative biography. The other, Karolina (Sobańska by marriage), insinuated herself ominously into the life of Pushkin.

Karolina Sobańska met with Pushkin during his southern exile. By that point, her destiny as a risk-taker had already become clear. In fact, having separated from her first husband, in Odessa Sobańska enjoyed a lifestyle unheard-of at the time. From 1821, she openly cohabitated with the chief of the southern military colonies, Lieutenant-General Jan Witt, flaunting her adultery. Such behavior was considered scandalous, yet it was in keeping with the Romantic image of the demonic beauty. Actually, Sobańska was not only Witt's lover, but also his secret agent.

Lieutenant-General Witt is one of the meanest personalities in the history of Russian political espionage. A spy not so much by appointment as by vocation, Witt harbored far-reaching, ambitious plans. On his own initiative, he started to surveille the ranks of the Decembrists: Alexander and Nikolay Raevsky, Mikhail Orlov, and others. He had an especially complicated relationship with Pavel Pestel.

Pestel was weighing the possibility of using the military outposts to the secret society's ends. He clearly saw both Witt's fondness for risk and his mean ambition, but Pestel was himself also inclined to separate the means of the struggle for society's aims from any strict moral rules—which brought him the Decembrists' reproach. He was ready to use Witt, much as he later hoped to turn the swindler I. Mayboroda into the secret societies' obedient weapon.

The mistrustful Alexander I had long delayed the advancement of Pestel's career by not granting him a separate military unit. And without one, any plans for a rebellion lost their footing. Pestel decided to use Witt—by marrying his daughter, an old maid, and receiving command of the military colonies in the south. In this case, the entire plan for a southern rebellion would rest on a revolt on the part of the settlers, whose "volatility" Pestel rated highly.

Witt's opposing "gambit" consisted of infiltrating the very center of the conspiracy, whose existence he sensed with a spy's intuition. Having received intelligence about a conspiracy within the Southern Army, he intended to use this trump card in a complicated, risk-filled scheme—to sell Pestel to Alexander, or Alexander to Pestel, depending on the circumstances.

Both Alexander I and Pestel despised Witt and were disgusted to have to come to his aid. But both sacrificed their aversion to the political game they were playing. Fate decided for itself: in the end, Alexander granted Pestel a regiment, and it became unnecessary for the Decembrists to turn to Witt.

Witt's far-reaching plans were not limited to his connections with Pestel. Both Pushkin and Mickiewicz fell among his special interests. But if he was making ready to lure Pestel with the prospect of receiving military outposts "as a dowry," there had to be another bait for Pushkin and Mickiewicz—and Witt's instrument was Karolina Sobańska. Both poets were tormented by feelings for the lovely intrigante. Pushkin suffered a difficult, genuine passion in the south, and afterwards he was overcome several times by short-lived paroxysms of this infatuation.

A few months before his wedding to Nataliya Nikolaevna Goncharova, on February 2, 1830, Pushkin, meeting Sobańska in Petersburg, wrote her the following letter in French:

> Today is the ninth anniversary of my seeing you for the first time. It was a decisive day in my life.
>
> The more I think about it, the more I am convinced that my existence is inextricably bound to yours; I was born to love you and to follow you—any other concern on my part is delusion or recklessness; far away from you, I am only gnawed by the thought of a happiness I have not managed to sate myself on. Sooner or later I will have to toss everything aside and fall at your feet. Among my somber regrets, but a single thought entices and revives me, that I will someday have a piece of land in Crimea (?). I will be able to make pilgrimages there, wander around your house, meet with you, see you in passing. ...[16]

The letter was never sent, because on the very same day Pushkin received a note from Sobańska written in a cold, aristocratic tone and postponing their meeting. Both the letter's tone and its content deliberately teased Pushkin's impatience: Sobańska was continuing her game from before. In response came a nervous letter from the poet, in which annoyance and passion merge into one:

You mock my impatience, it is as though you take pleasure in frustrating my expectations, and so I will see you only tomorrow—let it be so. In the meantime I can think only of you.

Though my happiness consists in seeing and hearing you, I prefer not to speak, but to write to you instead. There is an irony in you, an archness, that vexes me and plunges me into despair. My feelings are becoming agonizing, and sincere words transform into empty jokes in your presence. You are a demon, that is, *one who doubts and denies,* as the Holy Writ says.

Last time you spoke harshly of the past. You told me something I had tried not to believe—over the course of seven years. Why?

Happiness is so little made for me that I did not admit it when it was right before me. For Christ's sake, don't speak of it to me.—Pangs of conscience, if only I could experience them—in pangs of conscience there would be some delight—but such regret stirs only fierce and blasphemous thoughts in my soul.

Dear Ellénore, allow me to call you by this name, which reminds me of both the stinging reading of my youth and the tender phantom that charmed me back then, and of your own existence, so cruel and tempestuous, so different from what it ought to have been.—Dear Ellénore, you know that I have experienced all your power. I have you to thank for my knowing all that is most frantic and agonizing in the intoxication of love, and all that is most overwhelming. Of all this I am left with but the weakness of the convalescent, affection alone, quite tender, quite sincere, —and a little timidity that I cannot overcome.

I know very well what you will think if you eventually read this: how clumsy he is, he's ashamed of the past, that's all. He deserves to have me mock him again. He is full of himself, like his master—Satan. Is it not so?

Yet, in taking up the pen, I wanted to ask something of you—I no longer remember what—oh, yes—for your friendship. This request is quite banal, quite … It is as though a beggar were asking for bread—but the point is that I cannot stand not to be near you.

And meanwhile you are lovely as before, as much so as on the day of the crossing or even of the baptism, when your fingers touched my brow. I feel that touch to this day—cool, moist. You converted me into a Catholic.—But you will fade; that beauty will eventually slide downward like an avalanche. Your soul will hold out for some time among such

> numerous spent charms—and then it will disappear, and perhaps never will my soul, its timorous slave, meet it in boundless eternity.
>
> But what is the soul? It has neither a gaze, nor a melody—well, perhaps a melody ...[17]

Pushkin saw before him Ellénore, the heroine of Benjamin Constant's *Adolph*, but the person he was looking at was a spy, a secret agent of the police. Romantic literature from Eugène Sue to Victor Hugo had introduced the spy into the roster of demonic characters. And Karolina Sobańska, an opportunist and traitress, was not the kind of prosaic police agent familiar to us from the era of Nicholas I; her behavior was not without a distinctive demonism. But she reminded Pushkin of completely different literary heroines ...

... The image of the lovely spy-criminal could trouble the imagination of the Romantics, but Romantic spies were unnecessary to the Third Section. Afterwards, the Polish Karolina Sobańska did not get along with Benckendorff, fell into disfavor, and, accused of pro-Polish sympathies, was expelled from Russia.

Pushkin's letter was written in French and bears the imprint of French novelistic style. The choice of language here is made advisedly. Let us recall how in *Anna Karenina,* at just the point when the heroes' feelings have become clear to them but their relationship has not taken definitive shape, it became impossible for Anna and Vronsky to speak to each other in Russian: the Russian *vy* was too cold, but *ty* signified a perilous intimacy. The French language lent the conversation the neutrality of a high-society chat, and it could be variously interpreted depending on a gesture, smile, or intonation.

Another peculiarity characteristic of the Russian nobleman's letters in French is the widespread use of literary quotations. Quotation allowed one to lend the text an indeterminacy of meaning, to situate it between Romantic pathos and Sternean irony. Pushkin made broad use of the letter's stylistic possibilities. However, the abundance of literary reminiscences in no way signifies an absence of sincere and stirred-up emotion. A quotation does not diminish the sincerity, but only increases the shades of meaning. Both Tatyana's childishly sincere letter to Onegin and Onegin's letter to Tatyana in the eighth chapter, filled with tragic passion, disintegrate readily into quotations (as commentators have noted). Lensky's dying elegy consists of a mass of quotations (this provided scholars of the 1920s a pretext to reduce the entire episode to literary polemic). Meanwhile, the Romantic era employed quotations as other eras used the words of their natural language: far be it from us to accuse a person of insincerity for using words in conversation that have already been employed by others before him. Using quotations, a person of the Romantic era seemed to elevate himself to the level of a literary hero. But it would be strange to suspect General Raevsky of insincerity when he, wounded at the Battle of Leipzig, recited French verses from Voltaire's tragedy *Éryphile* to his adjutant, the poet Batyushkov.

In *The Queen of Spades* [*Pikovaia dama*], Hermann's first letter was "affectionate, respectful, and taken word-for-word from a German novel." In "The Blizzard" [Metel'], Burmin confesses his love, and for the heroine his confession brings to mind literary associations ("Maria Gavrilovna recalled St.-Preux's first letter"). It would seem that we have the very same phenomenon before us, but we are actually dealing with contradictory situations, and Pushkin draws a clear distinction between them. Formally, they are distinguished by the fact that Hermann transcribes a letter in full. His personal feelings are not reflected in his text (Pushkin explicitly stipulates that, later, when a sincere passion wells up in Hermann, his letters "are no longer translated from German"). But in "The Blizzard," Burmin does not copy a text that he has studied backwards and forwards, but improvises his confession, "imagining himself" the hero "of his favorite authors."

In the first instance, Hermann writes in a language that is foreign to him, and in this way he is uttering false feelings; in the second instance, the hero chooses an elevated literary language for the most precise expression of his elevated feelings.

At the end of Alexander Ostrovsky's drama *The Forest* [*Les*], Neshchastlivstev pronounces the pathetic monologue from Schiller's drama *The Robbers:* "People, people! A brood of crocodiles! Your tears are water! Your hearts, hard steel! Your kisses, daggers into the chest!" Milonov, the hero and a man of the world, who is right there, does not recognize the quotations and is about to make him answer for his sedition. Then Neshchastlivtsev answers: "I feel and speak like Schiller, and you—like some clerk!" What was in Ostrovsky's time the stuff of artists, of people of letters, belonged in the Romantic era to the everyday consciousness of the nobility. Tatyana, Onegin, Lensky, and other literary heroes, just like numerous heroes of real life, reconstructed their consciousness and built their own personality by making "of stranger's sorrow,/of stranger's rapture, her own plight."[xxviii] Everyday feelings were raised to the level of literary models.

xxviii Quotation from Pushkin's *Eugene Onegin*, Chapter 3, in reference to Tatyana.

Pushkin's letter to Sobańska makes for a vivid example. Whoever says that "this is the most passionate letter written by Pushkin" would be correct. Whoever says, "This is one of the most literary of Pushkin's letters," would also be correct. But whoever concludes that the letter is insincere would be mistaken.

Later, Lev Tolstoy would identify quotation with insincerity. Tolstoy will be interested in the structure of insincere speech: for him, it would also be citational and literarily executed. Its opposite is spontaneity, "yeah," "you, uh, yeah," as Akim utters in *The Power of Darkness*. The notion that "thought wrought in speech is a lie"[xxix] is deeply ingrained in Tolstoy. But the period from the eighteenth to the early nineteenth centuries had a different judgment. Truth is offered in elevated, heroic texts, in the words, gestures, and deeds of heroic people. A person approaches a higher truth by repeating these elevated models. One can compare this to how the heroes of the French Revolution adopted the names of "famous" Romans, striving to become their living embodiments.

Heinrich Heine wrote the characteristically Romantic poem "Nun ist es Zeit, daß ich mit Verstand":

It is now time I set aside,
With reason, acting the fool;
So long have I a comedian played
In a comedy played with you.

The splendid scene, which had been painted
In high Romantic style,
My knightly cape gold-decorated,
The finest feeling I felt ...

And with actual death in my breast
Have I the deadly swordsman played.[xxx]

Nun ist es Zeit, daß ich mit Verstand
Mich aller Torheit entledge;
Ich hab so lang als ein Komödiant
Mit dir gespielt die Komödie.

---

xxix Quotation from Tyutchev's poem "Silentium."

xxx Lotman's quotation of this poem is seriously mangled. We feature the poem here in a more faithful translation, quoting the first two stanzas and the concluding two lines, so that the quotation still conveys Lotman's idea.

Die prächtgen Kulissen, sie waren bemalt
Im hochromantischen Stile,
Mein Rittermantel hat goldig gestrahlt,
Ich fühlte die feinsten Gefühle ...

Ich hab mit dem Tod in der eignen Brust
Den sterbenden Fechter gespielet.

Heine recreates a characteristic Romantic situation: life and literature become confused, changing places, the game passes into death. Quotation is transformed into an actual howl of the soul, and actual sufferings are conveyed most precisely by the words of a quotation.

Having seen Sobańska in 1830, Pushkin experienced both a recurrence of a love that had burned out and a thirst for bold, decisive action. In this sense, running off to Crimea without permission in order to fall at the feet of a passionately beloved woman of doubtful repute, or else marrying a beautiful girl lacking in lived or worldly experience, money, or even, it would seem, any love for him—both of these acts were plot synonyms of sorts: like a flying leap into dark water, they cut off the path to the past and marked the beginning of something completely new, a desperate gamble in which Pushkin bet his happiness and his life on the turn of a card. Both acts were attractive for their daring.

But in Pushkin this intense sincerity pours out in readymade literary phrases, and we cannot even say what precedes what. The words "a happiness so little made for me" naturally calls to mind the words of Eugene Onegin: "But I was not for blissfulness made." One can draw other parallels as well. But they are not the point; the point is the general parallelism of the words and formulas used to express passionate feeling in life and literature.

The third life-and-literature image typical of the era is the woman-heroine. Its characteristic feature is the role it plays in the opposition between women's heroism and men's spiritual weakness. It may have been Alexander Radishchev who gave this representation its start by introducing, in his epic poem *A Historical Song* [*Pesn' istoricheskaia*, 1795–1796], the image of a heroic Roman woman who, by her own example, through suicide, encourages her weakened husband. It is important that, for Radishchev, heroic suicide was a manifestation of civic virtue: ready to perish, a person no longer fears the tyrant's power.[18]

In *A Historical Song,* the poet describes an episode from Roman history little-known in Russian culture, using it as a pretext to develop his own ideas. In 42 AD, Aulus Caecina Paetus was condemned to death for participating in the struggle against "the weakling tyrant," the Emperor Claudius. So as to avert dishonor, Paetus's wife, Arria, talked him into committing suicide, and then, wishing to overcome his indecision, pierced her own breast first and passed the dagger to her husband with the words, "No, it does not hurt":

> Behold, the man's wife, heroic
> In spirit, said to her dear spouse,
> Who was to evil death condemned,
> That he forestall the sentence foul
> By the strength of his own hard hand,
> But timid Paetus tarries on.
> And so bold Arria plunges
> the sharp steel into her own breast:
> "Take it, my obliging Paetus,
> No, it does not hurt ..." Man again,
> Paetus did stab his chest, and fell.
>
> Зри, жена иройска духа
> Осужденному к злой смерти
> Милому рекла супругу,
> Да рукою своей твердой
> Предварит он казнь поносну,
> Но Пет медлит и робеет.
> И се Арія сталь остру
> В грудь свою вонзает смело:
> «Приими, мой Пет любезной,
> Нет, не больно ...» Пет, мужаясь,
> Грудь пронзил и пал с супругой.

This is linked to the interest in the heroic woman in later Russian literature as well: Martha the Mayoress (Karamzin, Fyodor Ivanov), the Maid of Orleans (Zhukovsky), and let us also recall corresponding figures in the poetry of Lermontov and in the prose of Alexander Bestuzhev-Marlinsky.

The history of culture is frequently, traditionally, written "from a man's point of view." The eighteenth century, however, does not fit this tradition. Between the "masculine" and the "feminine" views there is a distinction that is by no means elementary in nature. The historian who works from sources written "from the man's perspective" sees before him a world of "grown-up" people.

He sees historical personages in their results, and not in the process of their formation, and the people before his eyes are a series of outcomes, as if they were a museum in which the immobile figures are arranged in chronological order.

When a person is mentioned, "the woman's gaze" first of all sees a child, and then the process of his formation. In people, "the man's gaze" underscores their deeds, what they have accomplished; the woman's, what they might have accomplished but lost, or else accomplished only partially. The man's gaze glorifies what has been done, the woman's mourns what has not. Blok sensed this acutely:

Of that star so very distant,
Mary, sing,
Sing of life from others hidden,
Lived alone.
Sing of what he has not done. ...[19]

Вон о той звезде далёкой,
Мэри, спой,
Спой о жизни, одиноко
Прожитой.
Спой о том, что не свершил он. ...

In this way, women's culture is not merely the culture of women. It is a particular view of culture, an indispensable element of its many-voicedness.[xxxi]

In his unfinished *Novel in Letters,* Pushkin addresses, through his heroine's lips, the functional difference between so-called masculine and feminine cultures. In a letter to her friend, Liza expresses the thoughts generated by her reading a novel from the previous century:

> Reading Richardson gave me cause for reflection. What an awful difference between the ideals of grandmothers and granddaughters. What do Lovelace and Adolph have in common? Meanwhile, the woman's role does not change. Clarissa, with the exception of her ceremonial curtseys, nevertheless resembles a heroine from the latest novels. Is it not because the

xxxi Here Lotman returns to the idea expressed in "Autocommunication: 'I' and 'Other' as Addressees" and in "Semiotic Space": that heterogeneity is at the heart of how a culture operates and can generate novelty.

> ways to please a man depend on fashion, on fleeting opinion ... but in women they are based in feeling and nature, which are eternal.

It is interesting, however, that the view characterized here as "feminine" Pushkin elsewhere took for his own, and in so doing he substantiated the idea of a kinship between how the world is perceived by women, who have preserved natural tastes, and by poets. In this way, the antithesis of a "masculine gaze" and a "feminine" one is replaced in Pushkin by an opposition between the historical and the eternal. The so-called feminine gaze becomes the realization of what is eternally human. It is revealing that here Pushkin approaches Dante, whom he felt deeply at this time, and in whose *Divine Comedy* the scenes of Hell, thickly saturated with political topicality, are provided in the assessments of Virgil, yet the passage into the world of eternal values demands a different judge: Virgil is replaced by Beatrice.

Notes

INTRODUCTION

1. The first pages of this introduction represent a revised version of my introduction to Andreas Schönle (ed.), *Lotman and Cultural Studies: Encounters and Extensions* (Madison: The University of Wisconsin Press, 2006). I have reused them here with the permission of the University of Wisconsin Press, which I gratefully acknowledge.
2. For a convenient synthesis in English of Lotman's semiotic and cultural theory, see Aleksei Semenenko, *The Texture of Culture: An Introduction to Yuri Lotman's Semiotic Theory* (New York: Palgrave Macmillan, 2012).
3. William Mills Todd III, *Fiction and Society in the Age of Pushkin* (Cambridge: Harvard University Press, 1986); Irina Paperno, *Chernyshevskii and the Age of Realism: A Study in the Semiotics of Behavior* (Stanford: Stanford University Press, 1988); Irina Paperno and Joan Grossman (eds.), *Creating Life: The Aesthetic Utopia of Russian Modernism* (Stanford: Stanford University Press, 1994); Svetlana Boym, *Death in Quotation Marks: Cultural Myths of Modern Poets* (Cambridge: Cambridge University Press, 1991); Svetlana Boym, *Common Places: Mythologies of Everday Life in Russia* (Cambridge: Harvard University Press, 1994); Monika Greenleaf, *Pushkin and Romantic Fashion. Fragment, Elegy, Orient, Irony* (Stanford: Stanford University Press, 1994). For a helpful discussion of the two modes of life emplotment which Lotman differentiates and of the creative role of codes, see David Bethea, "Bakhtinian Prosaics versus Lotmanian 'Poetic Thinking': The Code and Its Relation to Literary Biography," *Slavic and East European Journal* 41, no. 1 (1997): 1–15. For a critique of Lotman's concept of theatricality, see Michelle Lamarche Marrese, "'The Poetics of Everyday Behavior' Revisited: Lotman, Gender, and the Evolution of Russian Noble Identity," *Kritika: Explorations in Russian and Eurasian History* 11, no. 4 (2010): 701–739.
4. B. F. Egorov, *Zhizn' i tvorchestvo Iu. M. Lotmana* (Moscow: Novoe literaturnoe obozrenie, 1999), 31.
5. Egorov, *Zhizn'*, 46–48
6. Egorov, *Zhizn'*, 103–109.
7. This phrase, which Lotman used throughout the 1960s and 1970s, was proposed in 1964 by B. A. Uspensky as a euphemism for semiotics, a discipline that Soviet authorities considered undesirable, even though they tolerated structuralism. See "Tekst i poliglotism kul'tury," 142 and Egorov, *Zhizn'*, 119. "Primary modeling systems" would be natural languages, which classify, evaluate, and articulate reality for a given linguistic community. "Secondary modeling systems" are semiotic structures superimposed upon the primary system, such as culture or the arts. Semiotics as meta-language and music as art form would both fall under

the rubric of secondary modeling systems, which illustrates the elasticity, but also the haziness, of the concept.

8. The Tartu-Moscow School of Semiotics is a loose grouping of scholars from various disciplines—from linguistics and literary history to philosophy and folklore—who came together to study culture from a semiotic standpoint, but also to forge ahead with structuralist theory. For a history of the early years of the Tartu-Moscow school, see Peter Seyffert, *Soviet Literary Structuralism. Background. Debate. Issues* (Columbus, OH: Slavica, 1985) and Ann Shukman, *Literature and Semiotics: A Study of the Writings of Yu. M. Lotman* (Amsterdam: North-Holland Publishing Company, 1977). For a useful introduction to the school's subsequent work on the semiotics of culture, see Boris Gasparov, "Introduction," in *The Semiotics of Russian Cultural History: Essays by Iurii Lotman, Lidiia Ia. Ginzburg, Boris A. Uspenskii*, ed. A. D. and A. S. Nakhimovsky (Ithaca, NY: Cornell University Press, 1985), 13–29. For an excellent short critical overview of its history and doctrine, see William Mills Todd III, "Moscow-Tartu School," in *Routledge Encyclopedia of Philosophy*, ed. Edward Craig, vol. 6 (London: Routledge, 1998), 583–588.
9. For a bibliography of Lotman's works, see L. N. Kiseleva, "Spisok trudov Iu. M. Lotmana," in *Izbrannye stat'i*, vol. 3 (Tallinn: Aleksandra, 1993), 441–482. This bibliography features 813 entries. An expanded version, developed in 2004, is available at "Spisok pechatnykh trudov Iu. M. Lotmana," http://www.ruthenia.ru/lotman/biblio.html (accessed 6 July 2019). For a bibliography of English translations of works by Lotman up to 2011, see Kalevi Kull, "Juri Lotman in English: Bibliography," *Sign Systems Studies* 39, nos. 2/4 (2011): 343–356.
10. Egorov, *Zhizn'*, 224.
11. The journal is now published in open access, and most of the issues are available at http://www.sss.ut.ee/index.php/sss.
12. *Lotmanovskii sbornik*, vol. 1 (Moscow: Its-Garant, 1995); vol. 2 (Moscow: OGI, 1997); vol. 3 (Moscow: OGI, 2004); vol. 4 (Moscow: OGI, 2014).
13. See B. A. Uspenskii, "K probleme genezisa tartusko-moskovskoi semioticheskoi shkoly," *Uchenye zapiski Tartuskogo gosudsarstvennogo universiteta* 746 (1987): *Trudy po znakovym sistemam*, vol. 20, 18–29; B. M. Gasparov, "Tartuskaia shkola 60-kh godov kak semioticheskii fenomen," *Wiener Slawistischer Almanach* 23 (1989); and the series of articles published in *Novoe literaturnoe obozrenie* 3 (1994) and 8 (1994). See also Egorov, *Zhizn'*, 117–125. Most of these pieces (with a few additions) were republished in *Moskovsko-Tartuskaia semioticheskaia shkola. Istoriia, vospominaniia, razmyshleniia*, ed. S. Iu. Nekliudov (Moscow: Iazyki russkoi kul'tury, 1998). For later perspectives, see Maxim Waldstein, *The Soviet Empire of Signs: A History of the Tartu School of Semiotics* (Saarbrücken: Vdm Verlag Dr. Müller, 2008) and Semenenko, *The Texture of Culture*, 14–21.
14. See, for example, the publication of Lotman's unpublished penultimate work, Juri M. Lotman, *The Unpredictable Workings of Culture*, trans. Brian James Baer (Tallinn: TLU Press, 2013). For a preliminary study of Lotman's international networks and sources, see Igor Pilshchikov and Mikhail Trunin, "The Tartu-Moscow School of Semiotics: A Transnational Perspective," *Sign Systems Studies* 44, no. 3 (2016): 368–401.
15. Andrei Zorin, "Lotman's Karamzin and the Late Soviet Liberal intelligentsia," in Andreas Schönle (ed.), *Lotman and Cultural Studies: Encounters and Extensions* (Madison: University of Wisconsin Press, 2006), 208–226.

16. Aleksei Plutser-Sarno, "Sedoi shalun: shtrikhi k portretu Iu. M. Lotmana," *Na postu. Kul'tura/iskusstvo* 2 (July 1998): 18–23.
17. F. S. Sonkina, *Iurii Lotman v moei zhizni. Vospominaniia. Dnevniki. Pis'ma* (Moscow: Novoe literaturnoe obozrenie, 2016).
18. See Waldstein, *The Soviet Empire of Signs.*
19. Lotman absorbed some of Bakhtin's ideas, which helped loosen up his semiotic model, though he never fully accepted Bakhtin's phenomenological premises. See Bethea, "Bakhtinian Prosaics," 1–15, as well as Allan Reid, "Who is Lotman and Why is Bakhtin Saying Those Nasty Things About Him," *Discours social/Social discourse* 2 (Spring-Summer 1990): 311–324; P. Grzybek, "Bakhtinskaia semiotika i moskovsko-tartuskaia shkola," in *Lotmanovskii sbornik*, vol. 1, 240–259; as well as Kim Su Kvan, *Osnovnye aspekty tvorcheskoi evoliutsii Iu. M. Lotmana* (Moscow: Novoe literaturnoe obozrenie, 2003), 119–130, and Ann Shukman, "Semiotics of Culture and the Influence of M. M. Bakhtin," in *Issues in Slavic Literary and Cultural Theory*, ed. Karl Eiermacher et al. (Bochum: Brockmeyer, 1989), 193–207.
20. For a competent discussion of Lotman's reception in the English-speaking world and a comprehensive bibliography of works on the Tartu-Moscow school, see Henryk Baran, "Retseptsiia moskovsko-tartuskoi shkoly v SShA i Velikobritanii," in *Moskovsko-Tartuskaia semioticheskaia shkola. Istoriia, vospominaniia, razmyshleniia*, 246–275. Baran shows how the influence of Lotman and the Tartu-Moscow school of semiotics has been primarily confined to Slavicist circles, despite attempts, for example, to build bridges to cultural anthropology in the 1970s and 1980s. Baran's survey deemphasizes the latest works of Lotman and their reception. See also Artur Blaim, "Lotman in the West. An Ambiguous Complaint," in *Neo-Formalist Papers*, ed. Joe Andrew and Robert Reid (Amsterdam: Rodopi, 1998), 329–337. For an attempt to place Lotman in relation with broader intellectual frameworks, see Andreas Schönle, *Lotman and Cultural Studies.* For a recent bibliography of English translations of Lotman's works, see Kalevi Kull, "Juri Lotman in English: Bibliography."
21. Strangely enough (or characteristically enough?), even some Russianists have taken a dim view of Lotman's last theoretical move. See Vladimir E. Alexandrov, "Biology, Semiosis, and Cultural Difference in Lotman's Semiosphere," *Comparative Literature* 52 (2000): 339–362. Note, however, Edna Andrews's sympathetic reevaluation of Lotman's later theories in the context of semiotics, cognitive science, and psychology in Edna Andrews, *Conversations with Lotman: Cultural Semiotics in Languages, Literature, and Cognition* (Toronto: University of Toronto Press, 2003).
22. Galin Tihanov, "Do 'Minor Literatures' Still Exist?," *Forum for World Literature Studies* 7, no. 2 (June 2015): 226.
23. *Universe of the Mind* is, strictly speaking, not a monograph, but an authorized compilation and amalgamation of articles dating back to various periods. While the general thrust of the volume belongs to Lotman's post-structuralist phase, it incorporates inconsistent terminology and includes sections that cannot but suggest a sort of essentializing anthropological structuralism. Clearly, this conceptual inconsistency could not have helped its reception.
24. See Ilya Kliger, "World Literature beyond Hegemony in Yuri M. Lotman's Cultural Semiotics," *Comparative Critical Studies* 7, nos. 2–3 (2010): 257–274.

25. Caryl Emerson, "Bakhtin, Lotman, Vygotsky, and Lydia Ginzburg on Types of Selves: A Tribute," in *Self and Story in Russian History*, ed. Laura Engelstein and Stephanie Sandler (Ithaca, NY: Cornell University Press, 2000), 40.
26. See the cluster of articles on the subject of "Emotional Turn? Feelings in Russian History and Culture," *Slavic Review* 86, no. 2 (2009), in particular Jan Plamper's "Introduction," 229–239.
27. For a broader discussion of Lotman's conception of power, see Andreas Schönle, "Social Power and Individual Agency: The Self in Greenblatt and Lotman," *Slavic and East European Journal* 45, no. 1 (2001): 61–79.
28. Daniele Monticelli, "Critique of ideology or/and analysis of culture? Barthes and Lotman on secondary semiotic systems," *Sign Systems Studies* 44, no. 3 (2016): 432–451, and Patrick Sériot, "Barthes and Lotman: Ideology vs. culture," *Sign Systems Studies* 44, no. 3 (2016): 402–414.
29. Monticelli, "Critique of ideology," 445.
30. Roland Barthes, "From Work to Text," in *Image Music Text* (London: Fontana Press, 1971), 155–164.
31. In *Analysis of the Poetic Text* Lotman maintains that "the relationship of text and system in an artistic work is not the automatic realization of an abstract structure in concrete form, but is always a relationship of struggle, tension, and conflict." Iurii Lotman, *Analsis of the Poetic Text*, trans. by D. Barton Johnson (Ann Arbor: Ardis, 1976), 123–124.
32. On Lotman's binarism, see Semenenko, *The Texture of Culture*, 96–99.
33. Gary Marker, "The Enlightenment of Anna Labzina: Gender, Faith, and Public Life in Catherinian and Alexandrian Russia," *Slavic Review* 59, no. 2 (2000): 369–390.
34. Walter Benjamin, "The Task of the Translator" (1923), in *The Translation Studies Reader*, ed. Lawrence Venuti, 2nd ed. (London: Routledge, 2000), 75–82.
35. For a sophisticated discussion of "the domesticating movement involved in any foreignizing translation," that is, of the mutual interdependency between the two strategies, see Lawrence Venuti, *The Translator's Invisibility. A History of Translation*, 2nd ed. (Abingdon: Routledge, 2008), 10–34, quotation on 24.

FROM *UNIVERSE OF THE MIND*

Autocommunication: "I" and "Other" as Addressees

1. See Roman Jakobson, "Linguistics and Poetics," in *Style in Language* (Cambridge, MA, 1964), 353.
2. A. M. Piatigorskii, "Nekotorye obshchie zamechaniia otnositel'no rassmotreniia teksta kak raznovidnosti signala," in *Strukturno-tipologicheskie issledovaniia*, ed. T. N. Moloshnaia (Moscow, 1962), 149–150.
3. F. I. Tiutchev, *Lirika*, 2 vols., ed. K. V. Pigarev (Moscow, 1965), vol. 1, 51.
4. This and subsequent citations of Pushkin refer to A. S. Pushkin, *Polnoe sobranie sochinenii v shestnadtsati tomakh* (Moscow, Leningrad, 1937–1959), with the volume indicated in Roman numerals, the pages in Arabic.
5. See K. Saito and S. Wada, *The Magic of Trees and Stones: Secrets of Japanese Gardening* (New York, Rutland, Tokyo, 1970), 101–104.
6. See also Moloshnaia, *Strukturno-tipologicheskie issledovaniia*, 285.

7. L. S. Vygotskii, *Myshlenie i rech'. Psikhologicheskie issledovaniia,* ed. V. Kolbanovskii (Moscow, Leningrad, 1934), 285–292.
8. V. K. Kiukhel'beker. *Dnevnik V. K. Kiukhel'bekera. Materialy k istorii russkoi literaturnoi i obshchestvennoi zhizni 10–40-kh godov XIX veka,* ed. V. N. Orlov and S. I. Khmel'nitskii (Leningrad, 1929), 61–62. Küchelbecker was already in the sixth year of solitary confinement at the time he wrote this note.
9. *Koran,* ed. I. Iu. Krachkovskii (Moscow, 1963), 674. Lotman's emphasis.
10. L. N. Tolstoi, *Sobranie sochinenii v 22 tomakh,* vol. 8 (Moscow, 1981), 436.
11. M. A. Tsiavlovskii, L. B. Modzalevskii, T. G. Zenger (eds.), *Rukoiu Pushkina. Nesobrannye i neopublikovannye teksty* (Moscow, Leningrad, 1935), 307.
12. Tsiavlovskii et al., *Rukoiu Pushkina,* 314.
13. Peter I, *Iunosti chestnoe zertsalo, ili Pokazanie k zhiteiskomu obkhozhdeniiu* (St. Petersburg, 1717), 21.

Semiotic Space

1. R. Dekart, *Izbrannye proizvedeniia. K trekhsotletiiu so dnia smerti (1650–1950),* trans. and ed. V. V. Sokolov (Moscow, 1950), 272.
2. V. I. Vernadskii, *Izbrannye sochineniia v piati tomakh* (Moscow, 1960), vol. 5, 101.
3. V. I. Vernadskii, *Razmyshleniia naturalista,* ed. M. S. Bastrakova, V. S. Neopoletanskaia, N. F. Filippova (Moscow, 1977), book 2, 32.
4. V. I. Vernadskii, *Zametki filosofskogo kharaktera raznykh let,* ed. V. M. Fedorov (Moscow, 1988), vol. 15, 292.
5. *Opyt teorii partizanskogo deistviia. Sochinenie Denisa Davydova,* 2nd ed. (Moscow, 1822), 83.

The Idea of Boundary

1. L. A. Dmitriev and D. S. Likhachev (eds.), *Pamiatniki literatury Drevnei Rusi. Nachalo russkoi literatury: XI–nach. XII veka* (Moscow, 1978), 30.
2. F. Kardini, *Istoki srednevekovogo rytsarstva,* ed. V. I. Ukolova and L. A. Kotel'nikov, trans. V. P. Gaiduk (Moscow, 1987), 204.
3. "He who does not reach the summit falls quite low."
4. "A single ascent toward the summit suffices to fill the heart of man. One must imagine that Sisyphus is happy." See A. Kamiu, *Postoronnii. Chuma. Padenie. Rasskazy i esse,* ed. and trans. S. Velikovskii (Moscow, 1988), 354.
5. Dmitriev and Likhachev, *Pamiatniki literatury Drevnei Rusi. Nachalo russkoi literatury: XI–nach. XII veka,* 190, 192.
6. V. I. Vernadskii, *Khimicheskoe stroenie biosfery Zemli i ee okruzheniia,* ed. V. I. Baranov (Moscow, 1965), 201.
7. See B. A. Uspenkii, *Poetika kompozitsii: Struktura khudozhestvennogo teksta i tipologiia kompozitsionnoi formy* (Moscow, 1970), 203–206. Uspensky refers to Meyer Schapiro, "Style," in *Anthropology Today: An Encyclopedic Inventory,* ed. Alfred Louis Kroeber (Chicago, 1953), 293.
8. "If the word 'jargon' means only poor language that is a corruption of good, as perhaps, for example, that of lowly folk, it would scarcely be possible to speak of the jargon of the *Précieuses,*

for the *Précieuses* seek only what is most lovely, but this word also means affected language, and consequently the jargon of the *Précieuses* is a good manner of speech, it is not the true language spoken by those who call themselves *Précieuses,* these are sought-out phrases, made to order." Paul Tallemant, *Remarques et décisions de l'Académie française* (1698), 104–105.

9. See R. Lathuillère, *La préciosité: Étude historique et linguistique,* vol. 1 (Geneva, 1966), and B. A. Uspenskii, *Iz istorii russkogo literaturnogo iazyka XVIII–nach. XIX veka: Iazykovaia programma Karamzina i ee istoricheskie korni* (Moscow, 1985), 60–66.
10. "... there remain many testaments to these successes to this day, from Lima (as well as Panama and Manilla in the seventeenth century) to Zamość in Poland, from Valetta (in Malta) to Nancy, by way of Livorno, Gattinara (in Piedmont), Vallauris, Brouage, and Vitry-le-François." J. Delumeau, *La civilization de la Renaissance* (Paris, 1984), 264–265.
11. M. Iu. Lermontov, *Sochineniia v 6-ti tomakh* (Moscow, Leningrad, 1954), vol. 2, 33.
12. Among the numerous works on this subject, I would like to distinguish one for the clarity of its methodological approach to the question: R. Jakobson, *Russie, folie, poésie. Textes choisis et présentés par Tzvetan Todorov* (Paris, 1986), 157–168.
13. *Letters from a Lady, Who Has Resided Some Years in Russia, to Her Friend in England. With Historical Notes,* 2nd ed. (London: J. Dodsley, 1777), 65. [Lotman quotes from S. N. Shubinskii, ed., *Zapiski inostrantsev o Rossii v XVIII stoletii. Tom I. Pis'ma ledi Rondo, zheny angliiskogo residenta pri russkom dvore v tsarstvovanie imperatritsy Anny Ioannovny,* trans. E. I. Karnovich (St. Petersburg, 1874), 46].
14. *Mestnichestvo* in Muscovite Rus of the fifteenth to the seventeenth centuries was the policy of assigning administrative duties to boyars according to the nobility of their clan and to the importance of the roles fulfilled by their forebears (D. N. Ushakov, *Tolkovyi slovar' russkogo iazyka v 4 tomakh* [Moscow, 1938], vol. 2, 191). This assignment of duties, from one's place at a royal banquet to one's place in a campaign, embassy, or provincial government, was arranged by special order. *Mestnichestvo* provoked various disputes, since it was bound to family honor.
15. "Istoriia Rossii s drevneishikh vremen," in *Sochineniia Sergeia Mikhailovicha Solov'eva v shesti tomakh* (St. Petersburg, 1893–1895), vol. 3, 679.
16. Ibid., 682.
17. See O. Latimore, *Studies in Frontier History* (London, 1962); S. Piekarczyk, *Barbarzyńcy i chrześcijaństwo* (Warsaw, 1968); F. Kardini, *Istoki srednevekovogo rytsarstva.*

FROM *THE STRUCTURE OF THE ARTISTIC TEXT*

"Noise" and Artistic Information

1. Here we are always speaking about the perspective of the one receiving the information. The other side will be considered later.

The Problem of Plot

1. Insofar as "unlikely" surroundings are created on the basis of the writer's deepest imaginings about the unshakeable foundations of the world surrounding him, in fantasy literature in particular we find the fundamental features of that quotidian consciousness that one strives

to expel. When Khlestakov, in describing the balls that had been thrown for him in Petersburg, gets carried away in fantasies ("The soup had arrived in a saucepan by steamship, direct from Paris"), he is most exact in describing the daily life of a minor bureaucrat (the soup is served in a pot, the diner lifts the lid himself). In the words of Gogol, when a person tells a lie, "he shows himself within it precisely as he is." The very idea of fantasy is, in this way, relative.

2. B. Tomashevskii, *Teoriia literatury (Poetika)* (Leningrad, 1925), 137.
3. A. N. Veselovskii, *Istoricheskaia poetika* (Leningrad, 1940), 494.
4. V. Shklovskii, *Teoriia prozy* (Moscow, Leningrad, 1925), 50.
5. Ibid.
6. A. N. Veselovskii, *Izbrannye stat'i* (Leningrad, 1939), 35.
7. Starting from a naïve-realist notion of the correspondence between literature and reality, Alexander Veselovsky remains predictably confused by the fact that "fair hair ... is the favorite color among the Greeks and Romans; all the Homeric heroes except Hector are blond." A. N. Veselovskii, *Istoricheskaia poetika*, 75. "Are we dealing with the indifferent experience of ancient physiological impressions, or with an ethnic marker?" he asks. Yet it is hardly likely that the physiology of vision and the ethnic type of the inhabitants of the Mediterranean endured so much fundamental alteration over this historical period.
8. A. S. Pushkin, *Polnoe sobranie sochinenii*, vol. 12, 329.
9. L. N. Tolstoi, *Polnoe sobranie sochinenii v 14 tomakh*, (Moscow, 1951), vol. 3, 25.
10. N. V. Gogol', *Polnoe sobranie sochinenii* (Moscow, 1937), vol. 4, 75.
11. *Povest' vremennykh let* (Moscow, Leningrad, 1950), vol. 1, 165, 169.
12. *Polnoe sobranie russkikh letopisei* (St. Petersburg, 1908), vol. 2, 822.
13. See S. Iu. Nekliudov, "K voprosu o sviazi prostranstvenno-vremennykh otnoshenii s siuzhetnoi strukturoi v russkoi byline," in *Tezisy dokladov vo vtoroi letnei shkole po vtorichnym modeliruiushchim sistemam* (Tartu, 1966).

FROM *CULTURE AND EXPLOSION*

The Interrupted and the Uninterrupted

1. A. P. Chekhov, *Polnoe sobranie sochinenii i pisem v 30 tomakh* (Moscow, 1976), vol. 5, 271, 272–273.

Perspectives

1. M. E. Saltykov-Shchedrin, *Polnoe sobranie sochinenii i pisem v dvadtsati tomakh*, vol. 8 (Moscow, 1937), 423.
2. Owing to its graphic structure, the pause before the last verse lends it the character of an utterance summarizing the entire epic.
3. There is an earlier variant of this line: "He sang of mercifulness" (III, 1034). This line is connected to one that precedes it—"That, following Radishchev, it is freedom I have praised" (III, 1034)—uniting the ode "Liberty" and "I've raised myself a monument not made by hands" [Ia pamiatnik sebe vozdvig nerukotvornyi ...] as the beginning and the conclusion of a journey.

4. "Let justice be done, though the world perish"; "The law is hard, but it is the law." See also the ironic quote in Pushkin's poem "The Tsar, furrowing his brow …" [Brovi tsar' nakhmuria …]:

   And by the neck they hang you,
   But cruèl is the law. (II, 430)

   Вешают за шею,
   Но жесток закон.

   The juxtaposition with the Latin saying reveals the point of the verse as an attempt at self-justification.
5. N. V. Gogol', *Polnoe sobranie sochinenii,* vol. 8, 323.
6. L. N. Tolstoi, *Sobranie sochinenii,* vol. 11, 98–99.
7. O. E. Mandel'shtam, *Sobranie sochinenii v trekh tomakh,* 2nd ed. (Washington, New York, Paris, 1967), vol. 1, 178.
8. Is this perhaps where Bulgakov took the idea for Voland's visible globe-map? Pasquale Villari's two-volume biography of Savonarola, published in 1913 with a foreword by A. L. Volynskii, was within Bulgakov's purview.
9. P. Villari, *Dzhirolamo Savonarola i ego vremia,* 2 vols. (St. Petersburg, 1913), vol. 2, 251–252.
10. I. A. Krylov, *Polnoe sobranie sochinenii v 3 tomakh* (Moscow, 1946), vol. 3, 14.

Instead of Conclusions

1. This slogan, which was directed against state interference in the natural flow of economic processes, is most closely rendered by the expression "don't interfere," or "leave it to its own devices."

THE LANGUAGE OF THEATER

1. Of course, one cannot capture the multifarious ways of understanding the actor's intention, either; we are limited to the treatment of the play in regard to the performance at hand.

THE ROLE OF DUAL MODELS IN THE DYNAMICS OF RUSSIAN CULTURE

1. See Iu. M. Lotman and B. A. Uspenskii, "O semioticheskom mekhanizme kul'tury," *Uchenye zapiski Tartuskogo universiteta* 284 (1971): *Trudy po znakovym sistemam,* vol. 5, 147.
2. Here we do not address the disputed question of historical periodization from the contemporary researcher's perspective. What interests us is the segmentation that had been obvious to the bearers of culture themselves.
3. See Iu. M. Lotman, "Spory o iazyke v nachale XIX v. kak fakt russkoi kul'tury," in *Istoriia i tipologiia russkoi kul'tury* (St. Petersburg, 2002), 446–538.
4. *Povest' vremennykh let,* ed. V. P. Adrianova-Perets (Moscow, Leningrad, 1950), 81.

5. L. Müller, *Des Metropoliten Ilarion Lobrede auf Vladimir den Heiligen und Glaubensbekenntnis* (Wiesbaden, 1962), 87.
6. See E. V. Anichkov, *Iazychestvo i Drevniaia Rus'* (St. Petersburg, 1914).
7. Vladimir's graven images had been erected on a hill over the Dnieper—that is, *above*—and the Church of St. Ilya had been located in Podil, that is, *below*. Then Vladimir demonstratively *casts the idols down* into the Dnieper and builds the Christian Church of St. Vasily (his patron) on the hill, "on the very same mound where the idols of Perun and others had stood." *Povest' vremenykh let*, part 1, 81; see also 56. If the Church of St. Ilya stood "over the Ruchai," then Perun's idol was pulled down along what is today the slope of Kreshchatyk and Podil and into the Ruchai itself, and then into the Dnieper. See Anichkov, *Iazychestvo i Drevniaia Rus'*, 106.
8. See I. N. Zhdanov, "Slovo o Zakone i Blagodati i Pokhvala kaganu Vladimiru," in I. N. Zhdanov, *Sochineniia* (St. Petersburg, 1904), vol. 1, 70–80.
9. See N. F. Kapterev, *Kharakter otnoshenii Rossii k pravoslavnomu vostoku v XVI i XVII stoletiiakh* (Moscow, 1914). See also M. D. Priselkov, "Nekrolog N. F. Kaptereva," *Russkii istoricheskii zhurnal* 5 (1918): 315.
10. See O. Bodianskii, "Sobranie pamiatnikov, do deiatel'nosti sviatykh pervouchitelei slavianskikh plemen otnosiashchikhsia," *Chteniia v imp. obshchestve istorii i drevnostei rossiiskikh pri Moskovskom universitete* 2 (1863): 31. See also N. K. Nikol'skii, *"Povest' vremennykh let" kak istochnik dlia istorii nachal'nogo perioda russkoi pis'mennosti i kul'tury. K voprosu o drevneishem russkom letopisanii*, 1st ed. (Leningrad, 1930), 80, n. 2.
11. See B. A. Uspenskii, "Kul't Nikoly na Rusi v istoriko-kul'turnom osveshchenii. (Spetsifika vospriiatiia i transformatsiia iskhodnogo obraza)," *Uchenye zapiski Tartuskogo universiteta* 463 (1978).
12. See M. K. Gerasimov, "Slovar' uezdnogo Cherepovetskogo govora," *Sbornik Otdeleniia russkogo iazyka i slovesnosti imperatorskoi Akademii nauk* 87, no. 3 (St. Petersburg, 1910), 3, 56 (*mokoshá*, "impure spirit").
13. See Viach. Vs. Ivanov and V. N. Toporov, *Slavianskie iazykovye modeliruiushchie semioticheskie sistemy (Drevnii period)* (Moscow, 1965), 90, 150, 190; and V. N. Toporov, "K ob"iasneniiu nekotorykh slavianskikh slov mifologicheskogo kharaktera v sviazi s vozmozhnymi drevnimi mifologicheskimi paralleliami," *Slavianskoe i balkanskoe iazykoznanie. Problemy interpretatsii i iazykovykh kontaktov* (Moscow, 1975), 20.
14. See Toporov, "K ob"iasneniiu nekotorykh slavianskikh slov," 19–20; and V. I. Chicherov, *Zimnii period russkogo zemledel'cheskogo kalendaria XVI–XIX vekov (Ocherki po istorii narodnykh verovanii)* (Trudy Instituta etnografii AN SSSR, Novaia seriia, vol. 40) (Moscow, 1957), 55–62.
15. See "O bor'be khristianstva s iazychestvom v Rossii," *Pravoslavnyi sobesednik* (August 1865): 226.
16. See Adam Olearii, *Opisanie puteshestviia v Moskoviiu i cherez Moskovuiu v Persiiu i obratno*, trans. A. M. Loviagin (St. Petersburg, 1906), 128–129.
17. According to the chronicle, immediately after the baptism of Rus Vladimir turns to God in prayer: "… help me, Lord, against mine enemy, for it is in hoping upon You and Your might that I will run to smite him. And having thus spoken, he ordered that a church be hewn and raised in the places where their temples had stood." *Povest' vremennykh let*, part 1, 81.

And so the relevant actions are bound directly to the struggle against demonic forces. And elsewhere the chronicler cries out in rapture: "Where in days past the heathens sacrificed to their gods upon the hills, there the holy churches now stand, golden-roofed and stone-built, and monasteries filled with monks ceaselessly praising God in their prayer, in vigil, in fasting, and in tears, but it is for their prayers that the world stands." A. A. Shakhmatov, "Predislovie k Nachal'nomu Kievskomu svodu i Nestorova letopis'," *Izvestiia Otdeleniia russkogo iazyka i slovesnosti imperatorskoi Akademii nauk* 13, no. 1 (1908): 264.

18. See N. A. Nikitina, "K voprosu o russkikh koldunakh," *Sbornik Muzeia antropologii i etnografii AN SSSR* 7 (Leningrad, 1928): 311–312. In various songs about Grishka Otrep'ev, it is precisely on this basis that Grishka is characterized as a sorcerer.
19. See P. S. Efimenko, "Materialy po etnografii russkogo naseleniia Arkhangel'skoi gubernii," *Izvestiia Obshchestva liubitelei estestvoznaniia, antropologii i etnografii pri imperatorskom Moskovskom universitete* 30, no. 5, part 1 (Moscow, 1877): 104. See also I. Vahros, "Zur Geschichte und Folklore der grossrussischen Sauna," *Folklore Fellows Communications* 82, no. 197 (Helsinki, 1966): 199–200.
20. See P. Bessonov, *Belorusskie pesni s podrobnymi ob"iasneniiami ikh tvorchestva i iazyka, s ocherkami narodnogo obriada, obychaia, i vsego byta*, vol. 1 (Moscow, 1871), 29.
21. See B. A. Uspenskii, "Dualisticheskii kharakter russkoi srednevekovoi kul'tury. (Na materiale 'Khozhdeniia za tri moria' Afanasiia Nikitina)," in B. A. Uspenskii, *Izbrannye trudy*, vol. 1 (Moscow, 1994).
22. "Voproshenie kniazia Iziaslava, syna Iaroslavlia, vnuka Volodimirova, igumena Pecherskago velikago Feodosiia o Latine," in A. Popov, *Istoriko-literaturnyi obzor drevnerusskikh polemicheskikh sochinenii protiv latinian (XI–XV v.)* (Moscow, 1875), 79. The quote is drawn from the manuscript of the second redaction of Feodosii's speech, according to the sixteenth-century Rumiantsevskii Nomocanon [Kormchaia] of writing from southern Russia. The question of the text's authorship has sparked disagreement: some researchers ascribe it to Feodosii of Kiev, others to Theodosius the Greek, a twelfth-century writer.
23. See A. N. Afanas'ev, *Poeticheskie vozzreniia slavian na prirodu*, part 1 (Moscow, 1865), 250. Meanwhile, in Old Russian tales about the Slaughter of Mamai, as well as in the *Synopsis* of Innokentii Gizel' (in describing the Battle of Kulikovo), Perun appears as a *Tatar* god: "Then Mamai, beholding his own ruin, began to call upon his own empty gods, Perun, Savat, Irakli, Ghurak, and his supposedly great accomplice Muhammed." I. Gizel', *Sinopsis* (St. Petersburg, 1778), 163. See also S. Shambinago, "Povesti o Mamaevom poboishche," *Sbornik Otdeleniia russkogo iazyka i slovesnosti imperatorskoi Akademii nauk* 81, no. 7 (St. Petersburg, 1906): 67, 118, 160, 187.
24. See *Povest' vremennykh let*, part 1, 79. See also Popov, *Istoriko-literaturnyi obzor*, 17. This article, imported into the chronicle close to 988 AD, should have been attributed to a later time, given its content. For a broad range of parallels to the "heaven-father" and "earth-mother" opposition, see Ivanov and Toporov, *Slavianskie iazykovye modeliruiushchie semioticheskie sistemy (Drevnii period)*, 101, 207. See also S. Smirnov, *Drevnerusskii dukhovnik: Issledovanie po istorii tserkovnogo byta* (Moscow, 1914), 262–263, 266–268. It is curious that corresponding notions are reflected even in anthroponymy: "The Monk Selivestr, called Mother Earth," in the manuscript of the Rumiantsevskii collection (154, leaf 375). See A. Diuvernua, *Materialy dlia slovaria drevnerusskogo iazyka* (Moscow, 1894), 95. Quite

significant in this sense is the prohibition against men lying prone or on one's belly upon the ground, which figures not infrequently in Old Russian books of penance; in several texts, this rule is set out in greater detail: "If he has reproached his father or his mother, or beaten them, or lain prone upon the ground, as upon a woman, fifteen days [of penance]." A. I. Almazov, *Tainaia ispoved' v pravoslavnoi vostochnoi tserkvi* (Odessa, 1894), vol. 3, 151, n. 44, as well as 155, 195, 275, 279; S. Smirnov, *Drevnerusskii dukhovnik,* 273, as well as the appendix, 46, n. 15. Foul language was also regarded a feature of pagan behavior: it is no accident that, in his denunciation of ribaldry, the Old Russian preacher says that it is the Mother of God who is offended by foul language, then a person's actual birth mother, and "third, the mother-earth, from whom we are nourished ..."; the connection between obscene language and Mother Earth is clearly conditioned further by pre-Christian notions. In light of what we have said, the opinion that one finds in Old Russian instructive literature that crude obscenity "is Jewish speech" appears typical. Smirnov, *Drevnerusskii dukhovnik,* 274, 156.

25. Popov, *Istoriko-literaturnyi obzor,* 25. The quoted text is all the more revealing for its offering an apparent rethinking of the allusion to "Polovetsian vestments" and "Hungarian hats," which we find in other redactions of the given work (the tale of Pope Peter III, called "Mongus"). Ibid., 22, 26.
26. Ibid., 81. The point is imported into the *Voproshchenie kniazia Iziaslava,* which we have already quoted. It is not to be found, however, in other records of this composition and belongs, one must assume, to a later interpolator.
27. Extremely revealing in this regard are the various humorous sayings that are really quite often constructed according to a principle of parodically travestying one or another traditional sort of text. See also P. Shein, "Eshche o parodii v narodnykh tekstakh," *Etnograficheskoe obozrenie* 25, no. 2 (1895). In several cases of this kind, the travesty leads more or less organically to the actualization of pagan concepts. Compare, for example, the following humorous saying from Vologda: "This year new testaments arrived, a young courier ran from the post station bringing new testaments. Truth is dead, falsehood revived, lying left with a cane. It was written, and signed, from Uncle Boris, not written by Roman, all above board. Uncle Vlas showed up, had I such might and a flock of sheep then, I'd have become confessor over him, given him communion and confession, stuck him in the ground. On wheels I'd made, to the heavens I'd ride. In the heavens it's not like down here: church built out of swedes, guts for the doors. Got hold of some gut, to church I then hopped, in the church, it's not like down here: earthen gods, bald spot of wood. Slashed that spot, gobbled some oats, the crumbs I would find as Father Zevorot comes to mind. Father Zeverot, don't pass by my gate—or I'll gobble you up." G. N. Potanin, "Pesni i pribautki, zapisannye v derevne Alsent'evoi v 3-x ver[stakh] ot gor. Nikol'ska [Prilozhenie k stat'e G. N. Potanina 'Etnograficheskie zametki na puti ot g. Nikol'ska do g. Tot'my']," *Zhivaia starina* 9, no. 4 (1899): 523. The features of paganism ("falsehood revived") can be seen here in both the image of earthen god-idols and in the image of Vlas-Volos, protector of sheep, and so on. We feel obliged to express our gratitude to A. F. Belousov for pointing us to this text, as well as to references cited in the next note.
28. This is what they say about this in an anonymous foreign source, "A Report Concerning the Details of the Revolt Recently Led in Muscovy by Sten'ka Razin" [Soobshchenie kasatel'no

podrobnosti miatezha, nedavno proizvedennogo v Moskvovii Sten'koi Razinym], published in 1671:

> Afterwards he [Razin] and his confederates returned to the Don, where he again undertook to commit villainy against the church: he drove out many clergymen, placed restrictions on services, and interfered in church affairs. Here is an example of the magnificent ceremony established by Sten'ka, this Cossack Pope. Instead of the usual marriage rite performed in Russia by a clergyman, he forced those getting married to hop several times around a tree, after which they were considered married according to Sten'ka's way. And he went on shouting various blasphemies against the Savior. ...

In Razin's death sentence, which was read at the execution site on June 6, 1671, it was said:

> And in the year 7178 (1670), arriving at the Don, you, the evildoer, alongside your devoted Cossacks, having forgotten the fear of God, abandoning the Holy Catholic Apostolic Church, spoke all manner of blasphemy against Jesus Christ our Savior, and did not order that a church be erected on the Don to celebrate in those that were there, and drove out all the clergymen, and if someone wished to marry, you, instead of the customary wedding rite, ordered them to walk around a tree.

Zapiski inostrantsev o vosstanii Stepana Razina, ed. A. G. Man'kov (Leningrad, 1968), 108. See also the corresponding English text on 95 and 103.

29. See M. E. Sheremeteva, *Svad'ba v Gamaiunshchine Kaluzhskogo uezda* (Kaluga, 1928), 109. This is underscored by the expression "wed around the fir, around the bush" [*venchat' vkrug eli, vkrug kusta*], widely used in regard to an unmarried couple. See V. Dal', *Tolkovyi slovar' zhivogo velikorusskogo iazyka* (1880), vol. 1, 331. Dal' furnishes this expression with a note: "Is this a simple joke, or the memory of paganism?" Characteristic in this regard is the fate of "Wedding," a love song by A. V. Timofeev. The lyrics, written by a Romantic poet [Senkovsky dubbed him as belonging to the "Second Byrons"] and naively opposing the Romantic cult of Nature to the Christian rite of marriage, evidently—and, for the author himself, unexpectedly—resurrected several pagan ritual notions. The text, set to the music of Alexander Dargomyzhsky, which subsequently came to be interpreted through the prism of the idea of women's emancipation and the cult of George Sand, became a favorite song of the 1860s generation, and in the late nineteenth and early twentieth centuries passed from them into the repertoire of the Russian democratic intelligentsia.
30. P. I. Mel'nikov, "O sovremennom sostoianii raskola v Nizhegorodskoi gubernii (1854)," *Deistviia Nizhegorodskoi gubernskoi uchenoi arkhivnoi komissii,* vol. 9 (Nizhny Novgorod, 1910); *IX: Sbornik v Pamiat' P. I. Mel'nikova (Andreia Pecherskogo)* (Nizhny Novgorod, 1910), part 2, 275.
31. See D. K. Zelenin, *Opisanie rukopisei Uchenogo arkhiva imperatorskogo Russkogo geograficheskogo obshchestva,* vol. 2 (Petrograd, 1915), 581; V. Smirnov, "Narodnye pokhorony i prichitaniia v Kostromskom krae," *Vtoroi etnograficheskii sbornik, Trudy Kostromskogo nauchnogo obshchestva po izucheniiu mestnogo kraia* 15 (Kostroma, 1920): 39. Compare Smirnov's

discussion of how the Khlysts bury their corpses in a swamp, which also happens to be a site for burying the unclean dead. On the unclean dead and their burial, see D. K. Zelenin, *Ocherki russkoi mifologii*, vol. 1 (Petrograd, 1916).

32. Koz'ma Prazhskii, *Cheshskaia khronika* (Moscow, 1962), 107, 173. See also A. O. Kompliarevskii, "O pogrebal'nykh obychaiakh iazycheskikh slavian (Moscow, 1868), 93. Compare the related use of the word "growth" [*roshchenie*] to signify an ancient burial ground; this use is retained in Kostroma dialects. See Smirnov, "Narodnye pokhorony," 36; N. M. Bekarevich, "Dnevniki raskopok kurganov ...," *Kostromskaia starina* 5 (Kostroma, 1901): 335, 367, 396, 402, 406, 407, 416, 425.
33. V. S. Pecherin, *Zamogil'nye zapiski* (Moscow, 1932), 28.
34. One ought to bear in mind that as late as the sixteenth century one could find the dead being buried regularly not in Christian cemeteries, but in pagan burial mounds. Thus, in the Vodskaia District, as they informed Makarii, Archbishop of Novgorod (and future Metropolitan of Moscow), those who hold to the ancient (pagan) traditions did not visit the churches, they did not go to the priests for confession, instead summoning *arbui*—holy men—"and the Lord's dead they lay to rest in mounds among the villages and in burial grounds with the same holy men, and they do not bring those who have passed from them unto the yards of the Lord's churches to be buried." "Gramota Makariia v Vodskuiu piatinu ob iskorenenii iazycheskikh trebishch i obriadov," *Dopolneniia k Aktam istoricheskim, sobrannye i izdannye Arkheograficheskoi komissiei*, vol. 1 (St. Petersburg, 1846), 28. One can suppose that it was not only among the Finnish population that similar traditions were kept.
35. *Drevnie rossiiskie stikhotvoreniia, sobrannye Kirsheiu Danilovym* (Moscow, Leningrad, 1958), 9, 292.
36. Ibid., 181–182, 409.
37. Ibid., 259–260, 479.
38. *Pamiatniki istorii staroobriadchestva XVII v.*, book 1, part 1 (Russkaia istoricheskaia biblioteka, vol. 39) (Leningrad, 1927), cols. 192–193. Compare the same passage in other redactions of *Zhitie Avvakuma* [*The Life of Avvakum*], cols. 42, 119.
39. Ibid., col. 32. See also in other redactions, cols. 111, 186.
40. A particular manifestation of this was the fact that at the same time that cultures focused on "novelty" were creating an ideal of sophisticated and cultured behavior, "antiquity" was invariably associated with behavior that was "natural" and cultivated coarseness as the norm.
41. See also Iu. M. Lotman, "Zvoniachi v pradedniuiu slavu," in *O russkoi literature* (St. Petersburg, 1997).
42. *Pamiatniki istorii staroobriadchestva XVII*, book 1, part 1, cols. 268, 283. Analogously, in Kirsha Danilov's compendium, in the song "Where the Bukharians Fell Upon Us in the Mountains" [Tam na gorakh poekhali bukhary], we find transrational phrases like "Vesur, vesur valakhtantarakh-tarandarufu" taken simultaneously as Polish, Jewish, and "Bukharian" speech, evidently represented as a single "erroneous" (that is, magical) language. See *Drevnie rossiiskie stikhotvoreniia*, 275, 488–489.
43. We find a striking testament to such a notion in Gogol's "A Terrible Vengeance" [Strashnaia mest']: "An unheard-of wonder occurred outside Kiev. All the lords and hetmans gathered to marvel at this wonder: all ends of the earth suddenly became visible. Lake Liman shone

blue in the distance, and beyond Lake Liman spread the Black Sea. Well-traveled people also recognized Crimea rising as a mountain from the sea, and the swampy Syvash. *On the left,* one could see the land of Galicia." N. V. Gogol', *Polnoe sobranie sochinenii* (Moscow, 1940), vol. 1, 275, author's emphasis. If "well-traveled people" saw Crimea from Kiev, then they were undoubtedly facing south. For them, western Galicia ought to have been found *on the right.* But the West being to the left is, in the medieval Russian consciousness, a constant property, not a relative one, and Gogol, with his acute historical-psychological intuition, sensed this.

44. B. A. Uspenskii. "Historia sub specie semioticae," *Materialy Vsesoiuznogo simpoziuma po vtorichnym modeliruiushchim sistemam* 1, no. 5 (Tartu, 1975), reprinted in *Kul'turnoe nasledie Drevnei Rusi: Sbornik statei k 70-letiiu akademika D. S. Likhacheva* (Moscow, 1976). Quite significant in this respect is the attitude toward beards, which for many years sharply divided Russia into two antagonistically opposed parts. If, for one part of the population, a beard appeared as an indispensable attribute of Orthodoxy, and even of religiosity in general, then for the other part the beard becomes a symbol of "darkness." Just as the Old Believers would not allow the clean-shaven into their temples, on the contrary, the New Believers could not allow bearded men to take part in festive religious ceremonies. It was for this reason that they did not want to allow the famous Ilya Baikov, court coachman to Alexander I, into the Kremlin for the ceremony bidding farewell to the dead emperor's body. See N. K. Shil'der, *Imperator Aleksandr Pervyi, ego zhizn' i tsarstvovanie* (St. Petersburg, 1898), vol. 4, 436. In the same way, later they did not want to admit the artist Al. Ivanov into the consecration ceremony for St. Isaac's Cathedral, because, considering himself an icon-painter, he wore a beard and Russian dress. Count Guriev declared to him, "What are you, a Russian? There's no way I can let you into the ceremony with this costume and beard. A Frenchman would be another matter, but a Russian—hardly!" V. M. Zummer, "Problematika khudozhestvennogo stilia Al. Ivanova: Stil' 'bibleiskikh eskizov,'" *Izvestiia Azerbaidzhanskogo gosudarstvennogo universiteta* 2–3: *Obshchestvennye nauki* (Baku, 1925), 94. It is noteworthy that at this stage—specifically for a Russian, though not for a foreigner—a beard can turn out to be an obstacle to one's entry into an Orthodox church!

45. We must note that corresponding processes were observed even before the schism and thus, to some extend, affected the Old Belief as well. There, however, they were unable to develop further and have left no significant trace.

46. See I. I. Ioffe, "Russkii Renessans," *Uchenye zapiski Leningradskogo gosudarstvennogo universiteta* 72 (Seriia filogicheskikh nauk 9) (Leningrad, 1944–1945).

47. On the conflict over monophony, see, for example, N. F. Kapterev, *Patriarkh Nikon i tsar' Aleksei Mikhailovich* (Sergiev Posad, 1909), vol. 1, 8–9, 84–105. On *khomovoe* and *narechnoe* chanting, see B. A. Uspenskii, *Arkhaicheskaia sistema tserkovnoslavianskogo proiznosheniia. (Iz istorii liturgicheskogo proiznosheniia v Rossii)* (Moscow, 1968), 39–40, 61–65.

48. To this one could compare, on the one hand, medieval apprenticeship, in the course of which the future master is supposed to repeat the twists and challenges of his teacher's path, including his unproductive efforts, and, on the other hand, a pupil's rational instruction in the outcomes of knowledge using the shortest method. In the first case, they are teaching the *path*, in the second, the *outcome.*

49. *Feofana Prokopovicha, arkhiepiskopa Velikago Novagrada i Velikikh Luk, Sviateishago Pravitel'stvuiushchago Sinoda Vitse-prezidenta, a potom pervenstviiushchago Chlena Slova i rechi pouchitel'nyia, pokhval'nyia i pozdravitel'nyia,* vol. 1 (St. Petersburg, 1760), 145.
50. Ibid., 113.
51. S. M. Solov'ev, *Istoriia Rossii s drevneishikh vremen v 15 knigakh* (Moscow, 1963), vol. 9, 553.
52. Antiokh Kantemir, *Sobranie stikhotvorenii* (Leningrad, 1956), 75. Our emphasis.
53. On the deliberateness and semiotic character of Peter I's "sacrilege," see B. A. Uspenskii, *Historia sub specie semioticae.*
54. P. Alekseev, *Tserkovnyi slovar'* ... (St. Petersburg, 1818), part 3, 348.
55. Quoted in V. Sreznevskii, *Musin-Pushkinskii sbornik 1414 goda v kopi nachala XIX v.* (St. Petersbug, 1893) (Supplement 5 to *Zapiski Akademii nauk* 72), 69. Ivan the Terrible speaks in exactly this way in his first epistle to Andrey Kurbsky, writing of "the great Tsar Vladimir, who enlightened all the land of Russia with holy baptism." See *Poslaniia Ivana Groznogo* (Moscow, Leningrad, 1951), 9.
56. *Zhurnal ili Podennaia zapiska, blazhennyia i vechnodostoinyia pamiati gosudaria imperatora Petra Velikogo s 1698, dazhe do zakliucheniia Neishtatskago mira,* vol. 1 (St. Petersburg, 1770), 7. Connected to this is the introduction of the epithet "First-Called" into the order's name. This tendency was somewhat masked in the 1720 statute, and the order was presented as the (in fact, sham) continuation of the ancient Scottish Order of St. Andrew. It is extremely typical to take this fruit of one's own creation using ancient Russian models and try to present it *ex post facto* as the product of an all-the-more-prestigious Western influence.
57. F. Prokopovich, *Sochineniia* (Moscow, Leningrad, 1961), 178.
58. *Feofana Prokopovicha Slova i rechi,* part 2, 66–67.
59. D. I. Fonvizin, *Sobranie sochinenii v dvukh tomakh* (Moscow, Leningrad, 1959), vol. 2, 103.
60. Ibid., 102
61. Labzina's memoirs are exceptionally interesting in regard to how pre-Petrine norms and notions are "projected" through a Europeanized everyday. See A. E. Labzina, *Vospominaniia* (St. Petersburg, 1914).
62. The West was interpreted in Russia as anti-Christian, and thus any turn in everyday life toward the "infidel" was experienced as Europeanization, though objectively such "Europeanization" often moved away from the actual forms of European life.
63. Ia. M. Neverov, "Zapiski. 1810–1826 gg.," in *Pomeshchich'ia Rossiia po zapiskam sovremennikov,* ed. N. N. Rusov (Moscow, 1911), 138–143.
64. Ibid., 147–148.
65. V. V. Vinogradov, *Ocherki po istorii russkogo literaturnogo iazyka XVII–XIX vv.* (Moscow, 1938), 79.
66. A. V. Nikitenko, *Dnevnik v trekh tomakh* (Moscow, 1955), vol. 1, 154.
67. See Lotman and Uspenskii, "Spory o iazyke v nachale XIX v. kak fakt russkoi kul'tury," 200.
68. A. A. Kizevetter, "Novizna i starina v Rossii XVIII stoletiia: Rech' pered magisterskim disputom," in his *Istoricheskie ocherki* (Moscow, 1912), 268–269.
69. See Iu. M. Lotman, "O poniatii geograficheskogo prostranstva v russkikh srednevekovykh tekstakh," in his *O russkoi literature* (St. Petersburg, 1997), 112–117.
70. Tatishchev, *Izbrannye trudy po geografii Rossii* (Moscow, 1950), 214.
71. Fonvizin, *Sobranie sochinenii,* vol. 1, 163.

72. *Poslanie Ivana Groznogo* (Moscow, Leningrad, 1951), 9.
73. See Iu. M. Lotman and B. A. Uspenskii, "K semioticheskoi tipologii russkoi kul'tury XVIII veka," in *Khudozhestvennaia kul'tura XVIII veka (Gosudarstvennyi muzei izobrazitel'nykh iskusstv imeni A. S. Pushkina i Institut istorii iskusstva Ministerstva kul'tury SSSR. Materialy nauchnoi konferentsii 1973 g.)* (Moscow, 1974), 275–278.
74. A. S. Griboedov, *Sochineniia* (Moscow, 1956), 343.
75. This has its own logic: adherents to the idea of historical progress and the irreversibility of history's gradual march forward (the emergence of such a concept was one of the theoretical innovations of post-Petrine culture and falls beyond the scope of our article; an exponent of this real, not mythological, Europeanization was Karamzin in particular) think historically and study the past as historians. Adherents to "the return to antiquity" think, in theory, mythologically and see a beautiful tale in the past. The very idea of studying the past historically strikes them as offensive. Thus, for example, M. F. Orlov, protesting the monarchial conception of the origin of Russian state administration set forth by Karamzin, did not offer another interpretation of the sources, but demanded that they be replaced by a "splendid and credible hypothesis." See M. F. Orlov's letter to P. A. Viazemskii, dated July 4, 1818, in *Literaturnoe nasledstvo* 59 (1954): 567.
76. See Iu. M. Lotman, "*Slovo o polku Igoreve* i literaturnaia traditsiia XVIII–nachala XIX v.," in *Slovo o polku Igoreve—pamiatnik XI veka* (Moscow, Leningrad, 1962), 362–374.
77. See also N. A. Lvov's letter to G. R. Derzhavin, dated May 24, 1799, in *Poety XVIII veka* (Lengingrad, 1972), vol. 2, 246–247.
78. Ibid. At the same time, for N. A. Lvov the concepts "Russian song" and "Roma song" appear in certain respects as synonymous. See Z. Artamonova, "Neizdannye stikhi N. A. L'vova," *Literaturnoe nasledstvo* 9–10 (1933): 283.

THE SYMBOLISM OF PETERSBURG AND THE PROBLEMS OF SEMIOTICS OF THE CITY

1. Iu. M. Lotman and B. A. Uspenskii, "Otzvuki kontseptsii 'Moskva—tretii Rim' v ideologii Petra Pervogo," in *Khudozhestvennyi iazyk srednevekov'ia*, ed. V. A. Karpushin (Moscow, 1982).
2. For a comparison between this and the transfer of the capital to St. Petersburg, see A. Vakerbart, *Sravnenie Petra Velikogo s Karlom Velikim*, trans. Iakov Lizogub (St. Petersburg, 1809), 70, and E. F. Shmurlo, *Petr Velikii v russkoi literature* (St. Petersburg, 1889), 41.
3. Nikolai Tikhonravov (ed.), *Pamiatniki otrechennoi russkoi literatury*, vol. 2 (St. Petersburg, 1863), 262. See also "the great city of Edessa, having been flooded in the waters of rivers by God's wrath," in A. Popov, *Obzor khronografov russkoi redaktsii* (Moscow, 1869), 62, as well as the discussion of "the flooding of the city of Larissa," ibid. See also: V. Perets, "Neskol'ko dannykh k ob"iasneniiu skazanii o provalivshikhsia gorodakh," in *Sbornik istoriko-filologicheskogo obshchestva pri Khar'kovskom universitete*, 1895.
4. V. A. Sollogub, *Vospominaniia*, ed. S. P. Shesterikov (Moscow, Leningrad, 1931), 183–184. N. Pakhomov, researching Lermontov's artwork, characterized these drawings, unfortunately lost, as "views of flooding in Petersburg": "Zhivopisnoe nasledstvo Lermontova. Issledovanie N. Pakhomova," *Literaturnoe nasledstvo* (Moscow) 45/46, no. 2, 211–212. Of

course, these should be understood as eschatological portraits of the city in ruins, and not as views of flooding. See also Matvey Dmitriev-Mamonov's poem "The Underwater City" [Podvodnyi gorod], where the fisherman says to the boy:

See the spire? How we in weather
Tossed about, a year ago;
You recall it held the tether
To our boat, heaved to and fro?...

Once a city stood here, open,
Each was welcome, all were ruled;
Nowadays the belfry, spiring—
All that's left of what here stood.

Видишь шпиль? Как нас в погодку
Закачало с год тому,
Помнишь ты, как нашу лодку
Привязали мы к нему? ...

Тут был город всем привольный
И над всеми господин,
Нынче шпиль от колокольни
Виден из моря один.

M. A. Dmitriev, *Stikhotvoreniia* (Moscow, 1865), vol. 1, 176.

5. A. P. Sumarokov, *Izbrannye proizvedeniia*, ed. P. N. Berkov (Leningrad, 1957), 110. See his self-parody:

This mountain's not bread—it's of stone, not dough,
And hard to raise from the place it has known,
And yet it raised itself, and changing now its place,
It fell to the tail of our local bronze-cast horse.

Сия гора не хлеб—из камня, не из теста,
И трудно сдвигнуться со своего ей места,
Однако сдвинулась, а место променя,
Упала ко хвосту здесь медного коня.

Ibid., 111.

At the heart of the inscription is the theme of unnatural motion: the immobile (mountain) is endowed with the markers of motion ("raised itself," "changing now its place," "passed," "fell").

6. Tiutchev, *Lirika*, vol. 1, 103. Lotman's emphasis.
7. Romanovskii, "Peterburg s admiralteiskoi bashni. (K***)," *Sovremennik: Literaturnyi zhurnal A. S. Pushkina, izdannyi po smerti ego* 5 (1837): 292.
8. V. F. Odoevskii, *Russkie nochi*, ed. B. F. Egorov, E. A. Maimin, and M. I. Medova (Leningrad, 1975), 51–52.

9. See *L'image du monde renversé et ses représentations littéraires et para-littéraires de la fin du XVIe siècle au milieu du XVIIe. Colloque international. Tours, 17–19 novembre 1977*, ed. Jean Lafond and Augustin Redondo (Paris, 1979).
10. F. Delpech, *La mort des Pays de Cocagne. Comportements collectifs de la Renaissance à l'âge classique* (Paris, 1976); idem, "Aspects des Pays de Cocagne," in *L'image du monde renversé et ses représentations littéraires et para-littéraires de la fin du XVIe siècle au milieu du XVIIe. Colloque international. Tours, 17–19 novembre 1977*, 35–48.
11. See Lotman and Uspenskii, "Otzvuki kontseptsii 'Moskva—tretii Rim' v ideologii Petra Pervogo."
12. "Puteshestvie ot Peterburga do Beloozerska Pavla L'vova," *Severnyi vestnik* 4, no. 11 (1804): 187.
13. Tikhonravov, *Pamiatniki otrechennoi russkoi literatury*, vol. 2, 263.
14. From this perspective, culture and technology are in opposition: in culture, the entire depth of time is at work; in technology, only the last cross-section. It is no accident that the technicalization of the city that is proceeding so violently in the twentieth century inevitably leads to the demolition of the city as a *historical* organism.
15. On Petersburg as the utopian experience of building the Russia of the future, see D. Greyer, "Peter und St. Petersburg," *Jahrbücher für Geschichte Osteuropas* 10, no. 2 (1962): 181–200.
16. V. F. Odoevskii, *Sochineniia*, 2 vols., ed. V. I. Sakharov (Moscow, 1981), vol. 2, 146.
17. N. L. Oberkirch, *Memoires* (Paris, 1853), vol. 1, 357.
18. I. V. Selivanov, *Vospominaniia proshedshego. Byli, rasskazy, portrety, ocherki i prochee avtora provintsial'nykh vospominanii*, 2nd ed. (Moscow, 1868), 19–20.
19. See Titov's letter to A. V. Golovin, August 29, 1879, in A. I. Del'vig, *Moi vospominaniia*, 4 vols. (Moscow, 1912), 158. Delvig's death gave rise to an entire cycle of mysterious stories. His mother and sister told of how on the day he died, on his estate, which was located in the Tula Governorate, many hundreds of versts from Petersburg, their priest mistakenly prayed "not for the good health of Baron Anton, but that he should rest in peace." Reporting this, Delvig's nephew, an extremely rational person, notes, "I wouldn't mention this easily explainable mistake were it not that a great deal that seemed odd was always happening in Delvig's life." S. Ia. Shtraikh (ed.), *Polveka russkoi zhizni: Vospominaniia A. I. Del'viga 1820–1870*, 2 vols. (Moscow, Leningrad, 1930), vol. 1, 169. Mysterious stories were cultivated also in the house of the poet Kozlov, as well as in other literary salons in the 1830s. A. P. Kern was confused as to which almanac the tale had been published in, but she had a strong sense that Delvig had been the publisher. After publication, it was Delvig who recommended Titov to Zhukovsky as an emerging writer.
20. "At every step I marveled to see the ceaseless confusion of two arts so various as architecture and decoration: Peter the Great and his successors have taken their capital for a theater." *La Russie en 1839 par Le Marquis de Custine: I–IV*, 2nd ed. (Paris, 1843), vol. 1, 262.
21. "We were presented to the Emperor and the Empress. It was clear that the Emperor cannot forget for a moment either what he is or the constant attention he draws; he is *posing* incessantly, the result of which is that he is never natural, even when he is being sincere; his face has three expressions, not one of which is simply that of kindness. What strikes me most is his severity. Another expression, somewhat rarer, perhaps more suited to this fine figure, is

solemnity; a third is politeness. ... One might speak of a mask that he assumes and removes at will. ... Thus I wish to say that the Emperor is always in his role, and that he plays it like a great actor. ... The lack of freedom is painted on everything, including the face of the sovereign: he has many masks, he has no face. Do you seek the man? You always find the Emperor." Ibid., 351–353.

22. I. S. Turgenev, "Vstrecha moia s V. G. Belinskim," *Pis'ma k A. N. Ostrovskomu*, 250–251.
23. M. E. Saltykov-Shchedrin, *Sobranie sochinenii v dvadtsati tomakh*, vol. 14 (Leningrad, 1936), 161.
24. A. V. Nikitenko, *Dnevnik v trekh tomakh*, ed. I. Ia. Aizenshtok, vol. 1 (Moscow, 1955), 283.
25. N. I. Pirogov, *Sochineniia v dvukh tomakh*, vol. 1 (St. Petersburg, 1887), 496, 497. The last words clearly echo the lines of Alexei Tolstoy's "Popov's Dream" [Son Popova]:

   ... With a malicious stare
   He asked that Popov *put himself at ease,*
   And with a smile pointed to the chair ...

   A. K. Tolstoi, *Polnoe sobranie sochinenii v dvukh tomakh*, ed. E. I. Prokhorov, vol. 1 (Leningrad, 1984), 364. Lotman's emphasis.

   This is one of the sources that points to the connections between Krylov's story and urban talk. Also important is the semantic game that undoubtedly lends the story an air of artistic perfection. Since Feofan Prokopovich, an image has endured in apologetic literature: Peter I is a sculptor *hewing* a beautiful statue—Russia—from rough stone. Thus in the court homily of the times of Elizabeth Petrovna it was said that Peter "remade [Russia] into beauteous statues by his own hands." E. F. Shmurlo, *Petr Velikii v russkoi literature* (St. Petersburg, 1889), 13. Karamzin began a draft of a eulogy for Peter with the image of Phidias hewing Jupiter from "a featureless hunk of marble." See *Neizdannye sochineniia i perepiska Nikolaia Mikhailovicha Karamzina*, vol. 1 (St. Petersburg, 1862), 201. In Krylov's story, the function of "hewing Russia" is handed over to the Third Division, which in this way serves as Peter's successor and directs its creative energy toward him.

   Stories about "flogging" constituted the obligatory flip side of Petersburg folklore. Eschatological expectations and the mythology of the Bronze Horseman were complemented organically by "anecdotes" about the flogging of an innocent official. What S. V. Saltykov—a wealthy eccentric whose stories Pushkin loved—addressed to his wife had become a constant saying: "... today I saw *le grand bourgeois* [the tsar—*Y. L.*]. ... I assure you, *ma chère*, he *can* thrash you, *if he should want to*; I repeat: he *can*." *Trudy Gosudarstvennogo Rumiantsevskogo muzeia* 1 (1923): *Dnevnik A. S. Pushkina, 1833–1835*, ed. B. L. Modzalevskii, 143. The gossip about Pushkin being flogged by the police belongs to the same genre. The theme of "flogging" in Gogol grows out of the urban anecdote.
26. See P. Viazemskii, *Staraia zapisnaia knizhka*, ed. L. Ginzburg (Leningrad, 1929), 103. There would seem to be some connection between these kinds of urban anecdote and the vague intention of Pushkin's poem "The Tsar, furrowing his brow ..." [Brovi tsar' nakhmuria], which exhibits all the basic themes of this plot.

27. See Lotman and Uspenskii, "Otzvuki kontseptsii 'Moskva—tretii Rim' v ideologii Petra Pervogo," 239–240.
28. A. Griboedov, *Polnoe sobranie sochinenii v dvukh tomakh,* vol. 1 (St. Petersburg, 1889), 251.

THE DUEL

1. *Pamiatniki russkogo prava,* vol. 8, 459–460.
2. Ibid., 461.
3. N. L. Brodskii, *"Evgenii Onegin." Roman A. S. Pushkina* (Moscow, 1950), 239.
4. Quoted from A. S. Pushkin, *Pis'ma,* vol. 2: *1826–1830* (Moscow, Leningrad, 1928), 185.
5. Charles Montesquieu, *Dukh zakonov* (St. Petersburg, 1900), vol. 1, ch. 8.
6. This is how the duel was appraised in the anonymous brochure "A Gift to Mankind, or: A Cure for Dueling" (Saint Petersburg, 1826), 1; the foreword was signed, "Russkoi [A Russian]"
7. N. Strakhov, *Perepiska Mody, soderzhashchaia pis'ma bezrukikh Mod ...* (Moscow, 1791), 46.
8. "O poedinkakh," *Moskovskie ezhemesiachnye sochineniia* 2 (1781).
9. See *Dekabristy. Materialy dlia ikh kharakteristiki* (Moscow, 1907), 165.
10. The origins of this behavior were already noticeable in Petersburg in 1818–1820. However, no serious duel involving Pushkin is attested yet during this period. Pushkin had not taken his duel with Küchelbecker seriously. Having taken offense at Pushkin's epigram "What I Ate for Supper" [Za uzhinom ob"elsia ia ..., 1819], Küchelbecker challenged him to a duel. Pushkin accepted the challenge, but he shot into the air, after which the friends were reconciled. Vladimir Nabokov's suggestion of a duel with Ryleev nevertheless remains a poetic hypothesis.
11. *Razgovory Pushkina. Sobrali Sergei Gessen i Lev Modzalevskii* (Moscow, 1907), 165.
12. See V. I. Dal', "Zapiski," *Russkaia starina* 19 (1907): 64; P. I. Bartenev, *K biografii Pushkina,* vol. 2 (Moscow, 1885), 177.
13. Gédéon Tallemant des Réaux, *Zanimatel'nye istorii* (Leningrad, 1974), vol. 1, 159. See about this: Iu. M. Lotman, "Tri zametki k probleme 'Pushkin i frantsuzskaia kul'tura,'" *Problemy pushkinovedeniia* (Riga, 1983).
14. It happens that in my earlier work on *Eugene Onegin* I have written polemically about a book by Boris Ivanov (possibly a pseudonym; at any rate I do not have information about the author's actual name). See Iu. M. Lotman, *Dal' svobodnogo romana* (Moscow, 1959). While I maintain the essence of my critical remarks on the book's concept, I feel obliged to admit their one-sidedness. I should have noted that the author has demonstrated a strong familiarity with everyday life in Pushkin's era and combined a generally strange concept with a series of interesting observations that testify to his expansive knowledge. The harshness of my pronouncements, which I now regret, arose from the logic of polemic.
15. According to other rules, after one of the duel's participants has fired, the other could keep moving, and could also demand that his adversary approach his point. Bullies took advantage of this.
16. P. E. Shchegolev, *Duel' i smert' Pushkina* (Moscow, 1936), 191.
17. An expression signifying no wish to continue the conversation.

18. V. Durasov, *Duel'nyi kodeks* (1908), 56.
19. See also, in *A Hero of Our Time:* "'We have been waiting for you a long time already,' the dragoon captain said with an ironic smile. I took out my watch and showed him. He apologized, saying that his watch runs fast." The point of the episode is this: the dragoon captain, convinced that Pechorin is "a first-rate coward," is implicitly accusing him of wanting to call off the duel by being late.
20. *Mémoires de J. Casanova de Seingalt écrits par lui-même* (Paris, 1931), vol. 10, 163.
21. By participating in a duel, even as a second, one brought inevitable and unpleasant consequences upon oneself: as a rule, for an officer it was demotion and exile to the Caucasus (admittedly, superior officers often shielded those who were demoted for dueling). This created obvious difficulties in choosing seconds: as someone who had been handed another person's life and honor, the second should optimally have been a close friend. But this was contradicted by the desire not to draw a friend into an unpleasant affair, thereby destroying his career. For his part, the second likewise found himself in a difficult situation. The friendship and honor required that he accept the invitation to participate in the duel as a flattering sign of trust, but service and career demanded that he see in this the serious threat of ruining his advancement or, furthermore, of attracting the personal hostility of an unforgiving ruler.
22. *A. S. Griboedov, ego zhizn' i gibel' v memuarakh sovremennikov* (Leningrad, 1929), 278–279.
23. Ibid., 279–280.
24. Let us recall the rule of dueling: "Only the adversary who fires second has the right to fire into the air. An adversary who has fired first into the air, if his adversary has not answered the shot or has fired into the air as well, is considered to have backed out of the duel ..." Durasov, *Duel'nyi kodeks* (1908), 104. This rule is connected to the fact that when one of the adversaries fires into the air, it morally obligates the second to be magnanimous, usurping his right to determine his honorable conduct for himself.
25. This is what they called a duel wherein, after the adversaries had fired at each other, the seconds would as well.
26. *A. S. Griboedov, ego zhizn' i gibel' v memuarakh sovremennikov*, 112.
27. A. A. Bestuzhev (Marlinskii), *Noch' na korable. Povesti i rasskazy* (Moscow, 1988), 70–72.
28. A. I. Gertsen, *Sobranie sochinenii v 30-ti tomakh* (Moscow, 1956), vol. 7, 206.
29. The problem of automatization strongly preoccupied Pushkin. See Roman Jakobson, "Statuia v poeticheskoi mifologii Pushkina," in R. Jakobson, *Raboty po poetike* (Moscow, 1987), 145–180.
30. See Iu. M. Lotman, "Tema kart i kartochnoi igry v russkoi literature nachala XIX veka," *Uchenye zapiski Tartuskogo gosudarstvennogo universiteta* 365 (1975): *Trudy po znakovym sistemam*, vol. 7.
31. There were even harsher conditions. Thus Chernov (see above), avenging his sister's honor, demanded a duel at a distance of three (!) paces. In his dying note (which came in a copy in Alexander Bestushev's hand) he wrote: "I am taking up pistols at three paces, as befits a family matter; for, knowing my brothers, I wish to use up my life on him, on that offender of my family who, for the empty prattle of even emptier people, transgressed all the laws of honor, society, and mankind." *Deviatnadtsatyi vek*, book 1 (Moscow, 1872), 334. At the seconds' urging, the duel proceeded at a distance of eight paces, and both participants perished anyway.

32. These figures are taken from the book by Major General I. Mikulin, *Posobie dlia vedeniia del chesti v ofitserskoi srede* (St. Petersburg, 1912), part 1, table 1, 176–201.
33. The typical mechanism for a dueling pistol requires a double squeeze on the trigger, which protected against firing accidentally. The set trigger—*Schneller*—was a device that eliminated the preliminary squeeze of the trigger. The firing speed was increased as a result, but there was also a much greater potential for accidental discharge.
34. Bestuzhev (Marlinskii), *Noch' na korable,* 70–72.

A WOMAN'S WORLD

1. *Pamiatniki russkogo prava,* vol. 8: *Zakonodatel'nye akty Petra I* (Moscow, 1961), 186.
2. Women possessed their own rank only in their service at court. In the Table of Ranks, we find: "Ladies and maidens at court, who are performing real offices, have the following ranks ..." *Pamiatniki russkogo prava,* 8th ed., 186. They are subsequently enumerated.
3. L. N. Semenova, *Ocherki istorii byta i kul'turnoi zhizni Rossii: Pervaia polovina XVIII veka* (Leningrad, 1982), 114–115; "Perepiska kniagini E. P. Urusovoi so svoimi det'mi," in *Starina i novizna* 20 (Moscow, 1916); "Chastnaia perepiska kniazia Petra Ivanovicha Khovanskogo, ego sem'i i rodstvennikov," in *Starina i novizna* 10; *Gramotki XVII–nachala XVIII veka* (Moscow, 1969).
4. The medieval book was in manuscript. The book of the nineteenth century was, as a rule, printed (so long as we are not speaking of banned literature, of church culture, and without taking certain other special cases into account). The eighteenth century occupies a peculiar place: manuscript and printed books exist simultaneously, at times as allies, otherwise as rivals.
5. See the depiction of the merchant's wife in the "Novgorod" chapter of Alexander Radishchev's *Journey from Petersburg to Moscow* [*Puteshestvie iz Peterburga v Moskvu*]: "Praskov'ia Denisova, his new spouse, is white and rouged. Teeth like coal. Brows plucked, blacker than soot."
6. *Poety 1790–1810-kh godov* (Leningrad, 1971), 805.
7. In *Count Nulin* [Graf Nulin], Pushkin writes of these novels:

   A novel classic, outdated,
   Exceptionally long and long-winded,
   Didactical and sedated,
   Not Romantically intended.

   Natalia Pavlovna, the poem's heroine, still read such novels at the beginning of the nineteenth century: they remained in the provinces, but in the capitals they had been squeezed out by Romanticism, which had transformed readers' tastes. As Pushkin states in *Eugene Onegin*:

   All minds these days are a muddle,
   Morality brings us to yawn,
   Vice is as welcome in novels,
   And that's where its triumphs are won.
   (3, XII)

8. Nikolay Mikhailovich Karamzin's story "A Knight of Our Times" [Rytsar' nashego vremeni], our source in this instance, is an artistic work, not documentary evidence. One can suppose, however, that in these questions specifically Karamzin is close to biographical reality.
9. A letter in French to the sovereign or to high officials, when written by a man, would be taken for insolence: a subject was obliged to write in Russian and to follow the established form strictly. A lady was released from this ritual. The French language created a relationship between her and the sovereign similar to the ritual ties between a knight and a lady. The French king Louis XIV, whose behavior was still the ideal for all the kings of Europe, was pointedly chivalric in his conduct with women of all ages and social positions.

   It is interesting to note that, juridically, the level of social protection at a noblewoman's disposal in the era of Nicholas I can be correlated to the protection afforded to a foreigner visiting Russia. This coincidence is hardly accidental: in the world of the bureaucratic functionary, a world of rank and uniform, anyone who stands outside its bounds, one way or another, is a "foreigner."
10. In fact, unlike Saint-Preux from *The New Heloise,* Zhukovsky is a nobleman. Yet his nobility is doubtful: everyone around him knows that he is an illegitimate son with a nobility falsely procured. See N. I. Portnova and N. K. Fomin, "Delo o dvorianstve Zhukovskogo," in *Zhukovskii i russkaia kul'tura* (Leningrad, 1987), 346–350.
11. This was the common name for *Plutarch of Chaeronea's On Childrearing, or On the Education of Children: A Translation from the Helleno-Greek Language by S[tepan] P[isarev] [Plutarkha Kheroneiskogo O detovodstve, ili vospitanii detei nastavlenie. Perevedennoe s ellino-grecheskogo iazyka S[tepanom] P[isarevym]* (St. Petersburg, 1771).
12. *Dekabristy. Letopisi Gosudarstvennogo Literaturnogo muzeia* (Moscow, 1938), vol. 3, 484.
13. A. N. Murav'ev, "Avtobiograficheskie zapiski," in *Dekabristy. Novye materialy* (Moscow, 1955), 197–198.
14. Pushkin, *Polnoe sobranie sochinenii,* vol. 13, 24.
15. E. A. Baratynskii, *Polnoe sobranie stikhotvorenii v dvukh tomakh* (Leningrad, 1936), vol. 1, 49.
16. Pushkin, *Polnoe sobranie sochinenii,* vol. 14, 399.
17. Ibid., 400–401.
18. It is possible that Radishchev's attention was drawn to this episode by an event that immediately preceded the text's composition. The last of the Jacobins, Gilbert Romme and his confederates, with each other's encouragement, avoided execution by stabbing themselves with the same dagger, which they handed from one to the other. For the dating of the poem as 1795–1796, see A. N. Radishchev, *Stikhotvoreniia* (Leningrad, 1975), 244–245.
19. A. A. Blok, *Sobranie sochinenii v 8-mi tomakh.* (Moscow, Leningrad, 1960), vol. 3, 164.

Index

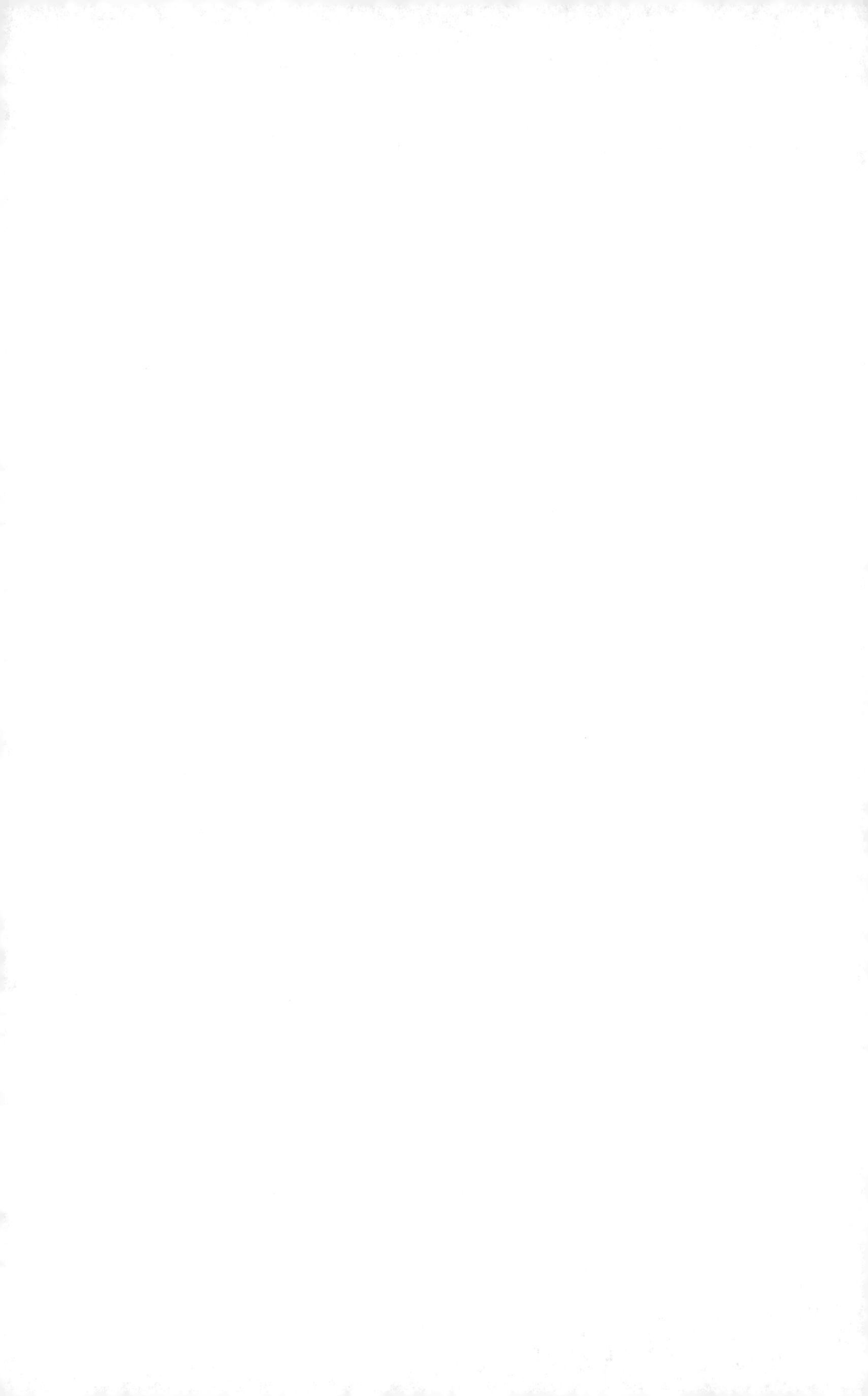

www.ingramcontent.com/pod-product-compliance
Lightning Source LLC
LaVergne TN
LVHW020508100826
845148LV00003B/726

* 9 7 8 1 6 4 4 6 9 3 8 7 2 *